P9-CKF-395

THE AGE OF ROCK

2

*Sights and Sounds of
the American Cultural Revolution
edited by Jonathan Eisen*

RANDOM HOUSE, NEW YORK

Copyright © 1970 by Jonathan Eisen. All rights reserved under International and Pan-American Copyright Conventions. Published in the United States by Random House, Inc., New York, and simultaneously in Canada by Random House of Canada Limited, Toronto. Library of Congress Catalog Card Number: 70–117675. Manufactured in the United States of America by H. Wolff, New York.

FIRST EDITION
9 8 7 6 5 4 3 2

Acknowledgment is gratefully extended to the following for permission to reprint from their works:

The Berkeley Tribe: For "To Dream," by Tari Reim, Vol. I, No. 18.

Crawdaddy: "The Acquiring of Musical Instruments," by Pete Stampfel; and "Apollo and Dionysus," by Walter Breen.

Esquire Magazine: "The Fifties," by Howard Junker. Copyright © 1969 by Esquire, Inc.

International Famous Agency, Inc.: "An Interview with Bob Dylan." Copyright © 1970 by Susan Edminston and Nora Ephron.

Andrew Kopkind: "Woodstock," from *Hard Times.* Copyright © 1969 by The News Weekly Project, Inc.

T. Procter Lippincott: "The Culture Vulture." © by T. Procter Lippincott.

Ramparts: "Rock for Sale," by Michael Lydon. Copyright © 1969 by Michael Lydon.

Fusion: "The Boston Sound Revisited," by Robert Somma; "West Coast Then . . . and Now," by Lars Tusb; "Check the Wiring!" by Bobby Abrams; "Interview: Sam the Sham," by B. Pfohlman (December 12, 1969); "The 'I Wanna Be with You, If You Wanna Be with Me' Fiction Interview," by Michael March; "Buffalo Springfield: A Round," by J. Oliphant; "No Expectations No. 2," by John Kreidl; "George Ratterman," by Borneo Jimmy (February 28, 1969); "Roto Rooter," by Sandy Perlman. © by New England Scenes, Inc.

United Press International: Altamont, California Rock Group article, from the December, 1969 edition of the *New York Daily News.*

The Village Voice: "I Quote," by Michael Zwerin, and "Nostalgia Is the Great Pretender," by Nick Browne. Copyright © 1969 by The Village Voice, Inc. "Bob Zimmerman," by Geoffrey Cannon also appeared in *The Village Voice.* Copyright © 1969 by Geoffrey Cannon.

Jazz and Pop Magazine: "The Best of Acapella," by Lenny Kaye. © Jazz and Pop Magazine.

THE AGE OF ROCK

2

Other Books by *Jonathan Eisen*

The California Dream, co-editor with Dennis Hale
The Age of Rock

CONTENTS

WITHDRAWN

B + T 10-71 (4054) 8.95

Yavapai College Library
Prescott, Arizona

Jonathan Eisen

INTRODUCTION

The volume you hold in your hands is the second Age of Rock. It bears no resemblance to the first Age of Rock which sold well enough for me to convince Random House that another one was in order. Like the first volume, however, this one also begins with music but soon meanders all over the map, trying gamely to get a handle on the culture generally, the rock culture more specifically, the people involved in making music and the people involved in packaging it and selling it to you. Alice Mayhew wanted to call the book *The Age of Rock Underbelly* which might have been a good title.

Nevertheless there is no central point, not even an order you're supposed to read the essays in, though in my mind there are connections between the various articles as you go along. Rockwrite itself is the most boring trash imaginable unless it is linked with other equally boring concepts about the way we live or think we're supposed to and then it makes for a more interesting time. However for those who want the straight rock stuff, there's some of that in here as well, plus some reviews of albums just in case you think you want some of that.

THE AGE OF ROCK

2

Michael Rossman

MAD MICHAEL'S SONG

With a burning spear and a horse of air
I wandered in the wilderness
too long, when I awoke the cities were
past their pride,

and the air was dark with their decay,
the lakes were sick and the fires banked
that brew new life at the verge of water
and waiting sky.

And the houses of the heart were let
in fragments to apartments fixed
to house apartness with thin walls
of helpless stranger pain.

And I saw the brothers start to build,
like timid light in mad morning's night,
not yet believed in in the mining
disaster soul.

For the dragon jaws of thunder fire
that blind the sky were upon them hard,

*advancing from dark lairs concealed
in roots of childhood dream.*

*And all our past was thus arrayed
in demon's guise in the mythic morning
where the* golem *clanks and ambles
his strange electric fire,*

*machine turned flesh at its secret core,
its song unknown as the children's laughter,
tinged with brassy overtones
of impatience and despair.*

*And birds and angels from half-remembered
brother cultures were rediscovered,
the flesh invented, the body worn
like bright new clothes,*

*while life guerrillas from old romance
cleared open space in the wilderness
for the love of their confusion
and the schools of our desire.*

*With a burning spear and a horse of air
I wandered in the wilderness
to dream of cities invisible
in the open leaves of man.*

*There's a knight of ghosts and shadow
who summons me to tourney there,
ten leagues beyond the wide world's end:
methinks it is no journey,
methinks it is no journey.*

With a burn-ing spear and a horse of air, I wan-dered in___ the

[verses 1, 2, 4, 8]

wil-der-ness too long, when I a-woke the cit-ies were past their prime.(And the)

[verses 3, 5-7, 9, 10]

walls   of   help-less stran-ger   pain

[last verse]

wide world's end,   me-thinks it is no jour-ney

Pete Stampfel

THE ACQUIRING OF
MUSICAL INSTRUMENTS

The acquiring of musical instruments has always been a strange business with me. When I was nine I got a fiddle from the old couple next door, who kindly allowed me to explore their attic & eat strawberries from their backyard.

This was in West Allis, Wisconsin.

That year I was sick from measles or something I caught from my brother or sister, who always got sick first. So there I was having delirious hallucinations, and so folks decided I should start playing music and the man came over with his book full of all the instruments so I could pick one. I was lying in bed, too sick to get up, hesitating between trumpet & violin (trumpet because Saber Dance was my personal ace number one hit that year) but picked the violin because the picture of the violin glowed more weirdly than the picture of the trumpet.

I took violin lessons on & off for seven years, mostly hated it & never got good. However in 1960 on the lower east side of New York, I taught myself to play old-timey country music. This time I learned by playing along with old 78-rpm records. In a month I was better than after seven years of lessons, and it was always fun. Me & two friends had a group called MacGrundy's Old Timey Wool Thumpers & we had one job, in a Jewish home for ex-Hillside girls in Brooklyn. Hillside was a posh flip house.

After that I played in the Strict Temperance String Band of Lower Delancey Street, which was a floating string band that existed when a quorum of three members played at one time. A lot of people were in it.

I traveled on to Berkeley, where I was in the Lower Telegraph Ave. Freedom Fighters String Band and the Merrie Order of St. Brigitte String Band. The latter two were the same band. We changed the name because we got bored with explaining we were fighting *against* freedom.

Later I was half of the Holy Modal Rounders. Prototype names for the Rounders were "Fast Lightning Kumquat" & "Rinky Dink Steve, the Tin Horn," "The Total Modal Rounders" (Holy spun off Total when a friend said our name while he was high), "The Temporal Worth High Steppers," "Flotsam Warp & Jetsam Woof," "The Total Quintessence Stomach Pumpers."

The Rounders made two records for Prestige, one for ESP, and we just did one for Elektra. *Buy them all.*

In summer 1958 I started playing banjo. I got my banjo from Herman the Hermit of Burbank, California, father of Cliffy Stone. Herman learned to play banjo from his father. Herman's father learned to play banjo from the slaves on his plantation. Herman was getting old & selling his banjos. The banjo I got was a Paramount style C whom I named Galadriel, from the Ring Trilogy—but I never called her that really.

To get money for her I sold my car—'46 Ford coupe decked, shaved, metallic blue, etc.

I never buy fiddles. People keep giving me fiddles from their attics.

My banjo died in 1964 saving my life. I was a passenger in a Volkswagen going to Boston & was playing the banjo because the chick who was driving was boring. I was uptight because she had already rolled two Land Rovers.

She swerved to avoid hitting a poor peasant & the car rolled over several times.

"Gee," I thought as we rolled, "I hope I don't get killed, blinded or paralyzed & my hands don't get hurt." I went through the window which God had considerably removed just before I went through it. I bumped my back on the way out & was in pretty much pain. Some priests came along & gravely gave me some extreme unction even though I told them I didn't want any. I had quit the Catholic church eight years previously. The chick who was driving ended up underneath the car & in a hospital for months, but her daddy sells diamonds.

When I could move I looked for my banjo. The neck was in four pieces. Also I couldn't find my duck call which I blew at people who wanted to know if I was a boy or a girl. For several hours Bob Dylan was in my head singing "Chimes of Freedom Flashing."

Thanks partially to the yoga exercises I had started earlier that year (it was October, two days before my birthday) I could stand on my head again in two weeks, normal. I had the neck of my banjo replaced with a fretless one but it wasn't, you know, the same.

A quick dimensional arc & here we are in early 1966 & my woman decides to get an electric guitar, and we bop all over New York waiting for one to leer at us from a window or something. A friend informs us of this strange Burns guitar in a pawn shop on Third Ave. He said it was priced cheap & expensive new, but it had been there for months. Many people went to buy it but never did.

The money for the guitar was from a special fund my woman had to run away to New Orleans with if it got real bad.

It was May when we got Burns. (We decided his name was Burns because that was the name on him: Burns London. We figured that was his full name.)

No less a guitar player than Mississippi John Hurt said that the best way to learn guitar (or any instrument) was to sleep with it near your head. The Merrie Order of St. Brigitte String Band guitar player used to do that. He would get up, yawn & stretch, and finger pick "Freight Train" or "Franklin St." or John Hurt's "Take This Hammer," etc., on his gold Klang guitar. (That's what it said on the peg head, which is where the pegs to turn the strings are.)

The way my old lady started to play guitar was by not touching him for two months. She wanted to give them time to get used to each other. I would play Burns (I started to play guitar in the summer of 1962) & we would work on music. We write songs. We work on music for long periods of time because we both love music.

We got this tiny old Gibson amplifier for fifteen dollars. After having Burns & the old Gibson amp for a while we decided to leave Burns turned on when he wasn't being played because Burns seemed to like that. After you get close to an instrument they make faces at you, especially electric ones. They sneer when you don't practice & sulk when you unplug them & they have their equivalent to a shit-eating grin & plenty others.

Burns's peg head was decorated with a triangle-shaped defraction grating pointed up because it's a blessing, upside down it's a curse. Also a button that was glued on that said BURN BABY BURN! because burn twice was Burns, and although not a baby Burns was quite young, about four yrs. old I'd say. (Eventually I'll check out the serial number with the company that made him & find out exactly. Then we can give him birthday parties, leaving him plugged in all day with full volume, fuzz tones & treble booster.)

We leave the radio on all the time except when records are playing or we're playing. Even when we're asleep. My old lady has been sleeping with the radio on since 1952 or '53 when she started listening to rhythm & blues. I have been doing it with her since 1962 when we met. It took me about four days to get used to it, then I liked it. We have suffered no ill effects except when WBAI broadcast a record of a bad LSD trip at 3 A.M. & we both had nightmares & woke up. We noticed after the guitar & amp were left on for several hours the guitar's tone would be enhanced. Richer, fuller, more resonant.

Once we left Burns on a long time while we had this argument/discussion we had been having lately. We would be figuring chords for a song & she would say the next chord should have This Note in it & I would say you can't have that note in the chord because it's right next to THIS note & if I played THAT, THIS note would be there & I could play THAT note or THIS note because as a rule either that would pre-empt the note from the chord needed on the next lower string &/or it would be too far to reach. Then she would say "Play another chord without that note in it" that made the necessary note by using harmonics so that the necessary note resulted from mixtures of other notes.

(Pianos never have this problem. That's why it's easier to make songs up on pianos.)

But when she would say that thing about making one note from other notes I would say, "IMPOSSIBLE," and that's basically about what we argued about. Sort of like the wine-wafer transubstantiation arguments, kind of. My old lady was raised Catholic but she never ever believed it. She used to think she was the only person in the world who never believed it when she was eight yrs. old.

Before I go on I shall give a short lecture on how not to get shocks while being electrified.

I'll do it because I asked plenty of electric players about how not to get shocks in 1965 & they all said "You don't get shocks." Bullshit. Like chicks saying getting your ears pierced—or cats saying getting tattooed—doesn't hurt. I know tattooing hurts because I got a trisected snake tattooed on my leg in 1958 & it hurt like hell.

Trisected because (1) I had just had my mind copped by Robert Graves's Triple Goddess concept, (2) the bellies of the three parts of the snake were going to be black, yellow & white, & there was going to be the word "Brotherhood" in Elvish Runes, but by the time the uncolored snake was finished I was so nauseated I rationalized, "Fuck it! by the 1960s Tolkien won't be esoteric." This isn't the place to go into reasons 3, 4 & 5. (My old lady's even better at prediction. She figured we'd be on the moon by 1970 in 1956.)

How you get shocks. Classic example: when Keith Richard was almost killed in early '66 because he hit an off-center microphone with a peg head. He got shocked because the guitar & the microphone were plugged into different amplifiers & they were not grounded. If both of them had been plugged into the same amplifier there would have been no shock. He almost got killed because the stage was covered with water.

About the most painful shock is when you're singing & playing & your tongue touches the microphone.

I heard about a guy who got electrocuted while playing an amplified Jew's harp, but that may be just a story.

So don't use your body to complete a circuit between two power sources not grounded. Three's a crowd, ha ha. But my old lady was right about making notes happen from the notes that preceded. Feedback, harmonics & the Holy Ghost are a railroad, and she's black.

That was a very interesting summer & we both learned a lot. During the first part of September we were both restless & had a feeling we were supposed to go to the Village (we lived on the lower east side), so we went.

We didn't know where we were supposed to go, so first off we went to the Night Owl, where Lothar & the Hand People were playing, because we like them & their music, but the Night Owl was closed. It was a weekday after three. Jimi Hendrix was at the Cafe Wha, only then he was called Jimmy James & his group was called the Blue Flames. We figured they'd be closed too, although they were usually open later than the Night Owl. We were right, so we went to Bleeker & MacDougal, which seemed like the very place for meditation.

While we meditated a procession of relatively straight people approached us & they all wanted to know where it was happening & we automatically told them "Try the Go-Go." After the third one we headed for the Go-Go ourselves, because if anything happens three times it's a prod from God!

We waited outside the Go-Go because the street was very strange there. People kept bopping by looking like they were looking for something, including a number of friends we hadn't seen in a long time, like Ed Saunders & Luke Faust. Then Dave, lead singer of a group called the Raves, passed by & asked me if I could play bass because they just lost a bass player. I had been wanting a bass for months but we were stone broke. But when God prods I boogie! "Right," says I, "I'll swap my banjo for a bass in the morning." Besides, the Raves are good, one of the best undiscovered groups on the planet. Dave was going to jam at the Go-Go with Jimi Hendrix & John Hammond so we thought this must be the place. Gee, we were right again. Wow!

Boy, was it weird at the Go-Go! Harmonics clusterfucked in

the air like the ghost of electric fireflies. Dave was drumming, John was singing, Jimi was making those neat noises he makes & there were a couple of other people playing too. The shadows of the jamming band merged on the wall in the form of a flashing prehistoric monster. In keeping with the prayerful vectors, Johnny had preceded the set by waving a censer of incense. As soon as the incense censer swaying stopped something happened. "I feel strange," several said suddenly. "That you, Burns?" my old lady asked Burns, who loves to be taken along, especially on subways. Burns seemed to be smirking inside his naugahyde case.

We were too excited to sleep that night, nor could Freddy, who at the time was going to be our rhythm guitarist (but that's another yarn). But anyway, at eight o'clock in the morning the phone rang & it was Freddy & he said, "You won't believe what happened last night. Listen," and he played a tape he had just made. It had a chorus in the background, his 12-string being foreground.

"Who's the chorus?" I asked.

"You heard it too?"

"Yup. Sounded like girls."

"I was just recording layers of guitars & all of a sudden . . ."

Obviously it was time to play music.

"Look, I'm gonna swap my banjo for a bass & I'll be right over." We took Burns & my banjo to Third Avenue.

Pawnshop creep gives heat cuz my banjo's fretless.

"Mashugena banjo, who needs a mashugena banjo?"

"The 'in' crowd," I hollered. "Look, I wanna swap this fine banjo for a cheezy electric bass. You can put frets on for ten dollars & sell it for three hundred dollars."

"Mashugena," he says & hands me a skyblue Hagstrom bass. I take it in back & try it out. He hangs around, giving me fisheye & taking his spitty cigar stub out of his mouth occasionally to say "Mashugena."

"Fire!"

The lights start acting crazy. Smell of burning rubber.

"Sic 'em, Burns," says my old lady. Burns hates pawn shops

'cause he spent seven months hanging in one like a side of meat. Of course they couldn't find the fire.

"I'll take the Hagstrom."

The burning rubber smell went away.

"It'll cost your banjo & fifty dollars," said Uncle Phleghm.

"I expected an even trade!" The burning rubber smell returned. Uncle Phleghm exits to this weird nook & returns with this grey Japanese St. George bass. I tried him. "Fine," says I. "Throw in a cord & e flatpicks & we're in business." They were still trying to find the fire when we split.

Two cabs passed us because St. George wrapped in brown paper looked like a weapon. A third cab approached & I said, "That's it!" The cabbie's name was George Burns.

Up the West Side Drive while the Byrds sing, "Hey, Mr. Spaceman, won't you please take me along, I won't do anything wrong," & up to Freddy's where a picture on the wall spooks me because it's like a picture in a horror comic book . . . painter pushed chick off roof for INSPIRATION! & she returns from frame for REVENGE!!

We set up the amps, one via extension cord from the kitchen. Freddy's tomcat lies at perfect right angles to the extension cord & remains for hours, purring. A beginning guitarist & old lady are there so my old lady gives helpful hints.

"Look, it's plugged in, just leave it in your lap while the radio or records are on for a while & get acquainted. It's a good exercise to get your heads together."

New guitarist & his old lady sat there with their arms around each other letting the guitar grope them & saying "Wow" softly.

We were doing freakout stuff 'cause I had never played a real bass before, I had been using the bottoms of guitars. Freeform stuff is of course less demanding. Suddenly new guitarist screamed. "The picture! It jumped at me!"

The picture that had spooked me was on the floor several yards from the wall. So we took a break & ate hamburgers while playing back the tape we just made. Freddy recorded everything.

I called the Wha to tell Dave I'd be late, but the music from the tape did a circuit thing over the telephone & buggered the

Wha's sound system. (My old lady had been doing experimental things along with the tape. She was teaching herself slide guitar.)

"Just a second," said Dave. "The sound system just went haywire."

"Oh well," I thought, & listened to the unbelievable sounds coming over the phone along with all these dismayed sounds— "What's wrong? What's happening?" After fifteen minutes I felt like playing again, so we did. Dave never came back to the phone.

And fate farts. This hood-type cat comes to visit Freddy. He starts giving Freddy a hard time. Now, Freddy had a gun because he said people were trying to kill him, mostly chicks he used to go with. Freddy loves power-play games, so he gets his gun & he & hood play power for a while. Then Freddy gets bored & puts the piece down & Baby Mafia grabs it. I don't like guns so I announce, "We're splitting." So B.M. points it at me & says "Play!"

So I sing my prayer song, which is called "Song of Courtship to Dame Fortune" (available on *The Moray Eels Eat the Holy Modal Rounders* on Elektra records) while Freddy happily accompanies me on bass (he had never played bass before) & my old lady plays slide guitar.

What the hell, I thought, the tape recorder's on & I've got to put some songs I wrote on tape to get them copyrighted. It's business time!

Baby Mafia takes turns pointing the gun at me, Freddy & my old lady. Doin' our thing at gunpoint, very heavy. Our thing involved using each other to experiment & learn on. Educational symbiosis. We'd been doing it for about two months. I had been learning bass on the bottom of a guitar, my old lady was learning slide guitar on Burns, and Freddy was learning to play with other people. Research! Any scientist can tell you research is mainly trying out all kinds of stuff, most of which won't work. You learn faster if mistakes are cool . . .

So we roll along, riding the wheel with an infinite number of spokes (wheels on fire), studying Music, Relationships, Science, Business, Kicks, Mathematics & Religion—at gunpoint . . .

And the songs are getting recorded—our songs are mainly pretty happy, good feeling songs. By the fifth one B.M. was smiling.

I had been mainly worrying about my old lady, because protecting her is my job, but when I'd look at her, she'd just smile. Freddy was doing okay, only he sure made a lot of mistakes. And I usually feel all right when I'm playing music.

So B.M. puts down his gun & starts to dance. And the tape gets finished, & I talk to B.M., whose name is Frankie.

"I always wanted to play music, but I never could," says Frankie, "but I love to dance."

I'm throwing the old mirror at him.

"I've never been able to dance, myself. I've always envied people who did."

Frankie grabs my arm. "Look, before you go you gotta watch me pantomime & Freddy has to play guitar. We've got a couple things worked out."

Freddy plays & narrates & Frankie pantomimes. They're very tight, I was surprised. Frankie had explained the two bits we did were not his. They both had the theme of having it, losing it, needing it to cope with an emergency, and getting it back. I enjoyed them thoroughly.

So finally we split & we're in the elevator & my old lady says, "I always wanted to play fastest gun in the west."

"Jesus," I said, "was I scared."

"You didn't look scared," she said.

"I didn't dare look scared as long as he had that revolver."

"What revolver?" she asked. I told her what revolver.

"How strange," she said. "I looked at him several times while we were playing & all I saw was an unarmed man."

Walter Breen

APOLLO AND DIONYSUS

To say that every trip is different can too easily be not only one of the most innumerable head clichés, but too often also a way of evading any attempt to understand in depth just what does happen on a major psychedelic experience—acid, mescaline, psilocybin, STP, etc. So far as I know, to date only Tim Leary has published anything really profound among would-be analyses of trip experience. The rest have for the most part produced either mere collections of case histories, catalogues of retinal circus visions, or descriptions of individual trips emphasizing the non-repeatable differences rather than the elements common to all. That is just about as useful as cataloguing cloud shapes.

If we are to make any sense out of the way in which music of any kind relates to trips (drug or nondrug), we have to understand first in what way trips resemble each other. This means that we need a new language to provide at least a reasonable analogy for describing them, since ordinary language obviously isn't enough and poetry could at best suggest some of the unique nonrepeatable features (aside from Tim's *Psychedelic Prayers*). The language for describing transcendent experiences has to be something almost equally unusual with the trips. Tim had to draw on Hindu, Indian Buddhist and Tibetan mystical systems for his own group of concepts. We won't need those here because the analysis I am trying to make has a different purpose and a different direction. If we compare a trip to a pie, Tim's analysis is most nearly that of a chemist, mine perhaps more nearly that of a Chinese pastry baker trying to reconstruct the recipe by taste alone.

Before getting down to music and how it can stimulate or affect trips, and what results it produces, we may as well consider two basic types of experience common to music and religion, which are at the same time also two basic components of a psychedelic trip. These are what Nietzsche, in *The Birth of Tragedy*, calls Apollo and Dionysus.

It is at the moment unimportant whether we refer to Apollo and Dionysus as cosmic forces, archetypes, gods, ideals, universal processes, energy levels, or paths to enlightenment. All such verbal labels are at best shadows, attempts to suggest an experience which might have been shared by you and me, attempts to adumbrate something genuinely larger than life, something of which we partake only in shallow sips lest we choke or drown, something quite beyond ordinary language's capacities. Whatever its context, any such experience is by definition transcendent; and insofar as it is associated with some alteration of consciousness (specifically with alteration in perceiving time, space, surroundings and self), it is correctly identified as psychedelic.

The ecstasy of Apollo is that of union ("tuning in") with the overriding pattern of order and design unfolding in the universe. One witnesses or even cooperates in creation of emergent pattern, of order out of chaos; one delights in the essential rightness, appropriateness, completeness, sheer excellence of something in itself, in the embracing of something exquisitely beautiful and worth knowing and grokking for its own sake. "Behold, I make all things new." Becoming part of this preeminent harmony is standing outside oneself—which is what the word ecstasy, ekstasis, actually means.

The touch of Apollo can be identified in the sense of wonder at its highest intensity. This is an essentially childlike trait ("Unless ye become as little children . . .") and it is correctly recognized that undamaged youngsters are naturally turned on. More specifically, the presence of Apollo is strong in experiences of sudden enlightenment, the Gestaltists' "Aha!" experiences, Maslowian peaks, in which one suddenly integrates what had seemed disparate, one sees how everything fits into a previously unrecognized pattern, one knows what it is all about. Examples in visual art include things like Pavel Tchelitchev's *Hide and Seek*, which is a lyrical evocation of the theme of the unity of all life and its cyclical rebirths. Examples in music are uncommon, but two that immediately come to mind are the slow movement of Mahler's *Fourth Symphony* (considered in context of the whole) and the climaxes of Ernest Bloch's *Schelomo*. (Rock, of course, is primarily Dionysiac.) At least some *satori* experiences are of this kind. It is not enough to say "Now I know what it is all about"—one must actually perceive it, but then words will probably be inadequate to communicate it. The best Japanese haiku, which do manage to convey much sensory-emotional impact in their seventeen syllables, presuppose at least a small taste of Apollo, even as seven *sumi* brushstrokes convey a wintry landscape viewed with the same intense feeling of "Oh, wow!" In another direction, the finger of Apollo can be felt in suddenly waking from mundane perceptions, suddenly being so deeply moved as to react with a gasp or even tears, "surprised by joy," at the sheer beauty of such things as a newly opened flower, the taste of an orange fresh from the tree, a baby, an ancient Greek sealstone, a sunset, a redwood tree or a Schubert song. This type of experience, as intense as it is often too brief, still awaits many who are alas too preoccupied to notice its proximity—and who have till now managed to miss such occasions, their senses or "doors of perception" remaining closed.

The ecstasy of Dionysus is that of being overwhelmed with the sheer glory of motion of what is beyond, being taken over by it, becoming no longer merely human but an instrument of the godhead, a part of the cosmic dance, a tongue of flame in the Sun. Patterns shift and pass away, almost too rapidly to be comprehended, certainly too fast to be communicated; the language of Dionysus is the dithyramb. One delights in the very activity, in the wild dancing (whether internal only or physically overt as well), in having laid down the burden of being human and surrendered to the overmastering cosmic forces.

The touch of Dionysus by and large has been most ambivalently regarded in western civilization. Its faint distorted echo is found in the perpetual search for escape from reality, for temporary respites—amphetamines, alcohol, tranquilizers, narcotics, hallucinogens such as datura stramonium (as distinct from psychedelics). A louder echo is in the often sexualized dancing stimulated by some jazz. Texas barrelhouse pianist-singer Robert Shaw was explicit enough about the latter: "When you listen to what I'm playing, you got to see in your mind all them gals out there swinging their butts and getting the mens excited. Otherwise you ain't got the music rightly understood. I could sit there and throw my hands down and make them gals do anything. I told them when to shake it, and when to hold it back. That's what this music is for." (Quoted on dustjacket of *Texas Barrelhouse Piano*, Almanac 10, 1967.) But this very quality—even aside from the eight-year association of jazzmen with New Orleans "Storyville" whorehouses—contributed to the bad reputation which jazz early received and which it never completely lost among the conventional. The very wildness of the Dionysus experience, today even as in the time of Euripides' King Pentheus, has been felt as a danger to the social order.

Stronger indications of Dionysus are principally religious. Primitive Christian love-feasts (small-scale ecstatic love-ins making participants seem to outsiders like people drunk on new wine) and celebrations of "receiving the Spirit" evidently embodied some such transcendent experience. Even today, on the one hand in Pentecostal and Holiness sects, and on the other in some outposts of the Church of England, there is once again ecstatic dancing and "speaking in tongues"—oddly reminiscent at times of tripping, of whirling dervishes' worship services, and of the "latihan" exercise of Subud initiates. But outside known religious contexts, Dionysiac experiences are usually believed a threat to the ruling minority: wild dancing represents an abandonment of mundane work, and might supposedly result in riots

or total withdrawal ("dropping out") from the prescribed games
or political loyalties. And the very unpredictability of whatever
superhuman force is surrendered to is felt as a peril; in such
topsy-turvy excitement everything falls or flees before the onrush.
This very threat, dimly perceived, is behind some of the opposition to psychedelics. It is also perhaps more inarticulately behind
some of the early opposition to rock-and-roll in the 1950s, as well
as that to much rock now.

Obviously Apollo and Dionysus are not mutually exclusive.
They are in fact less opposites than complementaries, two sides
of the same medallion. It would not be suitable even to call them
two distinctive regions in the same psychedelic spectrum, as
neither one is intrinsically "higher" (in any sense) than the other.
Each has its light and its dark side, each exists in primitive and
more highly developed forms, each manifests many gradations in
intensity and value.

It is too easy, even so, to fall into the essentially Manichean
error of identifying Apollo with intellect, Dionysus with emotion,
and elevating either at the expense of the other. That dualism
misled too many people into too much misery for far too long. A
more accurate view would be that the Apollo and Dionysus
experiences both go beyond intellect and emotion as normally
lived. Intellect and emotion themselves are complements, not
opposites, and accordingly a suitable mnemonic for their relation
in the human condition—as for the Apollo and Dionysus experiences—is the familiar yin-yang.

In experiences generally considered intellectual there is usually some admixture, sooner or later, of emotion; and in more
emotional experiences there is usually at least a possible ground
for intellectual activity, if only after the fact. (Not that many
people actually use the opportunity: "it is not given to man to
love and be wise.") So too in the Apollo experience there is much
quasi-intellectual (really intuitional, global, immediate) apper-
ception of pattern, vitalized by admixture of emotion seemingly
small by comparison though actually well beyond the mundane
norm. And in the Dionysus experience one retains awareness of a
kind of duality or divided consciousness, the selfpoint within

watching what is happening, the remainder of oneself behaving outside one's will as the instrument of the godhead—so that one can later recall in tranquility and perhaps verbalize what has been seen and what has been learned.

In the ecstasy of sexual union with love there is both Apollo and Dionysus, despite popular folklore which makes it the ultimate pure Dionysus kick. Apollo is the aspect of the experience which gives the delight of discovering "under me you so quite new," in the union with beauty, in grokking a personality in depth. Dionysus, of course, is felt in the surrendering of control to the wild swinging (at times involuntary) motions of sex. At the peak a man is no longer merely a man but the representative of all male humanity, of all animal maleness, of the primordial father and impregnator, thrusting toward the ultimate apocalyptic union with his polar complement in the woman who has become for him here and now the representative of all womankind, of the "Eternal Feminine [which] leads us onward," of the Great Mother archetype, of Aphrodite. I am of course describing an ideal occurrence; not nearly all mundane sex even approaches this level. Psychedelic or otherwise transcendent experience through sex is subject matter for another book. (It would draw heavily on Tantra and Alan Watts.) But even below the level of contact with archetypes as just described, the presence of Apollo and Dionysus components in ecstatic sex-love experience can be shown; and this is as it should be, for Apollo and Dionysus are as complementary as are the two partners in such experience.

In much the same way musical performance can have, for the performers, elements of Apollo and Dionysus in different proportions of emphasis. Apollo is more predominant in some classical music, Dionysus more in improvisatory music such as jazz and rock. Ragas in performance manifest both in varying measure according to the rhythmic pattern (Tala) chosen. But regrettably a musician who has lost enough of his Sense of Wonder so that a gig is merely something he is doing to pay rent will be lacking in the Apollo component—let alone Dionysus—and presumably the less capable of communicating either experience to even a turned-on audience; and this is the big pitfall for steadily employed musicians. They go stale and too often are without means to refresh themselves. The danger is less for musicians working in purely improvisatory techniques, still less for musicians who are themselves genuinely turned on. It is not zero even here; the amount of new meanings communicable through improvisation and derived from any single popular tune must remain limited.

On the other hand, the combinations rendered possible through an expanding repertory of pieces and techniques, and through combining these performances with other media in the multisensory experience of a San Francisco style dance-concert, are exponentially increased, and with them the possibilities for some kind of transcendent experience for the audiences. In practice these have more of Dionysus than of Apollo, though both are present. I find it significant that rock is described by some of its practitioners as the next thing to a religious ecstatic experience, and that David Crosby (when he was still with the Byrds) said that he preferred working at dance-concerts to any other context ("In Tune with Positives," interview with Ralph Metzner, in *The Ecstatic Adventure*, Macmillan, N.Y., 1968, p. 301). Metzner, in introducing that same interview, explicitly compared the atmosphere of a Fillmore or Avalon dance-concert to a revival meeting, in contrast to an "entertainment discothèque" such as Arthur's, Shepheard's or the West Village places (*Ibid.*, 296).

Music, poetry, pageantry, dance, and other verbal or non-verbal human patternings of experience can, singly or in combination, contribute to the ecstasy of Apollo or of Dionysus, or both, a fact known since antiquity when such early multimedia presentations formed part of the Greek mystery religions and more publicly part of the Festivals of Dionysus. In the mystery religions, says Robert Graves, they were used to program a Sacred Mushroom trip to tune the worshiper in to a profound mythic or archetypal system; in the nondrug Festivals of Dionysus, they achieved an overwhelming public impact subjectively experienced as purgation, what we would today call cleaning out one's head. Renaissance masques and early Venetian opera lacked the religious emphasis of their Greek congeners, but the impact on audiences appears to have been nearly as profound in some instances. Three hundred years later Wagner was trying for much the same thing on a still larger scale with still more overwhelming techniques, and the Bayreuth presentations of his operas definitely confronted audiences with something much vaster than mundane life. Some devotees appear to have been sent on trips by Wagner's own version of multimedia.

But in the ensuing generations people have had to turn themselves off increasingly, to armor themselves against misery, against overwhelming noises and foul odors of industry-polluted cities. As a result, increasingly extreme catalysts to psychedelic experience became necessary to enable anyone to get off the ground, until finally today we have the couple of dozen chemical keys ranging from the tetrahydrocannabinols all the way to acid and STP. Extensive experience of all these, described everywhere from scholarly journals to the underground papers, shows that in major trips of this kind Apollo and Dionysus experiences are present in high degree, in varying emphases. The sensitizing or turning on, the opening of the doors of perception, the renewed capacity to look at or listen to something as though for the first time, etc., all bespeak Apollo; the "flying" sensations, the shunting back and forth in time, the visits to widely separated regions of the cosmos, etc., all testify to Dionysus.

It has been discovered in the meantime that stimuli associated with acid trips can reactivate or restimulate some trip phenomena when presented in great enough intensity even without the chemical catalyst. An acid trip generates flicker internally; therefore supplying flicker from strobe lights can reactivate that and its other vibratory congeners; the wild colors of retinal circus can be recalled and restimulated by light show people who really know what is happening. Some of the abstract sounds produced internally by acid's stimulation of the auditory cortex resemble "musique concrete" creations realized directly on tape; therefore the latter are included in multimedia presentations. Snatches of remembered music from childhood, often associated with recovery of early memories, show up on trips; therefore similar taped fragments appear in long instrumental breaks by the Beatles, Stones, and other groups till now they threaten to become a cliché of studio rock. Examples can be multiplied to account for every feature of dance-concerts and much recorded rock. The ideas have been in the air for some years now; William Burroughs suggested experiments of this very kind in "Sedative and Consciousness-Expanding Drugs," in *The Marihuana Papers* (ed. David Solomon, Signet, N.Y., 1968, p. 440).

But clearly such experimentation is only at the beginning, as is understanding of psychedelic experience—and psychedelic music—as such. A fuller understanding of Apollo or Dionysus requires knowledge of both. Socrates realized in prison that one of his final tasks must be to learn the music of Dionysus, as he had neglected this side of religious experience too long to his own detriment. We may speculate that the wisdom he showed in the final dialogue (*Phaedo*) was at least in part gained from that late-born knowledge. Appreciation of many things is enhanced by exposure to their complementaries or even their opposites. This even holds true in music; late exposure to farther-out classics and nonwestern music such as ragas has benefited quite a few rock musicians and many devotees, and conversely.

Music known to have psychedelic effects naturally divides or classifies in several ways; the way I choose here is not the expected rock *vs.* non-rock division, but instead where the principal emphasis is, namely on effects comparable to those of the Apollo and Dionysus experiences respectively.

There are two basic types of effect of music on consciousness as distinct from mere memory stimulation or emotional catharsis. The first of these I call *mindstretching*. One is led to follow increasingly detailed, increasingly subtle and often increasingly rapid patterns of fantastic detail, requiring gradual entry into a different time-zone in order to keep up with what is going on. Such shifts of time-zone are themselves an essential part of a trip, and they are quickly followed by one or another form of ecstatic awareness, sometimes by other trip phenomena—specifically sensitization and later on retinal circus. Memories may flood in, sometimes events being relived, etc., though these deeper effects are more rare.

Mindstretching, of course, is the rationale behind the very

prolonged improvised performances of traditional ragas by Indian master musicians of the Tansen tradition. Both Ravi Shankar and the incomparable Ustad Ali Akbar Khan belong to that tradition, and in concert—especially when they are playing to Indian audiences—they normally prolong performance of any given raga to forty or fifty minutes, sometimes still longer. It takes much longer than one record side's worth of close, concentrated attention on such music to begin to experience trip phenomena. If your experience of ragas is confined to records, try to attend a live concert by Ravi or Ali even if you have to travel a couple of hundred miles to get there. You won't be disappointed.

The other psychedelic component in music is variously called *assault* or *impact*. Music principally emphasizing this aspect either insists on a rhythm extremely compelling and eventually matching one's heartbeat and alpha rhythms so that one's normal psychic screens are battered down and one is thrust into another time-zone; or else it confronts one with rapid shifts, crescendi, sensory overloads, etc., requiring entry into another time-zone to integrate as music. Furthermore, it prevents one's paying attention to anything else mundane (in a normal time-zone) while it goes on. There is thus a certain amount of surrender of the ego to outside forces.

Plainly enough, mindstretching tends to emphasize the Apollo experience, assault the Dionysus. This is the basic key to manipulating music for psychedelic effect.

Examples of nearly pure mindstretching are readily available: ragas, as earlier mentioned (though there is some Dionysus in the extremely rapid jhalas which climax jors and gats in many raga performances); some flamenco guitar performances; theme-and-doubles variations by some Renaissance lutenists; Balinese gamelans; some classical koto solos.

Examples of nearly pure assault are common enough in rock so that one need only mention a few groups who have experimented deliberately in this direction: Beatles, Byrds, Doors, the Who, the Grateful Dead, Clear Light, Traffic, Jimi Hendrix, etc. In other systems pure assault is less common, though some of the most powerful jazz belongs here, as does some "musique concrete." A very famous example in classical music, impossible to reproduce in a home recording because of the spatial effects and volume which would fail to come across on any existing hifi equipment, is the "Tuba mirum" from the Berlioz *Requiem.* Chorus members have repeatedly reported "flying" in live performance or rehearsal when the four brass choirs enter at this point. When the work was premiered, over a hundred years ago, audiences were stunned speechless. Berlioz was trying to depict the trumpet of Gabriel on Judgment Day—enough to wake the dead—and the sheer volume of sound literally surrounding the audience (and the chorus, soloists and orchestra) was unprecedented. It was in fact not equaled before the Grateful Dead; and in some ways it goes beyond them, as there is a richness of tone in live brass in a huge hall transcending that produced by a handful of electronically amplified instruments in a smaller hall. Also, the sheer spatial effect at 360 degrees of diverse sounds coming from brass choirs deployed around the auditorium is well beyond that which can be produced by a single group at one end of the Fillmore even if its manager has put up extra speakers for each instrumentalist. (Rock musicians might do well to experiment in this direction.)

Flicker-stimulating sounds in purely electronic music or "musique concrete" also belong to Dionysus or tend to bring on the Dionysus component of psychedelic experience, when they succeed in affecting consciousness at all. Some of the earlier experiments of this kind produced bad-trip phenomena, giving taped sonic experience a bad name for being full of sirens, nightmares, and cataclysms. The emotional range appears to have been fortunately broadened since.

More common in the Euro-American tradition, perhaps, than pure mindstretching or pure assault, are combinations of both. After all, a trip comprises Apollo and Dionysus. The names of Wagner, Mahler, Scriabin and Alan Hovhaness immediately come to mind, and it is noteworthy that Scriabin explicitly planned for his last works a multimedia presentation—specifically, light shows programmed by a "color organ" of his own invention. But to date nobody in professional music, so far as I know, has systematically explored these techniques. Rock people often take it for granted that the light show technicians will be familiar enough with their type of sound to choose and mix the visual presentations appropriately—not always is this the case, regrettably. Nor do many rock musicians attempt to do any mindstretching, preferring instead to rely for psychedelic effect on assault, ambience and contact highs. Coordination of music and light shows with live pantomime or the like is still only at its beginning, as is the integration of light shows with other types of music. There also needs to be more experimentation in timing and contrasts. Some musical numbers, classical, jazz and rock alike, show that a psychedelic effect was intended but they fail to produce it because they are too brief. It takes time to go up, to allow the cortical stimulation to spread out and reinforce itself by positive feedback. Early recognition of this fact may have underlain the prolongation of ragas in concert performance, and it was almost certainly the basis of prolonged instrumental breaks in much of the more advanced rock. Forty minutes of increasingly far-out improvisation is not too much, even on records. And if words are to be an important part of a rock number, one might well suggest that they not be indistinctly mouthed or allowed to drown in instrumental sound; the straining to understand them can sometimes be a bringdown, and if they are not important enough to be heard they hardly contribute to the total effect.

Even granting that to date there has not been a single piece of music produced which will be a turn-on for everyone, still we may be not too many years away from the discovery of techniques which will enable musicians to evoke psychedelic effects at will in even the straightest audiences.

WHY WON'T TEACHERS
TEACH ROCK?
SOME ANSWERS

To the Editor:

Rock music has not gone un-heard by the nation's music educa-tors, as Allen Hughes claims, any more than grade-C Westerns have gone unseen by the nation's movie critics. Many of us have protected our ears and hoped it would go away. It is not only "raucous and out of tune" but it lacks melodic variety, harmonic interest, dy-namic gradations and rhythmic originality. We have believed that our function as teachers was to introduce and foster the highest level of music, not the lowest. Rock music requires practically no training, because of its extreme simplicity, to be performed on the folk level.

But there *is* a place in the sec-ondary school curriculum for an art (?) form which appeals to so many teen-agers, just as there is a place for the examination of the appeal of comic books in language arts classes. First, I have used rock as motivation for the mastery of instrumental techniques and theory. Second, and even more important, a careful and disinter-ested examination of rock music reveals its shortcomings and leads to an appreciation of higher forms of music. There is bad rock and there is worse rock, and its prac-titioners should be able to dis-criminate.

Perhaps eventually from today's rock there will grow a true and original art form. More likely, the very respectability rock music would achieve by its general in-clusion in the curriculum might well cause its demise as a popular instrument of adolescent rebellion. The one danger of this highly-to-be-desired end would be this:

what even more repulsive outlet might take its place?

To the Editor:

Looking back on several years of music lessons (my own, those of my brothers and sister and those of many friends) it is my feeling that it is not the fault of music educators or their students that has led to the all but total lack of musical education available in rock music or almost any form of popular music, for that matter. Nor is it the fault of the thousands of young prodigies who demand such instruction.

It is, as far as I can tell, almost the total responsibility of a parental syndrome, among those parents who can afford music lessons for their children, which is based on the premise that if the kid is going to have good money spent on his music lessons, then he is going to learn good music.

Many were the times that I was told that if I wanted to play popular music on my clarinet I could go out and earn the money for the lessons or else stop taking lessons, but "I [my father] am paying for those lessons and you are not going to stop taking them."

To the Editor:

Let me give you some reasons why I, as a Music Departmental Chairman in the New York City High Schools, would not teach nor permit the teaching of "rock" in my classes.

I have always believed it to be the prime and major function of the school to open the minds of children to things above and beyond the meretricious and the temporal. In my fifty-odd years' association with music, twenty of which were spent in the profession, I have witnessed the passing of many musical fancies—ragtime, swing, blues, Dixieland, modern jazz and so on. They came and went as they always will come and go. Why, then, should I waste the taxpayers' money, the children's time and my energies teaching something which they could easily learn without my intervention— something about which, in all probability, they already know as much as there is to know?

The presumption that composers could learn something from jazz and rock is pure nonsense. Technically, these idioms are about fifty years behind the times. You will pardon me for adding that I consider myself pragmatically, academically and chronologically qualified to make that statement.

To the Editor:

As a music teacher of eleventh and twelfth grade high school students, I have asked myself the same question with which Allen Hughes ended his article: "Can music educators get along without rock?" While I might say that a music educator cannot and should not get along completely without rock, I am compelled to ask if today's students should be asked to get along with *only* rock.

In my opinion, the word "relevance" is the most overused word in educational jargon. It is precisely because of this emphasis on relevance that most of our children have little interest in the world that existed before they were born, as if to suggest that the ideas and attitudes they now espouse developed overnight. The same applies to music. Take away the rock beat and they are like three-year-olds whose "security blankets" have been taken away.

Further, they have little realization of the roots of the very music they embrace. Folk music for them is some guy (or girl) with long hair singing a protest song with a guitar accompaniment. They have not the slightest notion of the function of folk music in the daily lives of people around the world.

The large majority of my students have never been to a ballet, an opera or a concert and have no idea of the training and dedication involved in performing or composing. What do you tell a child who thinks Renata Tebaldi's singing sounds like screaming but thinks nothing of having her ear drums pounded by some of the decibels rock groups produce?

Must our children go through life without any understanding of the musical genius of the past? If

so, then let's stop teaching Shakespeare, Rembrandt or anything else that our children do not feel is "relevant." Let's not develop their sensitivity to other kinds of music, art and literature.

Unfortunately, too many teachers have "copped out." Well, I haven't—not yet, anyway.

To the Editor:

It can be agreed that rock is what the public (and not only the teen-agers) demands. Many of this summer's music festivals which feature our fine orchestras have been trying to bail themselves out of financial trouble by presenting additional concerts of pop and rock performers.

Educators need not ignore rock music's presence since it is relevant to our time, but is it valid? The educator has a perfectly sound (no pun intended) subject with the "classics" and "serious" music.

It is not the educator's job to present what his pupils want but to educate them to the "finer things in life." It is the educator's job to develop an interest, understanding and, ultimately, an appreciation of "serious music." One hopes that, in the future (if the educator does his job), the Philadelphia Orchestra will have enough public following so that it will not need The Association and The Fifth Dimension to make up the box-office deficit at the Saratoga Performing Arts Center.

To the Editor:

The conflict which exists in music education stems from those teachers who have been inadequately prepared to meet relevant needs in the schools. We play and sing the folk music of many countries. Somehow, we have neglected to see that American popular music is really the folk music of the large urban centers. Like other folk forms in our culture, it is related to the daily living of the people. If we can come to understand this music, from its crudest to its most sophisticated styles and forms, as another type of folk expression, it begins to take on new meaning for music educators.

Students with an interest in popular music should be encouraged to experiment with sound. Under the guidance of competent teachers, they can be taught to evaluate and improve their musicianship. Many of them make very exciting music without us. We should be able to set up a program where they can do even better with us. Interested, involved teachers can lead pupils to see that the rules for good musicianship apply here, also. The teachers who capitalize on the interest and excitement of the students can bring a group further ahead in the direction of greater sophistication, musicality and growth.

But most of our college and teacher training institutions certainly have not prepared potential teachers to organize popular music activities, and most teacher applicants are not tested for abilities along these lines. Teacher training institutions prepare applicants to teach concert music, and do little to equip them for teaching students who have been culturally deprived and underprivileged. It is unrealistic to send these teachers into music classrooms.

It is never too late to start correcting the situation. Let's get a large variety of music activities going, including rock. But let's make sure that we know where we are going. Let every student beware! We aim, eventually, to make better musicians of them, no matter where they plan to make music, in a neighborhood night spot or the New York Philharmonic.

To the Editor:

Allen Hughes's significant article points to a basic fault of most music educators in this country: our deliberate and insulting turning a deaf ear to the message rock and our young people are trying to tell us. Our excuse is the loudness of their music—and it is loud! The fact is, we sense the message that our teaching is out-of-date; we fear that it is and so we conveniently ignore rock.

We music teachers lose much by refusing to study the rock revolution. The flourishing of rock outside the school with little or no instruction demonstrates some exciting possibilities. First, we are *not* teaching musical know-nothings. In giving the respect to rock music that it deserves, we are giving respect to the students' good taste.

Finally, and most important, let us teachers lead in giving credit where credit is due and acknowledge that the source of rock is black culture. It is not enough in 1969 to teach spirituals or even the history of jazz. To many blacks, all that is in the past; rock is now. It is important for us to concede this for ourselves as well as for our students because it is only in the black ghetto that the basic changes in music education can be initiated. For the music teacher in the black ghetto is going to be forced to learn from his students as well as teach them.

To the Editor:

How does it happen that almost every writer for The Time's Sunday Arts and Leisure Section seems to have some kind of hang-up about looking at everything in terms of color—black and white (I mean race, not the TV picture tube). The complex seems to go pretty deep, because for some reason the b in black is usually capital B. The w in white is always small w, of course.

The latest sad example is Richard Goldstein's review of Elvis Presley's appearance in Las Vegas, titled "A White Boy with Black Hips." One wonders when the secret transplant took place. In the critics' headlong rush to be included among those who wish to be patted upon the back by the black ministers of information, whose dedication, it appears, is to convince us all that everything beautiful was first invented by blacks, and *is* black (Black) and everything ugly, banal, hypocritical, vicious, was invented by and is white, they have cast aside all pretense of even trying to use their own common sense.

I have been living in this country for almost fifty years, and I have yet to see any man, black or white, move his hips or any part of his body quite the way Elvis moves his hips and body. It would be just too much for Mr. Goldstein to credit Mr. Presley for moving in the way he does because of Elvis's marvelous feel for the music he performs. Mr. Goldstein seems to feel that to be a critic you must look for a race angle in everything.

Actually, Elvis's hip-swinging, if derived from *anyone's* previous efforts, is merely akin to what female dancers in America have been doing for a long, long time; particularly the interpretive dancers. Even so, Elvis has a grace and exciting flair all his own in his movements that set them apart from the hip movements of the girls.

Why did he choose a Black

(capital B) group to back him up, someone asked at Elvis's press conference (writes Mr. Goldstein). "Because they help to give me my feel," answers Elvis.

One is of course supposed to be convinced by that question and answer that there cannot possibly be any really good white groups around capable of generating the necessary "feel" for a white boy with Black hips.

There are still some people, though, who have resisted this brainwashing. Somehow, it seems to be a fact proven by watching any and all entertainers perform, whether black, Black, or white, that none of them move their hips like Presley at all. Watch James Brown. You see he has a movement of his own. Watch Wilson Pickett. He has his own movement. Watch Solomon Burke, and see that it resembles Brown or Pickett not at all. Watch Sly of the Family Stone. You see a different movement.

Then watch Elvis, and you will see that he is just Elvis. A dancer's hips, yes! Black, green, red, or yellow hips, no. It has nothing to do with race. It's about time The Times's Arts and Leisure critics started estimating an artist, or a show, on its merits and got out of the race rut.

Marc Eliot

"THIS, THEN, IS THE DEATH
OF THE AMERICAN"

*An account of
the Phil Ochs concert
at the Westbury Music Fair,
August 4, 1969*

The liner notes on the back of *Rehearsals for Retirement* begin, "This then is the death of the American/imprisoned by his paranoia." At Westbury, the funeral was held without Gypsy ritual, or religious sentiment.

Now he wanders unarmed, and the forty-year-olds can take their children to see him backstage, to argue with him, to put him down by tolerating his obscenities, and to force him to delve into himself when confronted with the question, "Yes, but what do you want the kids to do?"

He wants them to listen to him. Yet the old can't listen, because it isn't enough. The young can't listen, because it isn't pretty enough. His straining voice doesn't bind the Marxists and build them for combat anymore. It shows what will happen to you, young man, should you one day forsake your parents when they no longer "allow/that when I've got something to say, sir, I'm going to say it now."

It's 7:10, fifty minutes to concert. The kids are milling about Westbury, that tent (camp?) on the Island. Billboards boast Robert Goulet, Steve and Eydie, Mickey Rooney; but no folk singer, no Phil Ochs, no Monday. Can it be, everybody wonders, is it, the wrong night? The ticket sellers seem to have something happening this evening. But Mickey Rooney?

The earlier rain has dampened the grounds, and the parking lot is the last slog to go through to see him. Several people want to get his autograph. One young man waits to hand him some of his own poetry.

A cab pulls up, and out pops the American.

Smiling, lazy long hair, ruined brown suede jacket casually slung into his arms, and those same old black pants.

"Am I supposed to be here tonight?" The young man with the poetry is tempted to say, "It looks that way" but as the blur comes into focus, it is Ochs himself asking the question. The boy affirms with, "I hope so."

"I didn't see any signs. Maybe I'm Mickey Rooney."

The young man smiles at Ochs, and then blurts out, "I have some poetry, and a letter for you."

"Good. Where is the manager's office? Am I here tonight?"

"I have some tickets." He takes them out, but there isn't any name on them. They aren't real tickets; just computerized toothpicks.

Both of them now take his guitar, his overnight kit, and a green shirt that will not be worn, into the tent.

Inside, he is recognized by a few kids, and after looking as if he won't, he hesitantly signs autographs. Then he goes into the arena.

Ochs stands on the stage and circles about slowly, wondering how the show will go. He then starts another assault of questions on his new companion of the night, the young poet, who is still with him.

"Is it sold out? Do you think it will be a sellout? Do you think it will be the same audience as Carnegie? What did you think of 'All Quiet on the Western Front'? They say I'm copping out with that one. They'll think the same thing when they hear the new one tonight, 'There Are No More Songs.' I wrote it in two days, as I was coming to New York." He grins. "Every time I come to New York, I write a song. The same thing happened at Carnegie . . ."

The boy says that he couldn't hear all the words at Carnegie. This surprises Ochs, and he asks what was wrong. The boy tells him that there was too much bass in their sound system. He was sitting down-stage left, about fifteen rows into the audience, and he missed a lot of the words. So did his girlfriend.

Ochs puts down his gear and then walks around his dressing room; the one that has Mickey Rooney's name on it. There's a television, a sofa, and a motel bathroom.

"Let's get a drink," he suggests, and the two of them go to a local bowling alley, along the road, and walk into the bar. It's now seven thirty, just one half hour to showtime, and Ochs begins his preparation. He has four gins to the time of the boy's one. He shoots them down, not even bothering to be romantic about it anymore. He talks about Dylan with the young man, and laughs surprisingly when he hears him say that *John Wesley Harding* has, at least, a good cover. Ochs is redeemed for the moment. He still carries the burden of being the best. He confesses that he hasn't slept in two days. "I was in bed for sixteen hours, and I couldn't sleep. That's the worst kind of insomnia. That's when I wrote this song . . ."

Showtime.

The audience is spotty, with many empty seats. Maybe the show won't sell out. Maybe they all think that the curtain is eight thirty, and not eight. There wasn't a hell of a lot of publicity. No radio coverage. No air-play in New York. No TV exposure. Network TV almost once, this very week, but nothing.

The lights go out, and Ochs ramps up an aisle, to already thick applause. His people are here tonight. He won't say anything now, his music will speak for him. These kids want to watch him make an album. They want to squeeze their girlfriends' arms on that line in "Changes" that makes them all feel so sexy and dangerous. A few of them hope he won't sing "Highwayman" again as he begins its intro.

A few older people can be seen in the audience. It appears to be the youngest audience yet for one of his concerts. "I've heard that every time I give a concert. It's always supposed to be my youngest audience." Ochs doesn't appear to see anyone, not even the girl that gets ejected for taking his picture, right there in the first row. Everyone else sees it though, and it gets its moment of mumble throughout the tent. Someone says that if it had happened at Carnegie there would have been a riot. At Westbury the girl surrenders and returns to her seat without her camera, without Ochs even noticing.

Six lines into the concert he is faltering. His lines in "Bells" abort, and he is transposing them with the last stanza. Does he give a damn? It cost him twenty-four dollars to get out to Westbury by cab from Houston Street. No tip for the driver. "It was a flat fee we decided on. He looked it up in a book. I don't know if he took me or not."

The first half of the concert is, in Och's words, "the straight Marxist approach. All the crowd pleasers. 'I'm Going To Say It Now,' 'Is There Anybody Here,' 'Rhythms of Revolution.' I didn't do 'When I'm Gone' because I did it at Carnegie. I did 'Say It Now' instead." Yet during his best-known song, "I Ain't Marching Anymore," he forgets, and substitutes the start of the last stanza, instead of the second, and has to stop and go back. There is another round of encouragement from the audience. The song gets the first standing ovation of the night, and Ochs has to laugh to himself. It has to be inside of him, punching its way into his brain; "What if I was really on tonight, could I make them sit and listen, without a sound? Could I make them walk out, angry? Angry enough?"

Another nervous moment during "Say It Now"—every high note is greeted by the empty breath of a missing voice. Three or four strident notes come, and then three vacant ones in one line. Heads turn all around the arena. Ochs acknowledges, and parries with, "I could hit those notes in my younger days." He could hit those notes in his younger days. At twenty-eight, he sees them at a widening distance, evaporating, along with his balls talent, his thrilling shirtsleeves, and his cocky body. Now his stomach is hopelessly over his belt, filled with the alcohol of his adversaries, and he doesn't seem to give a damn. Let me get fat and die. It's their loss.

He ends the first half early, and is back in his dressing room. He is trying to get his "old Gibson" in tune. It kept on getting flat during the concert. He had to stop and tune it at least six times. The girls in the audience found it sexy; the boys, confusing.

The second half is different. "I went to the lyrical songs. I thought I had them in the first half. I wasn't sure how they responded to the second half. Did you like the John Wayne bit? Look"—he is recapping now, one of his bits from the concert, back in a New York apartment he still maintains—"when I was in France, someone told me that John Wayne said he was making the *Green Berets* in response to the music of Joan Baez and Phil Ochs. I was thrilled; Wayne's one of my childhood idols."

He goes to his "A&M" period, and the younger audience seems more at home with this music, knowing it, letting the words work. Ochs's voice doesn't strain now as much, and he settles into the euphoric security of his lyrics.

He has them now. Suddenly, he's proven legend, roaming from "Bound for Glory" to "Rehearsals for Retirement." He lives and breathes, endlessly, these same embattled songs, these same melodies, and don't they all sound alike anyway. He goes to his roots, so there is nothing to turn around and discover missing. He has respect for his older music, even though later in the evening the mention of a few of the earlier titles will bring a broad smile to his face, as if he was seeing his bare soul on a bear rug.

He has given someone in the audience his book to hold, which has the lyrics of "When in Rome" in it. He tells the boy to follow the lines, in case he forgets them. "It was either 'Rome' or the 'Crucifixion,'" he explains later, when he recounts how he rehearsed the program on the way to Westbury in the cab. He had to memorize all the songs, even those he hadn't sung in over a year ("Rome"), and he was definitely getting uptight about the whole evening. He was sure he was going to "sleep through the entire evening, or wake up around nine."

"I can't sleep on airplanes."

Yet when he forgets the lyrics to "Rome," it is in the last stanza, and the boy yells out, "back . . ." to get him on again. The applause is the kind that a pitcher gets after giving up six runs during a two-out rally and then finally throwing a strike, right down the middle.

The smattering is shattering.

The concert ends with a new piece, called "No More Songs." It is disturbingly foreboding. It tells of the moment in which

Ochs has now found himself—without anything left to say. This negative expression becomes in itself a positive statement, a new song, and he therefore finds himself at the end of a cycle, on the start of a circle.

Concert over, and the star clings to the "I can't go on" syndrome during the aftermath, when he can savor his small battle. Ironically, in his idiom he is now like Ché: tired, with mountain fatigue, pulsating inevitably toward a kind of death. While Fidel Dylan is finding new life in other directions, Ochs is dying in Argentina, or Long Island, with unimportant victories.

"How did you like it? What did you think of the last song? They're going to say I've copped out, right?" That unforgettable smile of his crosses his body as he absorbs a quart of Tanqueray, with little help from his friends. In the dressing room, there are no groupies looking for him. There is an older couple who once took some photos of him and who now follow him around, to be able to stand in his dressing room and stare at the man, and stare at the man, while he drinks and asks questions. "How did you like . . ."

"I never know what to say about these things . . ." they say, awkwardly inadequate.

"Say what you think."

"I . . . really don't know . . . you really can't say . . ."

He goes outside, and gives autographs. There are two women there who are telling him that his depression is coming because he's nearing thirty. "But don't worry, Phil. My husband says that you get over it in a year or two."

Another girl asks for his autograph on her shirt. He doesn't want to, but fuck it, give it to her. He signs, and there is a strange indifference about the act; no fainting, no screaming, no touch me addicts. It's done, and he goes on. The boy with the poetry has offered Ochs a lift home. He accepts, and promises to read the poetry. While this is happening, the manager is trying to clear the place out. Ochs won't give up. He wants to meet everyone, talk to all of them. One young man from the Mailer-Breslin campaign says something that catches his ear, and it means the boy will ride home in the car, and discuss politics, endlessly, with

Phil. Phil retires outside, and argues middle age with a middle-aged man. He has the kids with him, but one older boy finally snorts "shit" and leaves.

Back to New York in the riotous downpour; Ochs is still in politics. He believes that the cancer of Germany is now the cancer of America, and therefore the moonshot is a diseased crime. He really digs the film *True Grit.* "Here's Wayne, old, fat, one-eyed, and murderous. He shoots these rats, after doing a fantastic scene, for no other reason than he just doesn't like them. Beautiful. Did you know that when he wanted to make the *Green Berets* the big film co. that was supposedly behind him was afraid to invest in the movie because they thought it would lose money? Wayne, the country, the military, the economy's best friend, gets slapped in the face by his own comrades. You just can't hate the man!"

He says of L.A., "This is America. If I had a wounded Viet-Cong, and he asked me, 'What are you here for, in my country, fighting, I want to know what America is' I would put him in L.A. You don't breathe carbon monoxide, you breathe jet exhaust. You can hear the cops giving testimony. 'I pulled my gun, and shot him in the left shoulder. The first bullet entered his left shoulder. The second bullet pierced his heart. It appeared the suspect had a weapon in his hand, and later on it was discovered to be a piece of paper . . .'

"Yeah, I still can't get on TV. I was supposed to be on the Dick Cavett show. You know, I was coming in for Westbury, and they got in touch with me. I couldn't believe it. Then, well, it just didn't happen, and that was that. No Dick Cavett. The man in charge of casting just wasn't in this week and was having messages taken."

Later, back on Houston Street, he will say that sure, they're giving Joan a chance, letting her appear on TV. "But what does she sing? 'Stewball'?"

While he performs at Westbury, Baez is on the Dick Cavett show, network, prime time, across the country.

He says that they just won't touch him, that his music is still too strong, and they're still too scared. He did get on some local shows in the midwest and said that Johnson was a traitor. "Maybe they don't want the embarrassment of having to blip something out."

He decides that he wants a drink, and goes over to the Gaslight. It's closed. The Village is closed. He doesn't even recognize it. Like every trip before, it's gone even farther away than he would have believed. He winds up in the Hip-Bagel going into the third day without sleeping. He has a steak and two root beers. He is polite to the Asian waitress, and she smiles in appreciation. He looks around, crinkled up in the corner, and listens to the loud jazz on the jukebox, and says sadly, "It's like a piece of L.A."

When he leaves, he is a little fuller, and still walking with that mope of his, hoping to see somebody, anybody, in the street. Two spade cats come up and ask him for a dime. He walks away from them, disgusted by them.

Then he is in front of his building. It's the start of the third day. That third day. Strange things happen when he comes to New York. Who knows, maybe another song. He can't believe that he got through the concert. "It was important." Somebody, in a college campus next winter, when the snow has effectively seized the buildings, will discover a roommate's record collection, and will hear, "I'm Going To Say It Now" for the first time. Who is this Phil Ochs, he will ask. Does he write his own stuff? Is he still around? Are there any more songs?

WHAT MOTHERFUCKIN HEAVIES

1. Teleological ontology. Cyclic forms. The first is last and the middle too. Mythological fantasies of all ages, but especially the violent. Aggressive hostility in search of heightened hedonism. A form move that incorporates all into their *corpus operis, corpus delecti.* Demonic, satanic, swinish now in their advanced years. Decadence from the divine Marquis. At their press conference a string quartet where a guillotine would have been more appropriate.

2. Mick was born on July 26, 1944, the eldest of two sons, to Physical Education lecturer Joe Jagger and his wife, Eva. He was educated at Dartford Grammar School, Kent, and then spent two years at the London School of Economics before quitting to be a full-time rolling stone.

3. Like Mick Jagger, Keith was born in Dartford, Kent. He was the only son of Bert and Doris Richards and was born to them December 18, 1944. After completing his secondary education with no great enthusiasm, he moved to London and immediately immersed himself in the music scene.

Keith lives near Mick, in Chelsea, where they both own Georgian houses.

4. Is another Kent-born Stone. He was one of five children raised by William and Kathleen Wyman in Lewisham. He is twenty-eight years old and, before joining the Stones as their bass player, was a pupil of Beckenham Grammar School and a member of various local groups playing hybrids of blues, rock, and jazz.

A confirmed photographer, Bill lives in the country, in a fourteenth-century mansion formerly used as a monastery, complete with a moat he promises to stock with alligators one day. He has a son, Stephen, who is seven years old.

5. Is the drumming Stone. Born in Islington, North London, on June 2, 1942, to Charles and Lilly Watts. He was educated at Tylers Croft School, and graduated into the jazz/blues world in his teens.

Very happily married to his sculptress wife Shirley, Charlie is another country fanatic and owns an estate in Sussex. His house was built by the Archbishop of Canterbury, and was formerly owned by England's Chief Justice.

6. The youngest Stone, in every sense of the word, Mick Taylor, joined the group in July 1969.

Born on January 17, 1949, in Welwyn, Garden City, Hertfordshire, Mick was educated at Onslow Secondary Modern School, quit at fifteen, and started work with a local firm as an artist/engraver. He joined a local group called The Gods, and one night debuted with John Mayall when Mayall's then lead guitarist Eric Clapton failed to turn up at a gig. A few months later Mayall was looking for a new lead player, remembered Mick, and asked him to join.

7. The only one whose parents were musically inclined, he was born on February 28, 1944, in Cheltenham. An itinerant musician, he was the soul of the group. He met a tragic death on July 2, 1969.

8. The Rolling Stones. Long-haired, way out, uninhibited, tempestuous, avant-garde, blue or bluesy, filthy, subversive, sensuous, sensual, sexual, effeminate, beautiful. Five reflections of

today's children; no one who has ever listened to the group is without an opinion on their value, or lack thereof.

9. Five best Stones singles of all time and even longer: "Stoned" b/w "I Wanna Be Your Man"; "(I Can't Get No) Satisfaction" b/w "The Under Assistant West Coast Promotion Man"; "Have You Seen Your Mother, Baby Standing in the Shadow?" b/w "Who's Driving My Plane"; "Dandelion" b/w "We Love You"; "Jumpin' Jack Flash" b/w "Child of the Moon."

10. How did they get their name? Many stories. Mick Jagger wanted to honor his dear departed sainted uncle Roland Stoneham, a famous whipmaster in the town of Heidenheim. Another tale states that in a vision Brian saw the story of Sisyphus and decided that that had to form the basis of the group's future music. A tale told by Keith is that he was flipping through Bartlett's one day and hit upon the famous adage. The pedestrian claim they took it from a Muddy Waters song.

11. Ten best album cuts by length of playing time: "Surprise, Surprise"; "What to Do"; "Singer Not the Song"; "King Bee"; "Ride On, Baby"; "Sittin' On a Fence"; "I Can't Be Satisfied"; "Walking the Dog"; "It's All Over Now"; "Goin' Home."

12. "Are you a mod or a rocker?"
    "Neither, I'm a mocker."
    "I'm a rod."
    Perhaps that best sums up the difference between the two groups.

13. Van Morrison could've done it. As good a singer, and just as raunchy, he didn't have the life style. And when people talk about the sociology of rock, it's no new experience. The Stones embodied their songs and fantasies; that's what made them a big move. At the time they seemed successors to the fast-dying beatnik cult, but they were more and they knew it. Dylan has had to change images constantly; they've kept the same one and still managed to be relevant despite all the changes we went through this past decade. In this manner they can impose form on material and make it uniformly brilliant, allowing variation to be understated, and hence more effective.

14.

DEAR EDITOR,

Your reviewer has his head up his ass with regards to the latest Beatles and Stones albums . . . Ah c'mon, I mean it's cool to like the Stones, but you don't really listen to their albums do you? Mere dull trash. Sloppy, they can't play. Mick Jagger on harp, ho ho. And Watts has to be the worst drummer in rock. Wyman, why Wyman hasn't played but one bass line in seven years. The Beatles on the other hand are brilliant musicians. Where Ginger Baker is excessive, Ringo Starr has always been economical. Harrison's leads are the most melodic riffs coming out of England, a country saturated with superstar blues guitarists who don't even know what blues is all about. And the divine Lennon and McCartney—why, they're just the most together team of songwriters this century has seen. They are innovative geniuses who have introduced the finer elements of avant-garde, twentieth-century composition into music. On the third cut, notice the excellent reference to Varese's *Poème Electronique*. And in their thirteen-minute masterpiece, they employ techniques introduced by Cage, Stockhausen, Prokofiev, Berlioz and Gershwin. One is forced to conclude that your reviewer is a pompous ass who hasn't ever listened to the Beatles or the great masters.

Yours musically,
JOHN LOGAN (age 7)

15. Their first five albums are an education in rhythm and blues. The eclectic knowledge displayed on these albums would knock even such an expert as Jerry Wexler out, and indeed the Stones are one of his favorite groups. Using material from such greats as Buddy Holly, Chuck Berry, Muddy Waters, Howlin Wolf, Garrett Strong, Jimmy Reed, Willie Dixon, Slim Harpo, Marvin Gaye, Valentinos, Drifters, Coasters, Wilson Pickett, Solomon Burke, Bo Diddley, Otis Redding, Sam Cooke, Don Covay, Arthur Alexander and others. These albums demonstrate nothing if not that the Stones can play better than all these hallowed saints. The only time they miss is on Redding's "I've Been Loving You Too Long" and they miss only because that truly is the king's tune.

These early albums develop the themes of sadism and misogyny that are prevalent throughout their recorded history. Jagger is especially evil on these early sides. The early writing efforts are rather derivative in their chord progressions and lyric content (in particular Chuck Berry). By *Out of Our Heads*, Keith and Mick were starting to put it together; after they came into their own they have continually written the best lyrics in rock.

16. Ten best unknown Stones songs: "I've Had It"; "Monster Mash"; "Angel Baby"; "Speedo"; "Image of a Girl"; "Honey Love"; "Sea Cruise"; "A Rose and a Baby Ruth"; "Ankle Bracelet"; and "Just One Look."

17. The middle period, reminiscent of some guy's red period (or some chick's, I never paid much attention in school) is possibly the most profound in rock; certainly it is the most musical. Fully developed belief in existential absurdity. "Goin Home," rock's only long song and perhaps its only masterpiece. *Aftermath*, meaning the harvesting of the grass, and *Buttons*, meaning peyote or boobs, brilliant titles. The former, a railing at the fates; the latter a resolution through melancholy (and drugs and sex). The poignant Ruby, warning us that if we lose our dreams, we lose our minds. It is their Dylan period, and they best him, as, formerly, they bested the spade masters. *Flowers*, too, with the incredible "Ride On, Baby" (Pearlman claims it's about Jackie Kennedy Onassis) and "Sitting On a Fence," the most honest confession in twentieth-century literature. Another heavy from this time scheme is *Got Live If You Want It!* The only true live album, it should be included in a time capsule to show modern man's dependence on methamphetamine.

18. Mick has enormous stamina. He can go on singing for hours and hours non-stop—and always turning in a great performance.

19. "Of course I do occasionally arouse primeval instincts," he concedes, "but I mean, most men can do that. They can't do it to so many. I just happen to be able to do it to several thousand people. It's fun to do that. It's really just a game, isn't it? I mean these girls do it to themselves. They're all charged up. It's a dialogue of energy. They give you a lot of energy and take a lot away. Maybe they want something from life, from me. Maybe they think I can give it to them. I don't know."

20. Five best animal songs (alphabetically): "I'm a King Bee"; "Stray Cat Blues"; "My Girl Rover"; "Monkey Man"; "The Sheep in the Fence"; "The Spider and the Fly"; "Crustacean Lullaby"; "Little Red Rooster."

21. Around midnight, a black limousine carrying five shaggy-haired youths stopped at a gas station. Finding the restrooms closed, the boys pulled it out and answered nature's call on the side of the building. Charges were pressed by the attendant and this resulted in the Stones' famous piss bust.

22. "I have seen today the most disgusting sight I can remember in all my years as a television fan."

23. The late Mr. Jones was formerly a dustman. After achieving success with a rock-and-roll band known as the Rolling Stones, he purchased the estate of the late A. A. Milne.

24. "Well it's a very heady album, very spaced out."

25. The best, the absolute best. And it's what separated the men from the boys. *Their Satanic Majesties Request* is so solidly the Stones that Chuck Berry could have played on it. An album outspaced only by *Happy Trails* and *Piper at the Gate of Dawn*. Competition with the Beatles? No chance, this is so far superior in every way as to make comparisons insulting. Intelligent, tasteful use of the reference tongue, while the automatic pressure is constantly applied. And there's even a Bill Wyman song.

26. The best Dylan songs: "My Obsession"; "Who's Been Sleeping Here"; "Something Happened To Me Yesterday"; "2000 Man"; "Oxford Town"; "Jig Saw Puzzle"; "Revolution No. 9"; "Mind Gardens"; "Surprise, Surprise"; "Ballad of Hollis Brown"; "If I Had to Do It All Over Again, I'd Do It All Over You."

27.

DEAR MICK,

If I won a date with you, here's what we'd do. As we were exposing our bodies and secrets to each other, we'd be smoking some outrageous dope from Vera Cruz. As I whipped you with my platinum studded cat-o'-nine-tails, we'd sniff some coke and sympathy, all the while listening to Beethoven's *Eroica*. As we changed positions and records, I would moan indecently as my pink fleshy part was stimulated by bramble bushes, grooving to *In-A-Gadda-Da-Vida*. While I was giving you head, chewing on that famous piece of schlang, waiting for that creamy nectar to flow, you would be gouging my back with an icepick. Then, and only then, you could take me through any and all openings. I think it would be a perfect date, and we could go to the prom afterwards.

> With eternal love,
> GILLIAN WINTER (Age 11½)

28. Mick Jagger, in performance, is quite swinish, and yet he's still not the whole show. Not by a country mile. Topping the bill is Keith Richard, whose teased hair and fang tooth earring made the entire visual move. Mick Taylor, playing leads never heard before in Madison Square Garden, was flawless. I believe the group would be interesting without Jagger; more, they'd be almost as good. But Jagger is what we paid the money for, so here goes. Prancing and dancing on stage, he seems just about ready to play Peter Pan in a Living Theatre revival. Tossing a basket of roses as easily as a black power salute, he seems to have mellowed lately. But he's beautiful; as a unity, the Rolling Stones are the best rock and roll group.

29. "Do you want to live with me?"
"You ain't got the balls."

30. The most recent Stones albums show the art of the mythic readymade. First off, they've gone further back in the collective unconscious. Roots in Africa, derivatives in the Delta, integrations in Memphis. The lyrics now deal more with mythology than mere fantasy. Or, the individual has been made collective, all the while remaining universal. And of course it's great, 'cause if you buy the trip, you buy the trip. Raunch and outrage do not get to us jaded sophisticates, so what do the Stones do but keep right on being so obvious in the face of the supposed loss of innocence.

This tells us as much about the youth culture as any other set of parameters; i.e., the whole thing is a shuck, a sham, a hoax, and we ain't any different than that before us except for locus.

31. "Mick, what's your favorite shoe polish?"

"Here in America, I prefer Kiwi, but at home, it's Marianne's tongue."

"Keith, what do you do to relax?"

"I like to go down to Brighton with a few of me mates and some bob and chase the birds."

"Charlie, you are an acknowledged expert on jazz. What is your opinion on the Pops Brown Rhythm Kings?"

"Are you referring to their Chicago period, or their New York period, or their very early beginnings in Secaucus?"

32. It was reported today in a reliable English trade paper that pop star Mick Jagger will do a promotional tour for Mars bars.

33. Mick Jagger is probably the third best writer of English in this century. Joyce is the obvious No. 1 with a whole mess of creeps like Lawrence and Faulkner vying for the runner-up spot. And clearly by himself is Jagger, the best lyricist in the rock thing and that includes Dylan, the Moppets, Paul Simon, Donovan and any other limp tongues you might care to name.

34. "I get a strange feeling on stage. I feel all the energy coming from the audience.

"I feel quite violent sometimes. I quite often want to smash up the microphone or something because I don't feel the same person on stage as I am normally."

35. The beauty of the Stones is that they mean all things to all people. The radical protest movement has adopted "Street Fighting Man" as an anthem and yet the song points toward apathy as a way. Rebellious youth look on Jagger as a savior from the rotten Establishment, and yet the Stones have managed their finances the best of any rock group, and all live quite comfortably, if not to say excessively. Jagger is a big sex symbol, and married or not, has been dating (all right, living with is a better phrase) the same chick for the last five years. Ultimately, it seems

that the Stones, better than any other performers, can spin the right tales, tales that appeal to the taste brokers in this country. Because the Beatles' limited conception of the world is probably more accurate quantitatively, if not qualitatively.

36. God Bless the Rolling Stones!

ROCK FOR SALE

Businessmen they drink my wine
Plowmen dig my earth
None of them along the line
Know what any of it is worth
    —BOB DYLAN, "All Along the Watchtower"
                    (© 1968 Dwarf Music)

In 1956, when rock and roll was just about a year old, Frankie Lymon, lead singer of Frankie Lymon and the Teenagers, wrote and recorded a song called "Why Do Fools Fall in Love?" It was an immediate million-selling hit and has since become a rock classic, a true golden oldie of the sweet-voiced harmonizing genre. The group followed it up with other hits, starred in a movie, appeared on the Ed Sullivan Show, toured the country with Bill Haley and the Comets, and did a tour of Europe. Frankie, a black kid from Harlem, was then thirteen years old. Last year, at twenty-six, he died of an overdose of heroin.

Despite the massive publicity accorded to rock in the past several years, Frankie's death received little attention. It got a bit more publicity than the death in a federal prison of Little Willie John, the author of "Fever," another classic, but nothing compared to that lavished on the breakup of the Cream or on Janis Joplin's split with Big Brother and the Holding Company. Nor did many connect it with the complete musical stagnation of the Doors, a group which in 1967 seemed brilliantly promising, or to the dissolution of dozens of other groups who a year or two ago were not only making beautiful music but seemed to be the vanguard of a promising "youth cultural revolution."

In fact these events are all connected, and their common

denominator is hard cash. Since that wildly exciting spring of
1967, the spring of *Sgt. Pepper's Lonely Hearts Club Band,* of be-
ins and love-ins and flower-power, of the discovery of psychedelia, hippies and "doing your thing"—to all of which "New
Rock," as it then began to be called, was inextricably bound—
one basic fact has been consistently ignored: rock is a product
created, distributed and controlled for the profit of America (and
international) business. "The record companies sell rock and roll
records like they sell refrigerators," says Paul Kantner of the
Jefferson Airplane. "They don't care about the people who make
rock or what they're all about as human beings any more than
they care about the people who make refrigerators."

Recently, the promoters of a sleazy Southern California enterprise known as "Teen Fair" changed its name to "Teen Expo."
The purpose of the operation remains the same: to sell trash to
adolescents while impressing them with the joys of consumerism.
But nine years into the '60s, the backers decided that their '50s
image of nice-kid teenagerism had to go. In its place, they have
installed "New Rock" (with its constant companion, schlock
psychedelia) as the working image of the "all new!" Teen Expo.

By the time the word gets down to the avaricious cretins who
run teen fairs, everybody has the message: rock and roll sells. It
doesn't make money just for the entertainment industry—the
record companies, radio stations, TV networks, stereo and musical instrument manufacturers, etc.—but for law firms, clothing
manufacturers, the mass media, soft drink companies and car
dealers (the new Opel will "light your fire!"). Rock is the surest
way to the hearts and wallets of millions of Americans between
eight and thirty-five—the richest, most extravagant children in
the history of the world.

From the start, rock has been commercial in its very essence.
An American creation on the level of the hamburger or the billboard, it was never an art form that just happened to make
money, nor a commercial undertaking that sometimes became
art. Its art was synonymous with its business. The movies are
perhaps closest to rock in their aesthetic involvement with the
demands of profitability, but even they once had an arty tradition
which scorned the pleasing of the masses.

Yet paradoxically it was the unabashed commerciality of rock which gave rise to the hope that it would be a "revolutionary" cultural form of expression. For one thing, the companies that produce it and reap its profits have never understood it. Ford executives drive their company's cars but Sir Joseph Lockwood, chairman of EMI, the record company which, until Apple, released the Beatles' records, has always admitted that he doesn't like their music. The small companies like Sun and Chess Records which first discovered the early stars like Elvis Presley and Chuck Berry were run by middle-class whites who knew that kids and blacks liked this weird music, but they didn't know or really care why. As long as the music didn't offend the businessmen's sensibilities too much—they never allowed outright obscenity—and as long as it sold, they didn't care what it said. So within the commercial framework, rock has always had a certain freedom.

Moreover, rock's slavish devotion to commerciality gave it powerful aesthetic advantages. People had to like it for it to sell, so rock had to get to the things that the audience really cared about. Not only did it create a ritualized world of dances, slang, "the charts," fan magazines and "your favorite DJ coming your way" on the car radio, but it defined, reflected and glorified the listener's ordinary world. Rock fans can date their entire lives by rock; hearing a "golden oldie" can instantaneously evoke the whole flavor and detail of a summer or a romance.

When in 1963–64 the Pop Art movement said there was beauty in what had been thought to be a crass excreta of the Eisenhower Age, when the Beatles proved that shameless reveling in money could be a stone groove, and when the wistful puritanism of the protest-folk music movement came to a dead end, rock and roll, with all its unabashed carnality and worldliness, seemed a beautiful trip. Rock, the background music of growing up, was discovered as the common language of a generation. New Rock musicians could not only make the music, they could even make an aesthetic and social point by the very choice of rock as their medium.

That rock was commercial seemed only a benefit. It ensured wide distribution, the hope of a good and possibly grandiose living style, and the honesty of admitting that, yes, we are the children of affluence: don't deny it, man, dig it. As music, rock had an undeniably liberating effect; driving and sensual, it implicitly and explicitly presented an alternative to bourgeois insipidity. The freedom granted to rock by society seemed sufficient to allow its adherents to express their energies without inhibition. Rock pleasure had no pain attached; the outrageousness of Elvis' gold lamé suits and John Lennon's wildly painted Rolls Royce was a gas, a big joke on adult society. Rock was a way to beat the system, to gull grown-ups into paying you while you made faces behind their backs.

Sad but true, however, the grown-ups are having the last laugh. Rock and roll is a lovely playground, and within it kids have more power than they have anywhere else in society, but the playground's walls are carefully maintained and guarded by the corporate elite that set it up in the first place. While the White Panthers talk of "total assault upon the culture by any means necessary, including rock and roll, dope and fucking in the streets," *Billboard*, the music trade paper, announces with pride that in 1968 the record industry became a billion-dollar business.

> *Then it's time to go downtown*
> *Where the agent man won't let you down*
> *Sell your soul to the company*
> *Who are waiting there*
> *To sell plasticware*
> *And in a week or two*
> *If you make the charts*
> *The girls will tear you apart.*

> —ROGER McGUINN AND CHRIS HILLMAN,
> "So You Want to Be a Rock 'n' Roll Star"
> (© Tickson Music Co.)

Bob Dylan has described with a fiendish accuracy the pain of growing up in America, and millions have responded passionately to his vision. His song, "Maggie's Farm," contains the lines,

"He gives me a nickel, he gives me a dime, he asks me with a grin if I'm having a good time, and he fines me every time I slam the door, oh, I ain't gonna work on Maggie's farm no more." But along with Walter Cronkite and the New York Yankees, Dylan works for one of Maggie's biggest farms, the Columbia Broadcasting System.

Mick Jagger, another adept and vitriolic social critic, used rock to sneer at "the under assistant west coast promotion man" in his seersucker suit; but London Records used this "necessary talent for every rock and roll band" to sell that particular Rolling Stones record and all their other products. For all its liberating potential, rock is doomed to a bitter impotence by its ultimate subservience to those whom it attacks.

In fact, rock, rather than being an example of how freedom can be achieved within the capitalist structure, is an example of how capitalism can, almost without a conscious effort, deceive those whom it oppresses. Rather than being liberated heroes, rock and roll stars are captives on a leash, and their plight is but a metaphor for that of all young people and black people in America. All the talk of "rock revolution," talk that is assiduously cultivated by the rock industry, is an attempt to disguise that plight.

Despite the aura of wealth that has always surrounded the rock and roll star, and which for fans justified the high prices of records and concerts, very few stars really make much money— and for all but the stars and their backup musicians, rock is just another low-paying, insecure and very hard job. Legend says that wild spending sprees, drugs, and women account for the missing loot; what legend does not say is that most artists are paid very little for their work. The artist may receive a record royalty of two and one-half per cent, but the company often levies charges for studio time, promotion and advertising. It is not uncommon for the maker of a hit record to end up in debt to the company.

Not surprisingly, it is the black artists who suffer most. In his brilliant book, *Urban Blues*, Charles Keil describes in detail how the blues artist is at the mercy of the recording company. It is virtually impossible, he states, for an unknown artist to get an honest contract, but even an "honest" contract is only an inexpensive way for a company to own an artist body and soul.

A star's wealth may be not only nonexistent, but actually a fraud carefully perpetuated by the record company. Blues singer Bobby Bland's "clothes, limousine, valet, and plentiful pocket money," says Keil, "are image bolsterers from Duke Records (or perhaps a continual 'advance on royalties' that keeps him tied to the company) rather than real earnings." And even cash exploitation is not enough; Chess Records last year forced Muddy Waters to play his classic blues with a "psychedelic" band and called the humiliating record *Electric Mud.*

Until recently, only a very few stars made any real money from rock; their secret was managers shrewd to the point of unscrupulousness, who kept them under tight control. Colonel Parker molded the sexual country boy Elvis into a smooth ballad singer; Brian Epstein took four scruffy Liverpool rockers and transformed them into neatly tousled boys-next-door. "We were worried that friends might think we had sold out," John Lennon said recently, "which in a way we had."

The musicians of New Rock—most of them white, educated and middle-class—are spared much of what their black and lower-class counterparts have suffered. One of the much touted "revolutions" New Rock has brought, in fact, has been a drastic increase in the power of the artist vis-à-vis the record company. Contracts for New Rock bands regularly include almost complete artistic control, royalties as high as ten per cent, huge cash advances, free studio time, guaranteed amounts of company-bought promotion, and in some instances control over advertising design and placement in the media.

But such bargaining is at best a futile reformism which never challenges the essential power relationship that has contaminated rock since its inception. Sales expansion still gives the companies ample profits, and they maintain all the control they really need (even the "revolutionary" group, the MC5, agreed to remove the word "motherfucker" from an album and to record "brothers and sisters" in its place). New Rock musicians lost the battle for real freedom at the very moment they signed their contracts (whatever the clauses) and entered the big-time commercial sphere.

The Doors are a prime example. Like hundreds of New Rock musicians, the four Doors are intelligent people who in the early and mid-'60s dropped out into the emerging drug and hip underground. In endless rehearsals and on stage in Sunset Strip rock clubs, they developed a distinctively eerie and stringent sound. The band laid down a dynamo drive behind dramatically handsome lead singer Jim Morrison, who, dressed in black leather and writhing with anguish, screamed demonic invitations to sensual madness. "Break on through," was the message, "yeah, break on, break on through to the other side!"

It was great rock and roll, and by June 1967, when their "Light My Fire" was a number-one hit, it had become very successful rock. More hits followed and the Doors became the first New Rock group to garner a huge following among the young teens and pre-teens who were traditionally the mass rock audience. Jim Morrison became rock's number-one sex idol and the teeny-boppers' delight. The group played bigger and bigger halls—the Hollywood Bowl, the garish Forum in Los Angeles, and finally Madison Square Garden last winter in a concert that netted the group $52,000 for one night's work.

But the hit "Light My Fire" was a chopped-up version of the original album track, and after that castration of their art for immediate mass appeal (a castration encouraged by their "hip" company, Elektra Records), the Doors died musically. Later albums were pale imitations of the first; trying desperately to recapture the impact of their early days, they played louder and Morrison lost all subtlety: at a recent Miami concert he had to display his penis to make his point.

Exhausted by touring and recording demands, the Doors now seldom play or even spend much casual time together. Their latest single hit the depths; *Cashbox* magazine, in its profit-trained wisdom said, "The team's impact is newly channeled for even more than average young teen impact." "Maybe pretty soon we'll split, just go away to an island somewhere," Morrison said recently, fatigue and frustration in his voice, "get away by ourselves and start creating again."

But the Doors have made money, enough to be up-tight about it. "When I told them about this interview," said their manager, Bill Siddons, sitting in the office of the full-time accountant who manages the group's investments (mostly land and oil), "they said, 'Don't tell him how much we make.'" But Siddons, a personable young man, did his best to defend them. The Doors, he said, could make a lot more money if they toured more often and took less care in preparing each hall they play in for the best possible lighting and sound; none of the Doors lives lavishly, and the group has plans for a foundation to give money to artists and students ("It'll help our tax picture, too"). But, he said, "You get started in rock and you get locked into the cycle of success. It's funny, the group out there on stage preaching a revolutionary message, but to get the message to people, you gotta do it the establishment way. And you know everybody acquires a taste for comfortable living."

> *The price you paid*
> *For your riches and fame*
> *Was it a strange game*
> *You're a little insane*
> *All the money that came*
> *And the public acclaim—*
> *Don't forget who you are*
> *You're a rock 'n' roll star*
>
> —"So You Want to Be a Rock 'n' Roll Star"

Variations on the Doors' story are everywhere. The Cream started out in 1966 as a brilliant and influential blues-rock trio and ended, after two solid years of touring, with lead guitarist Eric Clapton on the edge of a nervous breakdown. After months of bitter fighting, Big Brother and the Holding Company split up, as did Country Joe and the Fish (who have since reorganized, with several replacements from Big Brother). The Steve Miller Band and the Quicksilver Messenger Service were given a total of $100,000 by Capitol Records; within a year neither one existed in its original form and the money had somehow disappeared.

Groups that manage to stay together are caught in endless

conflicts about how to make enough money to support their art and have it heard without getting entangled in the "success cycle." The Grateful Dead, who were house and bus minstrels for Ken Kesey's acid-magical crew and who have always been deeply involved in trying to create a real hip community, have been so uncommercial as to frustrate their attempts to spread the word of their joyful vision.

"The trouble is that the Grateful Dead is a more 'heard of' band than a 'heard' band," says manager Rock Scully, "and we want people to hear us. But we won't do what the system says— make single hits, take big gigs, do the success number. The summer of '67, when all the other groups were making it, we were playing free in the park, man, trying to cool the Haight-Ashbury. So we've never had enough bread to get beyond week-to-week survival, and now we're about $50,000 in debt. We won't play bad music for the bread because we decided a long time ago that money wasn't a high enough value to sacrifice anything for. But that means that not nearly enough people have heard our music."

The Jefferson Airplane have managed to take a middle route. A few early hits, a year of heavy touring (150 dates in 1967), a series of commercials for White Levis, and the hard-nosed management of entrepreneur Bill Graham gave them a solid money-making popular base. A year ago they left Graham's management, stopped touring almost entirely, bought a huge mansion in San Francisco and devoted their time to making records (all of them excellent), giving parties, and buying expensive toys like cars and color TVs. They've gone through enormous amounts of money and are now $30,000 in debt. But they're perfectly willing to go out and play a few jobs if the creditors start to press them. They resolve the commercial question by attempting not to care about it. "What I care about," says Paul Kantner, "is what I'm doing at the time—rolling a joint, balling a chick, writing a song. Start worrying about the ultimate effect of all your actions, and in the end you just have to say fuck it. Everybody in the world is getting fucked one way or another. All you can do is see that you aren't fucking them directly."

But the Airplane also profess political radicalism, and, says
Kantner, "The revolution is already happening, man. All those
kids dropping out, turning on—they add up." Singer Grace Slick
appeared in blackface on the Smothers Brothers show and gave
the Black Panther salute; in a front window of their mansion is a
sign that reads, "Eldridge Cleaver Welcome Here." But Kantner
said he hadn't really thought about what that meant: would he
really take Cleaver in and protect him against police attack, a
very likely necessity should Cleaver accept the welcome? "I don't
know, man. I'd have to wait until that happened."

Cleaver would be well-advised not to choose the Airplane's
mansion for his refuge. For Kantner's mushy politics—sort of a
turned-on liberalism that thinks the Panthers are "groovy" but
doesn't like to come to terms with the nasty American reality—
are the politics of the much touted "rock revolution." They add
up to a hazy belief in the power of art to change the world,
presuming that the place for the revolution to begin and end is
inside individual heads. The Beatles said it nicely in "Revolution": "You say that it's the institution, we-ll, you know, you
better free your mind instead."

Jac Holzman, president of Elektra Records, said it in businessman's prose: "I want to make it clear," he said, "that Elektra
is not the tool of anyone's revolution. We feel that the 'revolution'
will be won by poetics and not by politics—that poetics will
change the structure of the world. It's reached the kids and is
getting to them at the best possible level."

There is no secret boardroom conspiracy to divert antisocial
youthful energy into rock and thus render it harmless while
making a profit for the society it is rebelling against, but the
corporate system has acted in that direction with a uniformity
which a conspiracy probably could not have provided. And the
aware capitalists are worried about their ability to control where
kids are going: "There is something a bit spooky, from a business
point of view," a Fortune issue on youth said recently, ". . . in
youth's widespread rejection of middle-class life-styles ('Cheap is
in'). . . . If it . . . becomes a dominant orientation, will these
children of affluence grow up to be consumers on quite the
economy-moving scale as their parents?"

So the kids are talking revolution and smoking dope? Well, so are the companies, in massive advertising campaigns that co-opt the language of revolution so thoroughly that you'd think they were on the streets themselves. "The Man can't bust *our* music," read one Columbia ad; another urged (with a picture of a diverse group of kids apparently turning on): "Know who your friends are. And look and see and touch and be together. Then listen. *We* do." (Italics mine.)

More insidious than the ads themselves is the fact that ad money from the record companies is one of the main supports of the underground press. And the companies don't mind supporting these "revolutionary" sheets; the failure of Hearst's *Eye* magazine after a year showed that the establishment itself could not create new media to reach the kids, so squeamish is it about advocating revolution, drugs and sexual liberation. But it is glad to support the media the kids create themselves, and thereby, just as it did with rock, ultimately defang it.

The ramifications of control finally came full circle when *Rolling Stone*, the leading national rock newspaper, which began eighteen months ago on a shoestring, had enough money in the bank to afford a $7000 ad on the back page of *The New York Times*. Not only was this "hip rock" publication self-consciously taking its place among the communication giants ("NBC was the day before us and *Look* the day after," said the twenty-two-year-old editor), but the ad's copy made clear the paper's exploitive aim: "If you are a corporate executive trying to understand what is happening to youth today, you cannot afford to be without *Rolling Stone*. If you are a student, a professor, a parent, this is your life because you already know that rock and roll is more than just music; it is the energy center of the new culture and youth revolution." Such a neat reversal of the corporate-to-kids lie into a kids-to-corporate lie is only possible when the kids so believe the lie they have been fed that they want to pass it on.

But rock and roll musicians are in the end artists and entertainers, and were it not for all the talk of the "rock revolution," one would not be led to expect a clear political vision from them. The bitterest irony is that the "rock revolution" hype has come close to fatally limiting the revolutionary potential that rock does contain. So effective has the rock industry been in encouraging the spirit of optimistic youth take-over that rock's truly hard political edge, its constant exploration of the varieties of youthful frustration, has been ignored and softened. Rock musicians, like their followers, have always been torn between the obvious pleasures that America held out and the price paid for them. Rock and roll is not revolutionary music because it has never gotten beyond articulation of this paradox. At best it has offered the defiance of withdrawal; its violence never amounted to more than a cry of "Don't bother me."

"Leave me alone; anyway, I'm almost grown"; "Don't step on my blue suede shoes"; "There ain't no cure for the summertime blues"; "I can't get no satisfaction": the rock refrains that express despair could be strung out forever. But at least rock has offered an honest appraisal of where its makers and listeners are at, and that radical, if bitterly defeatist, honesty is a touchstone, a starting point. If the companies, as representatives of the corporate structure, can convince the rock world that their revolution is won or almost won, that the walls of the playground are crumbling, not only will the constituents of rock seal their fate by that fatal self-deception, but their music, one of the few things they actually do have going for them, will have been successfully corrupted and truly emasculated.

Nora Ephron & Susan Edmiston

BOB DYLAN INTERVIEW

This interview took place in late summer of 1965 in the office of Dylan's manager Albert Grossman. Dylan had just been booed in the historic Forest Hills concert where he abandoned folk purity to the use of electric accompaniment. He was wearing a red-and-navy op-art shirt, a navy blazer and pointy high-heeled boots. His face, so sharp and harsh when translated through the media, was then infinitely soft and delicate. His hair was not bushy or electric or Afro; it was fine-spun soft froth like the foam of a wave. He looked like an underfed angel with a nose from the land of the Chosen People.

Some American folk singers—Carolyn Hester, for example—say that what you're now doing, the new sound, "folk rock," is liberating them.

Did Carolyn say that? You tell her she can come around and see me any time now that she's liberated.

Does labeling, using the term "folk rock," tend to obscure what's happening?

Yes.

It's like "pop gospel." What does the term mean to you?

Yeah, classical gospel could be the next trend. There's country rock, rockabilly. What does it mean to me? Folk rock. I've never even said that word. It has a hard gutter sound. Circussy atmosphere. It's nose-thumbing. Sounds like you're looking down on what is . . . fantastic, great music.

The definition most often given of folk rock is the combination of the electronic sound of rock and roll with the meaningful lyrics of folk music. Does that sum up what you're doing?

Yes. It's very complicated to play with electricity. You play with other people. You're dealing with other people. Most people don't like to work with other people, it's more difficult. It takes a lot. Most people who don't like rock and roll can't relate to other people.

You mention the Apollo Theatre in Harlem on one of your album covers. Do you go there often?

Oh, I couldn't go up there. I used to go up there a lot about four years ago. I even wanted to play in one of the amateur nights, but I got scared. Bad things can happen to you. I saw what the audience did to a couple of guys they didn't like. And I would have had a couple of things against me right away when I stepped out on the stage.

Who is Mr. Jones in "Ballad of a Thin Man"?

He's a real person. You know him, but not by that name.

Like Mr. Charlie?

No. He's more than Mr. Charlie. He's actually a person. Like I saw him come into the room one night and he looked like a camel. He proceeded to put his eyes in his pocket. I asked this guy who he was and he said, "That's Mr. Jones." Then I asked this cat, "Doesn't he do anything but put his eyes in his pocket?" And he told me, "He puts his nose on the ground." It's all there, it's a true story.

Where did you get that shirt?

California. Do you like it? You should see my others. You can't get clothes like that here. There are a lot of things out there we haven't got here.

Isn't California on the way here?

It's uptight here compared to there. Hollywood I mean. It's not really breathable here. It's like there's air out there. The Sunset

Strip can't be compared to anything here, like 42nd Street. The people there look different, they look more like . . . you want to kiss them out there.

Do you spend a lot of time out there?

I don't have much time to spend anywhere. The same thing in England. In England everybody looks very hip East Side. They wear things . . . they don't wear things that bore you. They've got other hangups in other directions.

Do you consider yourself primarily a poet?

No. We have our ideas about poets. The word doesn't mean any more than the word "house." There are people who write *poems* and people who write po*ems*. Other people write *poems*. Everybody who writes poems do you call them a poet? There's a certain kind of rhythm in some kind of way that's visible. You don't necessarily have to write to be a poet. Some people work in gas stations and they're poets. I don't call myself a poet because I don't like the word. I'm a trapeze artist.

What I meant was, do you think your words stand without the music?

They would stand but I don't read them. I'd rather sing them. I write things that aren't songs—I have a book coming out.

What is it?

It's a book of words.

Is it like the back of your albums? It seemed to me that the album copy you write is a lot like the writing of William Burroughs. Some of the accidental sentences——

Cut-ups.

Yes, and some of the imagery and anecdotes. I wondered if you had read anything by him.

I haven't read *Naked Lunch* but I read some of his shorter things in little magazines, foreign magazines. I read one in Rome. I know him. I don't really know him—I just met him once. I think he's a great man.

Burroughs keeps an album, a collection of photographs that illustrate his writing. Do you have anything similar to that?

I do that too. I have photographs of "Gates of Eden" and "It's All Over Now, Baby Blue." I saw them after I wrote the songs. People send me a lot of things and a lot of the things are pictures, so other people must have that idea too. I gotta admit, maybe I wouldn't have chosen them, but I can see what it is about the pictures.

I heard you used to play the piano for Buddy Holly.

No. I used to play the rock and roll piano, but I don't want to say who it was for because the cat will try to get hold of me. I don't want to see the cat. He'll try to reclaim the friendship. I did it a long time ago, when I was seventeen years old. I used to play a country piano too.

This was before you became interested in folk music?

Yes. I became interested in folk music because I had to make it somehow. Obviously I'm not a hard-working cat. I played the guitar, that was all I did. I thought it was great music. Certainly I haven't turned my back on it or anything like that. There is— and I'm sure nobody realizes this, all the authorities who write about what it is and what it should be, when they say keep things simple, they should be easily understood—folk music is the only music where it isn't simple. It's never been simple. It's weird, man, full of legend, myth, Bible and ghosts. I've never written anything hard to understand, not in my head anyway, and nothing as far out as some of the old songs. They were out of sight.

Like what songs?

"Little Brown Dog." "I bought a little brown dog, its face is all gray. Now I'm going to Turkey flying on my bottle." And "Nottemun Town," that's like a herd of ghosts passing through on the way to Tangiers. "Lord Edward," "Barbara Allen," they're full of myth.

And contradictions?

Yeah, contradictions.

And chaos?

Chaos, watermelon, clocks, everything.

You wrote on the back on one album, "I accept chaos but does chaos accept me."

Chaos is a friend of mine. It's like I accept him, does he accept me.

Do you see the world as chaos?

Truth is chaos. Maybe beauty is chaos.

Poets like Eliot and Yeats—

I haven't read Yeats.

They saw the world as chaos, accepted it as chaos and attempted to bring order from it. Are you trying to do that?

No. It exists and that's all there is to it. It's been here longer than I have. What can I do about it? I don't know what the songs I write are. That's all I do is write songs, right? Write. I collect things too.

Monkey wrenches?

Where did you read about that? Has that been in print? I told this guy out on the coast that I collected monkey wrenches, all sizes and shapes of monkey wrenches, and he didn't believe me. I don't think you believe me either. And I collect the pictures too. Have you talked to Sonny and Cher?

No.

They're a drag. A cat gets kicked out of a restaurant and he went home and wrote a song about it.

They say your fan mail has radically increased since you switched sounds.

Yeah. I don't have time to read all of it, but I want you to put that I answer half of it. I don't really. A girl does that for me.

Does she save any for you—any particularly interesting letters?

She knows my head. Not the ones that just ask for pictures, there's a file for them. Not the ones that say, I want to make it with you, they go in another file. She saves two kinds. The violently put-down—

The ones that call you a sellout?

Yeah. Sellout, fink, Fascist, Red, everything in the book. I really dig those. And ones from old friends.

Like, "You don't remember me but I was in the fourth grade with you"?

No, I never had any friends then. These are letters from people who knew me in New York five, six years ago. My first fans. Not the people who call themselves my first fans. They came in three years ago, two years ago. They aren't really my first fans.

How do you feel about being booed at your concert at Forest Hills?

I thought it was great, I really did. If I said anything else I'd be a liar.

And at the Newport Folk Festival?

That was different. They twisted the sound. They didn't like what I was going to play and they twisted the sound on me before I began.

I hear you were wearing a sellout jacket.

What kind of jacket is a sellout jacket?

Black leather.

I've had black leather jackets since I was five years old. I've been wearing black leather all my life.

I wonder if we could talk about electronic music and what made you decide to use it.

I was doing fine, you know, singing and playing my guitar. It was a sure thing, don't you understand, it was a sure thing. I was getting very bored with that. I couldn't go out and play like that. I was thinking of quitting. Out front it was a sure thing. I knew what the audience was gonna do, how they would react. It was very automatic. Your mind just drifts unless you can find some way to get in there and remain totally there. It's so much of a fight remaining totally there all by yourself. It takes too much. I'm not ready to cut that much out of my life. You can't have nobody around. You can't be bothered with anybody else's world. And I like people. What I'm doing now—it's a whole other thing. We're not playing rock music. It's not a hard sound. These people call it folk rock—if they want to call it that, something that simple, it's good for selling the records. As far as it being what it is, I don't know what it is. I can't call it folk rock. It's a whole way of doing things. It has been picked up on, I've heard songs on the radio that have picked it up. I'm not talking about words. It's a certain feeling, and it's been on every single record I've ever made. That has not changed. I know it hasn't changed. As far as what I was totally, before, maybe I was pushing it a little then. I'm not pushing things now. I know it. I know very well how to do it. The problem of how I want to play something —I know it in front. I know what I'm going to say, what I'm going to do. I don't have to work it out. The band I work with— they wouldn't be playing with me if they didn't play like I want them to. I have this song, "Queen Jane Approximately"—

Who is Queen Jane?

Queen Jane is a man.

Was there something that made you decide to change sounds? Your trip to England?

I like the sound. I like what I'm doing now. I would have done it before. It wasn't practical to do it before. I spent most of my time writing. I wouldn't have had the time. I had to get where I was going all alone. I don't know what I'm going to do next. I probably will record with strings some time, but it doesn't necessarily change. It's just a different color. And I know that it's real. No matter what anybody says. They can boo till the end of time. I know that the music is real, more real than the boos.

How do you work?

Most of the time I work at night. I don't really like to think of it as work. I don't know how important it is. It's not important to the average cat who works eight hours a day. What does he care? The world can get along very well without it. I'm hip to that.

Sure, but the world can get along without any number of things.

I'll give you a comparison. Rudy Vallee. Now that was a lie, that was a downright lie. Rudy Vallee being popular. What kind of people could have dug him? You know, your grandmothers and mothers. But what kind of people were they? He was so sexless. If you want to find out about those times and you listen to his music you're not going to find out anything about the times. His music was a pipedream. All escapes. There are no more escapes. If you want to find out anything that's happening now, you have to listen to the music. I don't mean the words, although "Eve of Destruction" will tell you something about it. The words are not really gonna tell it, not really. You gotta listen to the Stapes Singers, Smokey and the Miracles, Martha and the Vandellas. That's scary to a lot of people. It's sex that's involved. It's not hidden. It's real. You can overdo it. It's not only sex, it's a whole beautiful feeling.

But Negro rhythm and blues has been around underground for at least twelve years. What brought it out now?

The English did that. They brought it out. They hipped everybody. You read an interview asking who the Beatles' favorite singer was and they said Chuck Berry. You never used to hear Chuck Berry records on the radio, hard blues. The English did that. England is great and beautiful, though in other ways kinda messy. Though not outside London.

In what way messy?

There's a snobbishness. What you see people doing to other people. It's not only class. It's not that simple. It's a kind of Queen kind of thing. Some people are royalty and some are not. Here, man, somebody don't like you he tells you. There it's very tight, tight kinds of expressions, their whole tone of speaking changes. It's an everyday kind of thing. But the kids are a whole other thing. Great. They're just more free. I hope you don't think I take this too seriously—I just have a headache.

I think you started out to say that music was more in tune with what's happening than other art forms.

Great paintings shouldn't be in museums. Have you ever been in a museum? Museums are cemeteries. Paintings should be on the walls of restaurants, in dime stores, in gas stations, in men's rooms. Great paintings should be where people hang out. The only thing where it's happening is on the radio and records, that's where people hang out. You can't see great paintings. You pay half a million and hang one in your house and one guest sees it. That's not art. That's a shame, a crime. Music is the only thing that's in tune with what's happening. It's not in book form, it's not on the stage. All this art they've been talking about is non-existent. It just remains on the shelf. It doesn't make anyone happier. Just think how many people would really feel great if they could see a Picasso in their daily diner. It's not the bomb that has to go, man, it's the museums.

I QUOTE

People squabble for power no matter how small or on which side of the crust. Under and overground alike use words. I found the Great Silent Minority . . . I quote:

> **FAG JOINT OWNER:** We want you to change all this.
> **LENNY BRUCE:** Gee man, I don't know . . . that's a big gig.

When the Red Mountain Tribe "liberated" the *Berkeley Barb,* they wrote: "We will no longer do [our job] for a capitalist profiteer who insists that the toughest radical underground newspaper in the nation is his own personal property . . . we will no longer work in a situation that funnels thousands of dollars every week into Max Scherr's personal, private, secret bank account . . ."

> *They are discovering new ways to divide us faster than we are discovering new ways to unite.*
> —ELDRIDGE CLEAVER

The *International Times* was liberated by a staff which just put out the *International Free Press* instead. Their side: "At 8

P.M. seven members of the staff accompanied by members of the London Street Commune entered the office of the paper . . . in order to carry on the next issue in freedom . . . Then—AND THIS REALLY HAPPENED . . . THEY CALLED THE FUZZ . . . They called the fuzz. THEY CALLED THE FUZZ . . ."

Those who speak of revolution without making it real in their everyday lives speak with a corpse in their mouth.
    —RAOUL VANEIGM

The latest palace revolution took place at the Hanover Square offices of British *Rolling Stone*. Hanover Square is a posh address. *Rolling Stone* covers underground music . . . whatever the hell that means.

The underground is a bunch of cats who can't pay their bills.
    —ANONYMOUS

THE CAST:

JANN WENNER—Editor of American *Rolling Stone*, published by Straight Arrow Publishers, Inc.

JANE NICHOLSON—Defunct Editor of British *Rolling Stone*, published by Trans-Oceanic Comic Company, Ltd.

ALAN MARCUSON—Current Editor of British *Rolling Stone*, soon to be named *Friends*, published by T. F. (for Too Fucking) Much and Company.

JON RATNER—Distributor of some *Rolling Stone* or other.

THE STAFF, SOLICITORS, ACCOUNTANTS, and BUSINESSMEN.

MICK JAGGER.

PROLOGUE:

A letter from Jann Wenner to Jane Nicholson. These extracts are to be read in an angry voice, loud, cranky as a child whose toy has just been broken.

". . . Your business practices are appalling . . . Is this some kind of joke? . . . You're a bunch of amateurs and kids playing at the game of publishing . . . taking a ride on the established reputation of *Rolling Stone* and Mick's bank account . . . Suspend operations and payroll . . . have a chartered accountant audit the books . . . I hope that Mick and I will have a solution . . . restructuring it from top to bottom . . ."

Beware of structure freaks.
    —ABBIE HOFFMAN

DIALOGUE ON HANOVER SQUARE:

"What a week! We beat the straights . . . beat them at their own game of hassling everybody."

"You mean Jann Wenner is a straight?"

"Yeah—sure. His whole approach to business is old-fashioned. I mean it's ridiculous that he should want the big control scene over this paper anyway. That's like some kind of American industrial expansionism or something: some little cat sitting in his San Francisco office biting his nails, laying a heavy scene on us. That's like some Jewish . . . that's like my old man would do it. We're supposed to want that to go . . . right?"

"When Wenner was here, you know, I quite liked the guy, but it was still an American businessman I was talking to. I couldn't really be straight with him. And he said some things that just blew our minds completely. Leaving this building one night . . . he'd been shopping on Carnaby Street or wherever . . . he said, 'There's not much for a pop star to do in London except go and buy clothes.' He's the pop star. Dig that?"

We had the best organization that the black has ever had in the United States—and niggers ruined it!
    —MALCOLM X

In Copenhagen a few weeks ago, I had breakfast with Bill Levy. Bill is a former editor of the *International Times*. He told me the story of how the staff revolted against his regime, saying it was too entrenched. Considering plans of action, Bill examined himself. He wanted to stay. Why? Power—partly—ego. He decided, "You got it."

You smash it—we'll build around it.
    —JOHN LENNON

Scene: spring, 1969. Mick Jagger's conference room on Maddox Street. Twenty or so long-haired representatives of the underground press and some observers. Mick is launching British *Rolling Stone* Magazine. Conversation buzzes with good vibes. Everybody wants to help. Nobody is afraid of competition. We are all drinking Jagger's wine.

JANN WENNER: in ruffled see-through blouse, calls the meeting to order: "Okay . . . okay . . . We're not here just to drink Mick Jagger's wine."

MICK JAGGER: "Hold it . . . that's exactly why we're here. To drink my wine."

Would there could be a blackout here. However the scene proceeds . . . problems common to the underground press are explored . . . printing, distribution, content . . . too many solutions are offered. Few listen. I leave them there . . .

Meetings are a pain in the ass.
    —ABBIE HOFFMAN

Nobody reads leaflets.
    —JERRY RUBIN

Scene: late fall, 1969. A stately office building on Hanover Square. Alan Marcuson raps: ". . . Our big hassle was that we had every two-bit hustler from here to Hong Kong between us and Mick. Everybody was wandering around and poncing about —nothing ever came out straight. Jann's letter kind of blew it all up. Three days before we were to go to print, we were told that we weren't going to get the negs of the American edition. Jann thought that would pull the carpet out from under us. But we all worked like fuckery and got a forty-page issue out on our own.

"There were all sorts of hassles. The check for the previous print had bounced for a start. The printers wouldn't touch us until they had the bread up front. So we are waiting for the money to go to print, getting everything together . . . nobody knew what the fuck was going on. Then it filters through to us—in a vague sort of way—that Mick wants to liquidate Trans-Oceanic Comics. We're supposed to be paid a month's salary and . . . that's it. But we had an issue ready. We were fucked if we were going to accept that decision.

"So we started pressuring Jon Ratner, who was distributing the magazine. We could have really made it tough for him, which we didn't want to do, but our backs were against the wall. We told Jon that if he didn't get Wenner to take the heat off and let us go to press we were going to pull every one in the book . . . We just kept this kind of constant pressure up. Eventually Wenner backed down and said all right, go to print this time.

"Before all this started, we'd talked to Mick about getting another investor in—which he agreed to and we have—and expanding the whole operation. Then he . . . I don't know what, but he decided to liquidate. I think it was mainly that the whole thing was becoming too much of a hassle and Mick didn't want a legal scene. I think Wenner must have pressured Mick and Mick bent, so he sent the order through not to print. Or someone did . . . Mick's lawyers maybe . . . we never knew . . .

"But now that we've been through all this, it's pulled us together. It's great. We know what we want to do and we're doing it."

What if at the last moment, when the banquet table is set and the cymbals clash, there should appear suddenly, and wholly without warning, a silver platter on which even the blind could see that there is nothing more, and nothing less, than two enormous lumps of shit.

—HENRY MILLER

Geoffrey Cannon

BOB ZIMMERMAN

Morning in the Royal Esplanade Hotel, Ryde, opposite the station and the hovercraft which takes people to the mainland. Through the night the road from the Isle of Wight Festival (four miles distant) has been crowded with people walking to the ferry. Now, in a three-quarter light, they wander up and down outside the hotel, shattered: wearing anoraks, ponchos, blankets, Afghan coats, etc. Inside the hotel, two white-jacketed waiters press up against the windows, trying for an idea of what is happening.

A late-middle-aged couple eat early breakfast: the toast is cut diagonally. The husband is practicing stern expressions, in a hotel full of alien journalists. But his lady is, wonderingly, sympathetic. "Of course, I wouldn't have gone, but I would like to have seen him, to say I'd been there." As if the concert had been a Passover, held in a Christian church.

These are people who are no doubt reached by the grotesque reports in the British popular press which dwelt, yet again, on drugs, freakouts, nakedness, hooliganism, and sex. After the concert ended the night before, Georgio Gomelsky, who is a friend and a pop manager with ten years in the music business, came out of the room where the journalists from the English popular press were telephoning their stories back to London. He retailed them to me with a faint amazed hysteria. Both the popular press and the inhabitants of the Royal Espanade Hotel were looking for clues. Men in brogues and flannels sat in the coffee lounge, pretending not to read the Daily Sketch and the Daily Mail. But they didn't find the story there.

What happened at the Bob Dylan concert was mental, not physical. By mental I don't mean intellectual. Its effect was, rather, sensual: one could feel it without reflection. I can only try to give an account of it by saying what was in my mind, and the minds of everyone I spoke to who was there.

For the train to leave for Portsmouth from Waterloo was appropriate: "Waterloo Sunset" is Ray Davies's most lyrical and idyllic song. He makes the gray, faded station pastoral; into an Eden blessed because it is ordinary.

The train is full of newly discovered companions. Everyone is humming a thesaurus of Dylan, switching from tune to tune as from mood to mood.

There are hundreds of Richie Havens fans on the ferry: so many spades that, perhaps, we're all going to a contest between Zeal and Magnanimity. But, five hours later, as Havens sings, there's no contest. His intensity catches the audience. His drummer's bongos sway, and almost bounce, to his celebration of Dylan: "Maggie's Farm," played with very fast cross-rhythms, Afro-style.

Previously, Julie Felix, stumbling through "Chimes of Freedom," showed only what a distance Dylan himself has traveled since such numbers and how mindless they sound if sung now as pointed, modern political statements. "Society just won't be the same after Julie's next number," camped a friend to Keith Richards, and he was right. It's not so simple to make one's fortune as a protest singer nowadays.

"And here's to you, my rambling boy: may all your rambling bring you joy." Tom Paxton sang the lines a little like Shirley Collins would; lightly and lovingly. The crowd was very quiet. Paxton had achieved the magic, surrounded by people half a mile deep, of making his song intimate as (to me) he, too, saluted Dylan.

Then he sang "Talking Vietnam Blues," a number which makes a pantomime out of the war with an effect like that of Brecht or a morality play. Paxton's Vietnam is peopled with bungling cardboard figures, further out in madness and monstrosity than the world of *Catch 22*. He finished the number, and the crowd rocked from the impact of its own roar.

The concert was full of Dylan numbers, sung by different singers in different styles, as if each were Dylan at a different age or mood. It's common enough, of course, for any concert to contain Dylan numbers; he's composed plenty. But on this occasion, if all the singers were interpreting Dylan songs, what would Dylan himself do? The fact of his presence, somewhere on the island, as the afternoon progressed, made his songs on other lips sound strange and disassociated. One imagined him in one of the helicopters or light aircraft that were constantly circling overhead, hearing himself, and watching the crowds listening to himself. There was danger that the experience of the day would be overwhelmed by its myth.

Around in the evening, the air tightened. Celebrities strolled in, with beautiful ladies, dressed as if they'd just stepped out of helicopters (which they had). The records played between gigs were a strange apposition: characteristically, "Honky Tonk Women" and "Hare Krishna." On stage, as night fell, the curtains were closed, in preparation for Dylan. They were tatty and creased, obviously hired hurriedly from some theatrical supplier. The stage was made into a lashed-up cardboard Parthenon. The atmosphere was that of the Walthamstow Supergrand, or of a hoedown in—well, perhaps in Hibbing, Minnesota.

The Band are what Blind Faith might have been, had the English group formed seven years ago. Robbie Robertson and Levon Helm, especially, know each other so well that as they sing and play together, interchanging instruments, their music becomes love's body, which they create, but which does not belong to them. They celebrate their own music, rather than invent it. As the playing passes from man to man, each is reminded of the hundreds of times they played together, privately, before.

They played numbers in every style from that of their old

band, the Hawks, to country music, to the solemnity of "I Shall Be Released" and their song of epic tribulation, "The Weight." The colossal p. a. system addressed not only the seated crowd but also people half asleep on the Downs, people swaying and smiling to each other in tents, and people sitting round small fires. And the voice of the band, dexterously intimate, became an amplified version of old stories told round a fire.

And, after all, everybody on the darkened slopes had traveled over water, undergone some (small) hardships to be there, and had walked a substantial distance to their places. Like the Band themselves, we had traveled and had arrived. We came to have confirmed and enlarged experiences, memories, images, which were already on our minds; to make joyful physical and mental encounters.

I became increasingly uninterested in noting what numbers the Band were playing, and, instead, attended to the effect their music was having on everyone. Despite the odd missile, or yells for Dylan or for a doctor, the Band's music was lifting the spirit. Their phrasing soars, and, accumulatively, successive phrases work above each other, as if collecting the strength of those before. This, to me, is their magic. It's not so much a matter of their musicianship, but of their ability to suffuse the mind with a radiant sense of space and happiness. They, like Paxton and Havens before them, had created a marvelous setting for Dylan.

I can tell you very quickly what Dylan did. He appeared in a white suit. He played a very loose-limbed acoustic guitar. And he worked through the Bob Dylan song book (leaving out the more gauche political numbers) from "She Belongs to Me" to "Maggie's Farm" to "Mr. Tambourine Man" to "Lay, Lady, Lay" to "Ramona" to "It Ain't Me Babe" to "Highway 61," to "Mighty Quinn" to "Rainy Day Women Nos. 12 & 35." Naturally, he sang in his new voice. He sang for an hour, walked off, gave no encore, and left.

But (as they say) there was more to it than that. Dylan's songs have lain in our minds for years now. And his relationship with society's view of itself has, over these years, become more and more complex and charged with meaning. There are certain events which cannot be disassociated from Dylan's own references to them. Television specials on race, Vietnam, bureaucratic violence, anomie, etc., don't need Dylan's songs as sound tracks: he's already made the point. For him to sing of these things now could only be a caption to a text he has already written. And his overt indifference to public affairs these last three years to me is because he knows he has made the points, which have made contact with everyone's perception of the disasters of peace, as well as ever he will be able.

His privacy, and the light personal style of "Nashville Skyline," are not merely a profitably tantalizing strategy. The analogy between a Dylan interview and the oracular remarks of religious prophets is close; not because, like a prophet, his words are searched so keenly, by so many people, that jokes and silence and games become the only way to escape interpretation. He can only be himself by being personal.

As he sang on Sunday, the voice of "Nashville Skyline" stretched out to cover songs which we'd only heard before sung by Dylan with high tension. Now he was so at ease. And his stance was his own version of the Johnny Cash stance: intonation underemphasized and flowing. "It Ain't Me, Babe," previously a number he wrenched out of himself, now had the simplicity and flow almost of "I Walk the Line."

It was essential to the concert that Dylan sung no new songs. New songs, in my view, are ruinous in concerts. A concert is a setting where, as a member of the audience, you want to start playing a song in your head as soon as you recognize it, so that you refresh and renew your experience by listening not to a copy of the song (as you would if you listened to a record) but to a version of it which is itself refreshed and renewed by its author.

The potency of the Dylan concert lay in his demonstration that his music can, indeed, be refreshed and renewed. (Unlike the early Byrds, for example, whose Apollonian style could only be repeated, not developed.)

Dylan's new voice is sinuous and self-confident. Electric music nowadays is often measured on Greek parameters: Apollonian or Dionysian. Dylan now is closer to the earth, further from the mind; and the content of his music is subtle, almost crafty. It didn't feel Greek. And, as he played, it seemed immaterial what songs he sang. In a way, he needed only introduce a song, as a preacher might a text, for us to hear his voice.

He was touching on a body of work—his own—so complex and so dense and so well known that his easy style seemed that of a consummate scholar. And I kept on thinking—what scholar? What text?

The Talmud. And Dylan's style is now Hasidic. Joyful, earthy: its value absolutely depending on constant recreation of itself (unlike Christian scholarship, which is by comparison inflexible and cerebral).

And Dylan himself looked and acted like a Hasidic scholar, too. He bobbed and weaved and swayed, smiling, in possession of an incalculable amount of potent knowledge, which was believed. I kept seeing his slight beard as plaited hair on his cheeks. He was happy, and full of life.

Bob Dylan has gone full circle. Now, he's wise; and he's also Bob Zimmerman. He has come to his people. And his people is us.

Tom Smucker

THE POLITICS OF ROCK:
Movement vs. Groovement

In my lifetime, which is exclusively post-World War II time, I have felt some interest and identity for two things: Rock and Roll, and "the Movement." One is a cultural form, and the other a political form, and both are peculiar to my generation.

Rock, and its constellation of associations—Dope, Hippie Ideals and Styles—gave a form for our middle-class avant-garde rebellion against tedium and repression that wasn't associated with the irrelevant and abhorrent situations of the past. I remember, when I was in high school, via my Advanced College Prep English Class I developed an attachment to the poets of the '20s who lived in Paris, particularly e. e. cummings. Eventually, of course, I had to see that as a dead allegiance to a time gone by whose attempts at freedom were largely failures, as my own fucked-up life could prove.

Eventually, of course, I *had* to see that the Beach Boys, of course, had been my avant-garde all along. That they were dealing with the context that I lived in.

Likewise, somehow, the Movement, or the New Left, has usually been described as a political alternative for our generation. "Don't Trust Anyone Over Thirty" used to be a popular motto. And for a while (less so now I think), it was in vogue to give present-day America a totally new political interpretation related to its advanced technology.

Both of the above generalizations, actually, aren't really true.
And that's why they sound a little hackneyed.

Rock and Roll has reached such a level of success that it is
almost boring, and is becoming so old that it can spawn a revival
of itself. The promises of Haight-Ashbury, if you didn't guess,
haven't been fulfilled. Not many of us, though we tried, were
able to live like the Beatles, and now many of us aren't sure we'd
want to. The kids beginning to buy records now are the same age
as Elvis Presley's recording career.

The New Left and/or Movement is going through some
heavy convolutions relating heavier to its middle-aged and aged
heritage. We are seemingly at a moment of disintegration and
crystallization, to the point where it isn't clear whether the term
New Left is appropriate anymore, and that vague sense of a
social "Movement" doesn't seem enough.

Nevertheless, outside of the institutions connected with home
and the Establishment (school, church, psychotherapy, the draft,
the Stu Erwin Show, *Time* magazine), my life has swung back
and forth between Rock and Roll and the Movement, and it's
only *their* failures that I can feel responsible for and sad about.

I would imagine, too, that if most post-Hiroshima people look
at their lives they will see the same thing.

The problem, of course, is that there seems to be some sort of
connection between the two—they get entangled in your life—
but it isn't clear what the connection is. They both developed at
the same time, and both, in some ways, dealt with the same
problems—Race, Sex, Repression, Class (remember when Rock
was low-class unrespectable?). But they are both so new
that . . .

On the one hand you have cats like Lennon who have really
gotten into their thing and are *forced* to prove that there is no
connection. That Rock is Politics. Or the third-rate ideology of
the movie *Wild in the Streets*. Or far-out jive like Marshall Mc-
Luhan runs down to give a set of symptoms and tools credit for
all social reality.

On the other hand you have the politicos seeing all those kids
smoking dope, tired of school, into something, and the idea of

course is how do you pick up on that. Even if they aren't class-conscious.

Well, lately, to be simple, I've been into my political phase. I was planning to go up to Woodstock anyway since it sounded like An Event, plus a lot of good groups (which is why I imagine most people went). But I was wondering, well, is that *responsible*, shouldn't I stay in New York City handing out useless leaflets convincing nobody to be radical instead? Or attend a meeting? And then I had my excuse. Somehow Abbie Hoffman had coerced, conned, or threatened the festival promoters into giving him space at the festival and bread for the Movement. Various groups in New York were getting together and planning to go up to Woodstock to organize. I could have my weekend *and* be political.

It also seemed like a chance to resolve the Rock-New Left contradiction in my life. Here was a large, organized (the first attempt at a coalition between New York groups) attempt to relate politically to a Rock Event.

What happened was instructive.

First off, everyone knew that this was something new. A test to see if the Movement could relate to something hip.

Here were the approaches I heard suggested:

1) Point out to people that what they were doing wasn't fun, free, warm, wet, or whatever, that it was happening under Capitalism, and therefore bad.

2) Point out to people that what they were doing isn't real. Bread and Circuses, Co-optation, The Plastic Straitjacket, that it was happening under Capitalism and therefore phony.

3) Talk to the Natives in Their Language Approach—Be Elitist but Don't Show It. Talk hip to hide your straight ideas.

4) Point out to people that Rock and Roll is good, that it's "Ours," but it's run by capitalist corporations and thus mis-treated, stolen from "US," fucked-over, etc. That it's happening under Capitalism and therefore suppressed. That, of all things, the Promoters were trying to make money off this.

All of these were interpretations of the event. All of them are wrong as far as I can see. But nevertheless, no matter what we thought, the preparations for the Festival were mainly the printing of literature, banners and posters, and preparations for doing more printing up at the festival.

The promoters had also given us a section of the grounds, across the woods by the Hog Farm, to camp out and set up booths: Movement City. All these people, see, will walk over to Movement City, go to the booths of the different groups, scoop up literature . . .

The old campus lit table approach.

The other plan was to go around to the different campsites and rap with people.

Rap means talk, the same old verbal-intellectual bullshit. But it sounds hipper.

Well, we got up there with our literature. And we set up our booth (I'm in MDS) with the others. And behind it was this $1,000 printing press that was going to run off a newspaper each day.

As you may know by now, having read it in *Time-Life-Newsweek*-Special Issue *Life-Times-Post-Rolling Stone-Fusion*-On the Radio-TV, Woodstock wasn't like that. It was big (I have my big anecdotes), it was far-out (I have my far-out anecdotes). (But I'm not going to use them.)

Besides the fact that our analysis and preparations were all wrong, the Festival, at that time, which seems a long time gone, . . . was a mind blower.

I was there, Abbie Hoffman was there, SDS, MDS, Mother fuckers, Peaceniks, Swamis, Mehr Babaites, the Hot Chow Mein truck guys, we were all there, trying to pick up on it, but nobody got all the energy. Not even the performers. Not even Janis Joplin, who I once saw DANCE with 3,000 people—she couldn't really relate to the whole audience. Too big, too far-out.

The one good tactic planned (to storm the gates and let everyone in free) was never used. Everyone was already in. The gates weren't even ever put up.

The booths were never used. The scene was so far-out people started leaving right away. Literature got rained on or was never distributed. The plates for the printing press never showed up, so it couldn't be used.

Friday night the rain was a very bad scene for the many people there without cars or tents to get into. We awoke to hear the U.S. Committee to Aid the National Liberation Front announcing over their loudspeaker: "Get Your Dry Che Guevara T-Shirts: Only Two Dollars."

The T-shirts had cost them, so I heard, about 5–10 percent of that, maybe, and were silk-screened earlier in New York.

That's called Radical Politics.

The next day, Sunday, when it started raining, we rushed back from the concert to save our sleeping bags and saw it, the thousand-dollar printing press, standing in the rain, unattended. We covered it, a little amazed, and that stayed my symbol of all our political activity—leaflets blowing through a field, a printing press in the rain that was never used.

The Movement failed at Woodstock, in a small way because the event was basically incomprehensible to everyone up there. The incredibly mind-blowing aspect of *that* weekend, however, only helped expose and render useless an approach that usually appears just irrelevant.

Once again the Movement approached things from a stagnant, formalized position *exterior* to what was happening, while managing to be both uncomprehending *and* elitist about it. This was shown by our inability to think of anything to do except write things down on a piece of paper and hand them out to people. And our acceptance of a campsite that put us in a particular location, distinct from those where just plain old campers were.

This was to be expected, since the Movement must, really, set itself in opposition to the existing order, and must constantly be creating positions of opposition. That's the idea. In this case, though, it was clear to everyone that the opposition was meaningless, and the alternative position was swept away immediately by the monster energy and eventual good vibes of the event itself.

The problem remains though, because Rock and Roll, in spite of what the hip theorists say, whether they are Leftist-hip or Buddhist-hip, works in a constant process of assimilation of contradictions.

What does assimilation of contradictions mean?

It means, first off, that Rock and Roll, Rock culture, hip, pop, and youth culture all spring out of middle-class reality, and spring out of capitalism, and all spring out of affluence.

That Rock and Roll wasn't created (like the Port Huron Statement) by a bunch of smart-asses sitting around saying, "Let's make an alternative revolutionary culture;" it was made by some businessmen who began to understand that the recreation of black music (blues, rhythm and blues) into a white context made money.

Of course they never understood the total significance of it. And that's why we all like Rock and Roll.

Because it contains both the respectable reality of its own position and the suggestion of something destructive to that reality. So it was never really clear whether Elvis was a good guy or a bad guy. That's the idea.

Just like the ever-continuing dialectic of black/white that everyone *knows* is the staple of Rock and Roll. And will continue to be as long as it, racism, and repression (sexually) continue to exist here.

Well, all I'm trying to say with this muddled theory is that Rock and Roll, like you and me, is a child of capitalism. Listening to Rock and Roll can be pro, anti, non, or a-capitalist, also like you and me.

To me Woodstock was another Rock and Roll adventure. Since, lately, the music has become slightly boring (who has been excited about a record or a concert lately?) Rock and Roll created an event that transcended the music, and that event was definitely exciting and incomprehensible, the way Rock music used to be.

A higher plane of assimilated contradictions.

What this meant, however, was that it was necessary to have money behind it, i.e., capitalist promoters, be they dumb, smart, hip, or piggish. It also meant that it would be a middle-class experience, not a revolutionary one, although there would be revolutionary implications or seeds in what happened.

That is to say, the kids (including us, finally) were up there to have a good time. And would have it Goddamit, no matter what. The possibilities for a good time were there, and so the possibilities for a bad time were ignored.

This is how you survive in affluent middle-class adolescence, and beyond. You take the good things, which are lying here or there, and turn them into something you can dig or turn yourself into someone who can dig them. You ignore the rest.

It worked beautifully at Woodstock. You took the massive energy, the freedom (dope, going nude), all the good music, and general friendliness, and dug that. You ignored whether or not someone was making money from it. You ignored the rain and mud, lack of water, toilets, food, and too much sun, and assumed that on some level people would provide.

They did. It never became a crisis.

In fact, the few inconveniences gave everyone something to do, and developed a reason for cooperation, which made you feel good, although it can hardly be said that the audience themselves solved the problems of food, medical supplies, and water.

Now at the time, seeing the total meaninglessness of our "political" attempts, and digging the good vibes, from the crowd, the music, and being in the country, we were hip to the idea that the Movement was missing the whole thing.

We camped near the Hog Farm, the commune that served the free food and helped the people on bummers. Our line going up there was that they were co-opted sell-outs and so on who were going to con people into thinking that COPS WERE GOOD IF THEY WERE HIPPIES. (They had been hired by the Festival.)

Well so on and so forth for that shit. I ended up eating Hog Farm food (mainly grains) that was cheap and good, admiring their productivity and good vibes and comparing them to the politicians and their leaflets.

In the rain and mud, water shortages, heat and cold, the Hog Farm served the people, whatever their ideology, while others were trying to point out that if there wasn't enough water, that meant capitalism was bad.

At the time, I went away from the weekend with hordes of good vibes. Sharing with people, being in the country, not relating to possessions. Being able to smoke anywhere you wanted.

And I was thinking that this good-vibes stuff is where it's at.

Since then, however, I have heard and read (and yes, written) so much about Woodstock that I'm sick of it. WMCA has a special Woodstock record selection. *Life* magazine has a special issue. Someone on the block has a "We Proved It at Woodstock" bumper sticker.

The only thing I'm thankful for is that no one sent Norman Mailer there.

And, as we all know, the good vibes don't last.

We were all out in the country around nothing but white middle-class kids (notice that intentional lack of soul acts or more proletarian acts up there). We were in the country. And entertainment, food, and water was being provided, at least minimally.

We didn't build the city, that's for sure.

Sometimes I wonder if it can ever happen again. Whether anyone will be able to pull off a super-Festival again where things are run just well enough to keep everyone happy and just poorly enough to give everyone something to do.

It was interesting, you know, when we went over to the concert area, how eager people were to take our leaflets. Out of boredom and lack of fear.

If one is sufficiently well run, I bet it will get as boring as the Fillmore concert-light show thing has become. Nothing to do but watch it run.

And when I think about it now, in tranquility, after the original rush of good feelings, I can recall my bad moment anecdotes, too, which only go to prove that one far-out weekend can't turn around twenty crummy years of middle-class life. (A bunch of kids on Mescaline, next to us, spending the evening insulting each other, laughing, not bad.)

Finally, no one really had anything to say about what was going on. You were just sitting on your blanket. And at some point that becomes a drag. If you aren't a personal friend of Jimi Hendrix and aren't at the performers' party eating strawberries and cream, but in a blanket sharing a Coca-Cola it took an hour to get.

Well, it was a limited game, and someone should have run down the limits to people. But it had to be someone who understood the game, and related to it, and knew why people were playing it, and what the payoff was or might be.

Sandy Perlman

VAN DYKE PARKS

Van Dyke Parks's new release has a title (*Song Cycle,* Warner Bros. W1727/WS1727) in the tradition of Schubert or Mahler and a cover not unlike all those groovy moldy Westminster or Vox classical music albums recorded in Europe (often by native Europeans—we bought the tapes) and put out here in the late 1950s and early 1960s. (You know the period, wherein record cover art generally passed from mere graphic to photographic.) This is a cover lusciously heavy in the browns. But as for the record, that's certainly a direct function of American information density. It had to happen here. More eclectic than the new one by the Buffalo Springfield, and with more all-American nationalism than the first one by the Doors (whose nationalism was mostly Southern Californian anyway), its main connection with histori-cal Rock 'n' Roll is probably in the intention (a matter of ideas rather than execution). Also there's guilt by association due to the fact that Van Dyke played on the Byrds' *5-D* and the first Buckley album, collaborated with Brian Wilson on *Smile* (which wound up later on as *Smiley Smile*) and produced the fabulous Mojo Men hit cover version of "Sit Down I Think I Love You." But who exactly is Van Dyke Parks?

Born ("on base") in Hattiesburg, Mississippi, he once lived in Bayside, Long Island, Queens, New York City. Now he lives in a

garage apartment close to a big old L.A. Freeway in which city
he's served time as a super-session man, educated by Carnegie
Tech, and from the fourth through ninth grades by the Columbus
Boys Choir School. Today—since this even bears on the album—
his interest is in Thoreau, Emerson and the conservation problem. Enough. Enough.

Now, about Marcel Duchamp we've gotta say this (at this
time 'cause it also bears): his ready-made move looms large in
the history of the potentiality of objects. It's well known that this
person's self-conscious placement of an ordinary urinal in the
midst of a pretty fancy early twentieth-century art show simultaneously created an extraordinary art historical urinal and
added the artist's intention to the dimensions within which
objects could be manipulated. But his use of this ready-made
was questionable. The art show wasn't its rightful spot. It was
out of place/out of phase. So Marcel Duchamp wound up a very
nasty comedian, i.e., both funny and disturbing. Setting a pattern.
And, in fact, it's only been recently that the presence of a ready-
made (anyone at all, anywhere at all) has become blatantly
hackneyed enough to prove not always hilarious, not always
scary, but sometimes just potentially comforting. R. Meltzer's
term, "academic beauty," encompassing such truck as Steve
Noonan, Tim Buckley, Simon and Garfunkel, The Bee-Gees, and
Pearls Before Swine, implicates this newer role for the ready-
made: the formal one of modular component. Ready-mades can
be taken from anywhere and plugged in anywhere. Their neutral-
ity is violated only by the intention of their manipulators (and
this intention, of course, controls where they wind up). Something becomes a ready-made when your manipulative intention
takes it from one context to another. When it is intentionally
recontextualized. And when these new and old contexts are
equivalent, then the ready-made could seem comfortable and
comforting. (In phase.) Back to the academically beautiful, and
we note that the ideal for this stuff's words is most of the poetry
we had to learn in the seventh through twelfth grades. Perhaps
that explains its high dullness potential. Not only over-familiarity,
but bad associations and bad Karma even. I mean, I mean that

the academically beautiful is obvious clichés. Although they are, to tell the truth, mainly of the Bizzaro variety. Formally rather than exactly reproductive. Only reproducing styles which seem to refer to (evoke) all that junior high and high-school stuff. Bizzaro ready-mades can pass for the real clichés because of this acute formal accuracy. Information density (force-fed here by the schools, there by public communications) can impose some absolute standards for the beautiful. And the case of the Pearls Before Swine makes clear how effective the pressure of the cultural pool (i.e., information density acting environmentally) can be. The Swine's first album is dedicated to Dick Sommer who spins the disk on WBZ way up in Boston. But where these Swine come from is the vicinity of Cape Kennedy (née Canaveral) way down in Florida. How? And you've the right to ask. Because it seems that WBZ's transmissions are bouncing offa the ionosphere, which makes them heard in Florida. Where the Swine heard them and developed (influenced) a style reminiscent of something as particular as Dick Sommer's favorites (Tom Rush, "The Urge for Going," etc.) during the late fall and winter of 1966.

Now, as for Van Dyke Parks's own move, it required prior modularization and neutralization of ready-mades to deprive them of their ever-implicit protest function. Contemporary ready-mades can be taken for granted. *Can be.* Allowing them to serve lots of simultaneous functions. Rather than merely protest (a simple out-of-phase position), they can be the locus for really complex interference networks. *Smiley Smile* was an early step toward postcynical interference effects wherein many on-the-face-of-it contradictions were embodied in smooth eggs that at once did away with and preserved these very contradictions. Nobody fails to be somehow amazed by the "Woody Woodpecker Symphony" (instrumentally in the same league with The Who's "Waltz for a Pig"), "Vegetables," and "Heroes and Villains." And yet there's been confusion. Critics like Dickie Goldstein take a "spiritual" view of *Smiley Smile,* while others compare it to Frank Zappa's G. A. P. O. humor. And certainly there are many rampant physiological references. ("Vegetables"—digestive tract indications maybe?) In England, where the Beach Boys were voted last year's big group, the album got up to right near the top of the charts, probably as an automatic reaction, only to be greeted later with significant consumer nausea. Perhaps a problem was too much emphasis, or put otherwise, a delicacy deficiency. The Beach Boys employed an enormous stock of ready-mades (including many of their own), manipulated via a nice and self-conscious production job—but the idée fixé having to do with the primacy of contradiction was finally overwhelming.

Sure enough Van Dyke Parks starts with many of the same intentions. (Wasn't he Brian's collaborator?) But he's got a softer touch (like in basketball). He thinks art is rooted in the anonymous. And that ideas and intentions are getting up in the saddle. Leaving imagination as manipulative, synthetic and sort of irresponsible. Altogether this means that imagination synthesizes ready-mades that have been turned into anonymous clichés via the information density route of overexposure through constant appearances on your radio (Top 40 and others), your TV and your tradition (folk songs, for example). As with the cynics (later Stones, Kinks, Who) there's an emphasis on positioning—but not to get things all questionable. Rather Van Dyke's synthetic move is toward a whole new order of stability, restabilization within a new context. So his *Song Cycle* is at once synthetic, derivative, funny, out of and back into phase, cliché-ridden, filled with ready-mades, overly familiar and unfamiliar, manipulative, anonymous, pretty pretty and manufactured with an all-time autonomous and superior production job. Clearly this finished product isn't a canned version of anything. Nor even an approximation. Today the sound effect isn't merely convenient. (Organized sound has achieved autonomous integrity!) And if it took seven months and the seventy-eight persons named on the back cover to do all this, then it's been worth it.

But what does it manage to sound like? Taking side one as a sequential example: beginning with Steve Young of Gadsen, Alabama, singing "Black Jack Daisy," a bluegrass (folk); then "Vine Street" (by Randy Newman, soon-to-be-famous) with a big Broadway Pop-Swill influence, a lot of strings and prominent snatches of Beethoven's Ninth; "Palm Desert" syncopated with horns from Mahler; "Widows Walk" sung by Van Dyke with even more mince to his voice than Mick's had on the *Got Live If You Want It* "Lady Jane"; "Laurel Canyon Blvd.," a very short automotive traffic song, completely unrelated to the Beatles, Beach Boys or Chuck Berry; "The All Golden," a song in the American style about Steve Young, it includes "Glory, Glory Hallelujah!" amidst itself. In a Mahleresque arrangement hinting at Charles Ives. Ended by a train noise sequence, reminiscent of the great train arrival nostalgia scene in "Chappaqua"; finally "Van Dyke Parks" (a song in the public domain) with some more of that American folk tradition sung in combo with equally traditional "Star Spangled Banner" war sounds (appropriate to these lines: "And the rocket's red glare, the bombs bursting in air . . .").

But this sequential evaluation just won't do and perchance only the analytical mode will. Outside of the appearance (on side two as an intermezzo) of the long-rumored-but-hard-to-get great George Washington Brown version of "Donovan's Colours" (a version wherein the skippy treble ideal of the xylophone is the rule; also a very mechanical-musical toy-sound version, wound up and down by a *ratchet*), the single most immediately striking thing about the record is its intimate relationship to silence. First a justificatory statistical note: there are only three fadeouts: "Black Jack Daisy" to "Vine Street," "Palm Desert" to "Widows Walk," "The Attic" to "Laurel Canyon Blvd." Leaving us with very little heard silence and Van Dyke with maybe the most significant use of silence rendered absolutely significant by its merest absence since Mahler and Bruckner. Thus a destruction of silence, by noise, which makes silence into the ever-implicit (but never-present) comparative. (Subtly evoked by its absence. Always present but never there.) The closest thing in the history of Rock 'n' Roll is, of course, the Bronx Genius Phil Spector and his fantastic ground theory-silence denial hits: from the Ronettes to the Righteous Brothers to Ike and Tina Turner. But Van Dyke sustains this trick for so much longer than anyone has before. And like all good silence denial stuff the eventual cumulative impression is oceanic and homogeneous (wavelike sound motion dropping hints of secretive submarine cycles. Exactly.). Of course there aren't any unknown tongues. Oceanic music is so homogeneous as to be quite vulnerable to the excruciating breakthrough of the tongue. Rather, there's an active tongue avoidance principle.

In conclusion, who is to say that this isn't one of the greatest of Muzak albums? Joining Phil Spector's greatest, Herb Alpert, Procol Harum, Bob Dylan (*Blonde on Blonde* and *Highway 61*), Mantovani and others too, too numerous. And this select company makes it not only (above all) traditional in every possible sense, not only a true idealization of the Muzak idea (i.e., universally eclectic silence denial), but also such an acceptance of so many disparate elements as to cancel out all interference and render this most up-to-date cynicism postcynical, i.e., absolutely accepting. (His arms are open wide.)

Howard Junker

THE FIFTIES

When the time comes, it may not be easy, despite the rebirth of Richard Nixon and Elvis Presley, to muster nostalgia for the Fifties. (Davy Crockett and Roy Cohn, Grace Kelly and the Playboy Bunny, *My Fair Lady* and adult Westerns, filter tips and instant coffee, Zen and the art of the Roller Derby, Ban the Bomb and togetherness, Harry Belafonte, Jack Kerouac, Dr. Kinsey, and The Golden Age of Television.)

But some of the words we used to use already have the power to charm, so great is the distance between then and now.

Jargonwise, the Fifties spoke a finalized version of advertisingese. (Let's run it up the flagpole and see who salutes.) Euphemists offered: the Police Action, peaceful coexistence, nuclear blackmail, freedom fighter, creeping Momism, desegregation, payola, cleavage, recession, pinko. Korea did little to enrich the language (brainwashing, gook). But from Russia came Sputnik, hence beatnik.

One kind of nostalgia for the Eisenhower Era looks back to an age of innocence. But this apparent innocence was protected at a cost. Irony, ambiguity, complexity were academic passwords that sophomores enacted as apathy. The common language was designed to not say what was meant: Would you like to have a cup of coffee/come up for a drink? (In the Sixties, *pace* Lenny

Bruce: "Let's ball.") Sarcasm (Wanna lose ten ugly pounds? Cut off your head) and innuendo (I have here the names) were basic modes of conversation. Much literary imagination went toward developing acceptable variations on Mailer's (1948) fuggin, as in effing, frigging. Sick jokes finally mentioned other unmentionables, and with *Lady Chatterly's Lover* (1959) the unprintable became available in drugstores and at your local supermarket.

Beneath much of the (dirty) white buck, saccharine, other-directed innocence of the Fifties lurked smug obliviousness. You could still say colored. (Ixnay, ofay.) Niggerlipping didn't seem such a terrible way to describe wetting the end of a cigarette. A riot was really funny. A soul kiss involved the tongue. The ghetto was where (some of) the Jews had escaped from. Race as in arms, rat and drag. A pill was like a dope. A bust was a pair of knockers, bazooms, lamps, as in M.M., B.B. and Diana Dors. Crash as in going to a party without an invite. A joint was maybe a bar.

Getting stoned meant hitting the hard stuff (not horse, booze). A quick brew: quaff a foamy. Whales' tails, Thumper. Here's to the Cardinal once. Chug-a-lug. Getting blotto, stinko, shit-faced, loaded, smashed, plowed, bombed out of your ever-loving mind. Then: heaving, tossing, blowing your lunch (cookies). Upchuck, barf, puke. The problem of youth was getting served. Do you have proof (an I.D.)? Churchkey.

In short, in the Fifties, culture still enjoyed a literary base. Words (the novel) still mattered. Awareness was limited, not electronically total. And regionalisms, celebrated during the Thirties when the middle class stayed home, were not yet erased by television, which went coast to coast in 1951, and commercial jets, which crossed the Atlantic in 1958. Have gun, will travel.

In the Fifties, it was dangerous to take anyone at face value. (Are you for real?) In conformist times, you worried about Image (status), doubly anxious because words functioned as costume: are you hip?

Now you're talking (speaking my language). Certain key terms, dig, became juvenile gestures: L7 (index fingers together, pointing outward, extended horizontally, descended an equal distance, rejoined) equaled square (cube or octagon meant supersquare). The three-ring sign indicated cool; screwy was the finger twirled at the temple, then flung at the nut.

Status was divvied up into geographical dualisms: in, out; with it, from squaresville. Hepcat. Beat/Jazz contributed: daddy-o, pad, bread, gig, slip me some skin. And all that, like, well, you know, man, incoherence. (Holden Caulfield, Marty, Brando and the Method, action painting, the silent generation, Nichols and May, taking the fifth).

Don't hand me any of that jazz. (Take five.) Built-in shit detector. And the farmer took another load away.

Alienation was the absurd egghead bit. (Did Adlai sell out?) Psychology was Krazy, man, like, I nearly flipped. The best minds. The orgone box, Or, as the get-well card said: I'm glad you're sick, but I'm sorry you're ill. You only got hung up when somebody flaked out on you. If you psyched a test, you had it made. What, me worry?

Yes, above all, anti-frantic. Stay cool. Hang loose. No sweat (negative perspiration). Under control. Made in the shade. Big deal.

Duhhhh!

You're so dumb, you think manual labor is President of Cuba. You think Sherlock Holmes is a housing project. If brains were dynamite, you couldn't blow your nose.

Well, I'll be a dirty bird.

The antithesis of cool was the slow burn, indicated by touching the index finger to the tongue, extending it toward the unfortunate victim and announcing "Psss" as if touching a hot stove. A variation: same gesture: Chalk one up for me! Tuftittie. The way the cookie crumbles, The Royal Screw, hence The Royal Shaft, hence The King's Elevator. Up the creek without a paddle.

Cruising for a bruising. Don't give me any grief. You want a knuckle sandwich. Get Bent. Your ass is grass. Blast off. Suck gas. Wise up. Don't bug me. Drop dead. DDT. Finally gonna shut you down. Dump all over you. How's that grab you? Forty lashes with a wet noodle.

Who cut the cheese? The true clue: he who smelt it dealt it. Silent but deadly.

Hardeeharhar.

Antlers in the Treetop or Who Goosed the Moose.

That went over like a pregnant pole vaulter with a broken stick.

What a fake-out.

Almost everything was a drag (negative attitude, like it or lump it, better dead than red). Some guys did get a charge (some kicks). Have a blast. Really hairy. Going ape. Bad, Mean, Wicked, Evil. Bitchin. I eat her up. She sends me. Gone, man, gone. Into the air, junior birdmen.

If you weren't grounded, you could take off. And hack, screw, mess around. Goof off.

Where did you go? (Take me to your leader.) I dunno, whaddya wanna do? Catch some rays. (Shades.) Play charades, spin-the-bottle, Frisbee, pogo stick, Hula-Hoop, bowling, knock-knock, why did the moron?

Precisely at age thirteen, you became a teen-ager. And there were pajama parties and sock hops with a thumbful of 45's. Only bird dogs cut in on a slow dance. Every party has a pooper, that's why we invited you. They tried to tell us we're too young. Grow up.

Certain college studs stuffed phone booths, smashed pianos and, from automobiles, displayed their naked asses to passersby, an act variously called dropping trou, mooning, handing out the b.a., gotcha. Slipping them some pressed ham involved pressing one's bare butt against the window. Driving around with your penis hanging out the window was trolling for faggots. In the city, you could nerf a cab, i.e., bump it gently at a light. On the highway: chicken. Five points for a pregnant nun.

M*I*C*K*E*Y*M*O*U*S*E

The J.D.'s emerged. The hood. The Rock. (Don't knock the Rock.) Baddass. Tough an nails. Switchblade and zip gun for stomping, mixing it up, rumbles. (Squeezing a beer can.) Pegged pants and a greasy D.A.

Or: butch, crew cut, flat top, Princeton. Charcoal-grey flannel, belt-in-the-back, paisley, Shetland, Madras, bermudas. Our fine-quality pink button-down. Tweedy and preppy. Collegiate.

The common ground: blue jeans, as in the one and only

Levi's. (I'm wise to the rise in your Levi's.) As in shrink 'em in the bathrub. As in James Dean lives. As in engineer boots. Classy.

With a digression to honor circle pins, knee socks, saddle shoes, fruit boots, straight skirts, ponytails. Which came first, the sack or the chemise? On the one hand. On the other: beards, sandals and leotards—not yet called tights. Who wears short shorts? If you wore green on Thursday. . . .

As for sex, there was going steady (I.D. bracelet, ring-on-the-necklace, letter sweater or jacket). SWAK. And breaking up. But mostly the eternal search for a little quiff, quim, ginch, snatch, pussy, tail, nookey, poontang, action, etc. Bedroom eyes. Hot lips.

(The 4-F Club: findem, feelem, fuckem, forgetem.)

The first thing a make-out artist asked: is she fast? (Nice or good.) Does she put out? Lay it on the line? Do the deed?

He, of course, was always horny. (Blue balls.) When really hard up, he would even overlook her b.o., cooties, flat chest. (Scuzzy, grungy.) Her zits. Put a flag over her face and fuck her for Old Glory.

It was suspected that sometimes she, too, was climbing up the wall. Hot to trot.

In that case, if he didn't get shot down (stood up), he might suggest catching a flick. The passion pit. Parking. Let's go watch the submarines race.

For openers, a snow job. Coming on like Gang Busters. Are you trying to feed me a line?

She might come across if he were a big wheel, a B.M.O.C. On the ball, divine, clean cut, casual, snazzy, a really good (great) guy, the living end. Cute. Neat. Smooth. Sensitive. Peachy keen. A hunk. Hey, bobo. She would certainly be turned off if he were grubby, a phony, a sex fiend, bad news, out to lunch, a banana, weenie, yo-yo, turkey, spastic, nebbish. Gross. A fink. With a bad case of the uglies. A dumb cluck. A loser, creep, simp. A nothing. Of course, if he were a straight arrow, there'd be no danger of his trying to go too far. (Goodnight kiss. Heavy petting.) Meanwhile, awaiting his chance to go all the way, a circular bulge (rubber, safe, skin [going in bareback]; sophisticates referred to *her* device as a flying saucer) etched itself into his wallet.

Back with the guys, who had probably been wacking (jacking) off, beating the meat, flogging the log. (Keep it bent in Lent.) Pounding or pulling their collective pud, wang, schlong, dong, skin flute, meat horn, beef tube, pecker, as in pecker tracks in bed or, in the shower after gym, pecker checker (about yay! big). In other words, circle jerk, pocket pool, home and away. (Gang bang.) After a date they would ask, especially if he had a rep as a hot ticket, an ass man: Get much? Bare tit? In her panties? Your rocks off? Zilch!

And at school next day, where the brains were grinds and usually brown-nosers, her friends noticed the hickey on her neck. And the guys asked, how they hanging? (Lover's nuts.) One in front, for speed, he said.

Which brings us to that ultimate, fabulous Fifties experience: wheels.

Bombing around.

In a '49 Ford.

A '55 Chevy.

A Merc.

T-Bird.

Vette.

Coming and going in a Studey.

(Edsel.)

Stick shift, as in grind me a pound. Hang a left.

Fins and tails and two-tone and one year there was three-tone.

Raked and flamed, decked and lowered, chopped and channeled.

Duals.

Glass pack. Overhead cams.

Fuelie. Frenched lights. Coon tail.

I don't care if it rains or freezes, long as I've got my plastic Jesus.

A 4.56 rear end. Zero to sixty.

Driver ed.

I got cut out. Peel out, lay rubber.
Take it easy.
Anyway I can get it.
See you later, alligator.

Nick Browne

NOSTALGIA IS
THE GREAT PRETENDER

Nostalgia is a wretched witness who cannot describe the accident, gets the details all wrong, and is very likely in the pay of an interested party.

Yet at the Felt Forum, Saturday night, they bought her some new clothes, had her hair done, and hoped she'd get her lines right. The evening was called the 1950s Rock Revival, headlined by Chuck Berry, the Platters, and Bill Haley and the Comets. Although it was emceed by Scott Muni, he was just another boy friend and all she talked about was Alan Freed, her first and best old man.

"Who's Alan Freed?" asked a bouffant graduate bopper but no one answered her. Someone shouted "The Big Bopper Lives" as the show got underway. Anyone who wasn't with that was either a date or picked up the wrong tickets.

Both shows were sellouts with the overflow lining the stairs. The ads for the show had tried to hype interest, with a typographical montage of phrases of the '50s—staying cool, pegged pants, making out—but that was unnecessary, for memory has stronger cues than catch phrases.

In a late-night, near-empty saloon, a contemporary talking about the show stared at the whiskey-colored walls and said, "I

wonder if Bill Haley knows what he did? I wonder if he really
knows what he did?" The speaker then fell asleep.

What did he do? The same friend answered the question
later. " 'Rock Around the Clock' had already hit the top of the
charts and disappeared when they used it for that movie 'The
Blackboard Jungle.' How was it . . . the screen was blank and
then boom, the soundtrack explodes up every amp they can crank
out . . . one o'clock, two o'clock, three o'clock ROCK. He gave
us hard rock, he showed us how rock had to be. Without Haley
there'd be no Beatles."

Well, more than that. He gave all those young existentialists
up in the suburban farmlands south of Boston one terrifying
glimpse of what was afoot in the great urban jungles and life
styles on the battlefronts of youth.

The motorcycles and Chevy manifolds snarled by the night
river at the line where the edge of the city touched open country.
No basketball game or Holy Name dance without its confronta-
tion of gangs. These usually ended in negotiated withdrawal with
mutual honor, for those gangs were ersatz groups hastily assembled and nobody made much bones about standing opposite
the smallest, most pacific-looking individual until the leaders had
found reason to forget about it. This led occasionally to some
runty younger brother dragged along for the evening finding
himself casually surrounded by huge concentrations of enemy
troops while his burly elder brother had trouble finding takers.

Haley said with the sadness of too long exile that in recent
years he had been playing in Europe and South America, had
heard about the rock revival in these far-off places, but would not
believe in it until it happened in New York. Now here he was
headlining a sellout show . . . Well, doubtless there will be
more of these when other promoters count Saturday's house, but
being a popular period piece and selling your stuff in those two
for $5.98 stores are separate matters. Haley's group looked tired
and not really with it and they futzed about with lesser hits and a
couple of songs that weren't really theirs until going out with the
big one, what the people had come to hear. They rocked around
the clock and they got a standing ovation. As they went off, the

Garden Specials filed out to protect the stage. They were too late. About ten years too late. The men had promising jobs and balding tired guitar players started no juices simmering in the groins of their ladies.

The other acts, too, had the down value of retreads. Mention was made of some of the other great groups, and stars that couldn't be with us this night and you wondered how many of those singers and groups who had scored with one or two hits could be found in state hospitals, or holding down hotel desks, or with a little luck making a living picking a guitar back where it had all begun.

Dropped like discarded friends because they can do nothing more for me are Joni James, Kay Starr, Little Anthony and His Imperials, Fats the Man Domino, and the rest of that old gang of mine.

"This stuff used to turn me on right away," the lady said. "Now I need a drink."

Then Chuck Berry came out and plugged himself in. Old Chuck, it is said, wants his money in a roll which he puts in his pocket before going on stage. He goes through the motions, the duck walk, plays his axe upside down or something, and talks easy to the audience, but you know he's there for the payday. He came out strong with "Maybelline" and after that he had them. The automobile race mixed with an unspecified sexy regret. . . .

"Rainwater blowin' back under my hood, I knew it was doin' my motor good . . . Maybelline why can't you be true, you started back doin' the things you used to do . . ."

We raced and chased those old Fords and Chevys through the backroads of Eastern Massachusetts, spun them out into trees and haystacks, made varieties of inexpert love in them in a dozen woodsy roads and golf courses, and sat up sick nights with them tinkering with carburetors for they were all our patrimony. A man with wheels all his own was a cavalier with a retinue of the wheelless, with a passport to foreign towns.

On a snowy morning the street is silent, the elms and pines heavy with snow. You stand under a street light with your hockey bag and stick and wait, listening to the quiet and the hiss of the falling snow. You identify Ronnie's car in the dark coming down the street because he had added fog lights this year, a prince's flourish from Western Auto.

Hockey in the Boston Arena at 4 A.M., the clack of sticks and thump of bodies slammed against the boards . . . in class weariness is a badge of honor. There has been nothing so elitist since the Lafayette Escadrille.

In summers there was a tradition. On the fourth of July the boys from Dedham took wagons purloined from neighboring farms and rolled them downhill into a bonfire in Oakdale Square. By the mid-'50s this was increasingly difficult as you had to go two, three towns away to find enough farms with wagons left on them. It was also, of course, absolutely forbidden by the police, and the highest diplomatic honor I shall ever obtain was sitting in council with the chief of police who said that this year it was all over and that he was forced to crack down entirely and this being the case here were the things he would tolerate when we did it and here were the things he would not.

I doubt if it is done now because the last time I was through the area our richest source of wagons, the connecting roads, were superhighways and, looking at the terrain with the eye of an old partisan, I saw how certain essential roads were cut off and swamps that were way stations and holding areas had been drained to make bowling alleys and electronics firms. All this was less than fifteen years ago and today such a tale is as much a period piece as a Booth Tarkington novel.

Well, we have all come a piece since the '50s and nostalgia is the great pretender. If those '50s lyrics summon mellow recollections of maturing bodies whose sweets were still unknown, of cars parked by winter ponds and well-tuned engines humming down bleak New England roads, there is much that it chooses to conceal.

You know it all. It was a time of waiting, of endless becoming and the agony of lack of choice. There are few of us who would want to go back again.

So we left the Felt Forum when the Platters, the best preserved of the groups, sang "The Great Pretender," the national anthem of the youth of the '50s. They were to be followed by a group of college students who, the word had it, were very popular reviving songs of the '50s. We feared camp.

She'd be damned, the lady said, if she'd be mocked at the wake of her own childhood.

Ian Whitcomb

THE ROCKERS

*A Study of Rock's
Scourge of God—The Guardians
of the Balls in Big Beat*

If you asked me where rock's beginning was exactly I'd put my
finger on Bill Haley's kiss curl.

Don't worry. I know all about the pre-history—the underground of race records, legendary blues singers with one eye and
no leg, Kansas City R&B shouters of the thirties and forties. I
know that Fats Domino hit the charts even as long ago as 1948.
And that Haley covered black Joe Turner. I know what whitey
done . . .

I know that rock and roll was a hybrid, raping, snatching,
robbing like Baron Frankenstein in order to end up with Rock 'n'
Roll.

Nevertheless, the myth cannot be changed. At least, not in
England where we knew none of this stormy historical background. Here rock 'n' roll struck Britain suddenly in its sleep, so
that it seemed all fresh and gleaming. Where had it come from?
Why, AMERICA!—the land of dreams, where real life happened
and there was never any powdered egg, kirby grips, Sunday
dinners, cinema queues, cloth caps, liberty bodices, tea cosies . . .

In Britain we got Haley, Presley, Jerry Lee Lewis, Little
Richard, Fats Domino on nice, safe, thick 78s from a High Street
record shop, just near the sweet shop. We got rockabilly without
rednecks; R&B without racism.

This neatly packaged bundle for Britain formed the bible for the grand order of rockers—sweat students of classic rock who still guard the beat of pop. No one knows exactly how many there are. Like homosexuals, many remain hidden, working quietly by day in ordinary white-collar jobs. But when a rock idol gives a concert—SHAZAM!—into their leather gear or teddy boy outfits they clamber, onto their motor bikes they climb, into the show they march—arm in arm—cloggy boots hammering the floor. Metal studs glitter and reason hops out the exit door.

In an age in which the good old Kinks can be described as "musique concrète" and likened to "fine wine" (Paul Williams), when the Pink Floyd lay "surfaces of sound one upon another in symphonic thunder" (John Peel), when orchestra leaders fall over each other trying to get pop groups to join them in Art/Straight/Rock-grafting concerts—in an age of rather heady intellectualism—there is a real need for the rockers, to bash us on the head with a brick, clobber us with a studded belt, violate us back to rock roots. The rockers are necessary and evil. I'm glad that most of the time they stay undercover—under stones, as it were. But they are rock's scourge of God and somewhere in most rock musicians is a little rocker beating away—he is in John Lennon, Paul McCartney, Ringo, Bill Wyman, the Fleetwood Mac, Eric Clapton.

A BRIEF HISTORY OF ROCKERS

The rocker evolved from the teddy boy, who in turn had evolved from the cosh boy, who was distantly related to the thirties race-track razor lout (see Pinkie in Graham Greene's *Brighton Rock*). All these were juvenile delinquents but none, except the rocker, had any musical accompaniment. This was what made him different.

Of course, many teds became rockers. The new music burst into Britain right in the middle of the teddy boy movement and was eagerly adopted by most teds and most civilian kids. The teddy boys, curiously, wore an Edwardian garb. This assertion of Britishness was contrary to the trend toward Americanization that had been conquering Great Britain ever since ragtime ousted the music hall song during the First World War.

Mostly, it was the movie that fixed the U.S. image. In particular, the gangster and the cowboy. Like rock 'n' roll the image came trailing no grim, grey reality. (We didn't see ugly, sweaty and boozy Calamity Jane but pleasant, wholesome Doris Day portraying her.) America was framed, like fine art, by the silver screen and viewed in the cosy warmth of our gallery the Picture Palace.

The teds wore tight, drainpipe trousers, long drape jackets that often reached below the knees. Their lapels were velvet; their shoes had inches of thick crepe. Their ties were boot-lace. Their long hair was greased back by metal comb.

Mainly, the teds came from South London and were rough, common, lower class. They were more sinister than the swing jitterbuggers (baggy sweaters, billowing slacks, mechanized fun to spectacled Benny and spectacled Glenn) and quite different from the bright young things of the roaring twenties who'd been middle-class rebels and who threw rolls rather than knives.

The teds liked to fight and smash—for no particular reason. And "Rock Around the Clock," as record and then movie, provided music as an accompaniment to the mayhem. The record was released in 1955 and topped the Hit Parade in January 1956. That year was one of enormous upheaval: not only was it the year of rock 'n' roll, but also the year of the Suez fiasco ("It's GREAT Britain again!" bannered the Daily Sketch), of Colin Wilson (the coffee-bar philosopher and genius author of *The Outsider*), and of John Osborne's *Look Back in Anger* (the play about an "angry young man"). Right in the middle of the "serious" young men came the jolly rockers.

In September, 1956, the quickie flickie *Rock Around the Clock* was released, gathering rockers together just as a Hyde Park Stones concert would gather together progressive Thinkies. They ripped seats out of cinemas to make more room for the jiving. On the screen—Bill Haley, one eye looking at the balcony and the other at the stalls.

Rockers, teds and ordinary kids, let all hell loose in response to the portly, benign Haley. In several cities the movie was banned. Rioting increased: on September 12 there was a field day of window smashing, garden urinating, and car overturning when three thousand rock lovers roamed the streets of South London.

But Haley was only the first man on the scene. His success opened the way to a horde of wilder rock stars, mostly dredged from southern hick towns, reeking of rockabilly. What was great was that they didn't come dressed in overalls and chewing straw. They appeared in gold lamé and shiny boots. Elvis had a gold Cadillac, Jerry Lee Lewis a huge brass comb. Little Richard in his barrage balloon of a suit. Fats Domino's fingers were wrapped in rings. These were just the sort of people to counter kirby grips and grey pullovers.

Of course, most of these rock maniacs—who in real life would have been bounced into the nearest jail or loony bin—were confined to disc or film at first. In 1956 we were left to make our own rock scene—with the help of Oxford-educated Jack Good and his pioneering television rock shows. He was the first to gild the boy-next-door singer into a super-boy and to introduce the black leather evil belter. He was the first person to realize the great theatrical potential of rock 'n' roll. Perhaps it was inevitable that it was to be an educated foreigner who saw rock 'n' roll as All-American, vital, new, exciting, contemporary: in the short history of pop music outsiders have nearly always been the first to applaud (the London *Times* in 1913 recognized ragtime, Hughes Panassie became the first spokesman for jazz in his 1936 book *Le Jazz Hot*, Paul Oliver—of the Architectural Association, London—researched the blues more fully than anyone before).

In 1957 Good took over the B.B.C.'s jolly rock frolic called The Six-Five Special, a Saturday high-tea time show full of healthy sorts in baggy jeans and playtex check shirts, whiffs of firewood, scout knots and Ralph Reader's Gang Show.

Six-Five did serve one important purpose: rock groups of the future watched the ordinary blokes strumming guitars and thought if that idiot can do it so can I. And they did, helped by the vogue for skiffle music (tea-chest basses, scrubbed guitars, songs about life on the cotton plantation), which was a real do-it-yourself music and was popular at the same time as early rock 'n' roll.

But Good wasn't satisfied with ordinary blokes and tea-chest basses. His eyes were on the theatrical possibilities of Elvis's Cadillac and Jerry Lee's comb. His next rock shows (Oh Boy! Boy Meets Girl, Wham!) were much slicker and professional. They raised the barrier between viewer and performer. Good was arch-wizard performing magic for the gaping public. Gone was the camp-fire folksiness of the old Six-Five show with dear Josephine Douglas fluffing her lines. Now it was smooth Jimmy Henney rattling off "It's Oh Boy—the *fastest* show on television!!!" and a rapid-fire collection of zippy rock acts carefully shot and lit by ace cameramen. Performers were rigorously rehearsed, films of Elvis carefully studied and Cliff Richard, one of Good's regulars, taught exactly how to flicker his eyelids in tight close-up as he pouted into camera two. Good was keen on the untouchability of the artist. For instance, once Cliff Richard was trapped by fans in the men's lavatory of the Hackney Empire. Chains of men were organized to link arms and form a barrier in order to get him out and safely into the limousine.

The transformation of Gene Vincent from nice to nasty was a major triumph for Jack Good and established the uniform of the rocker for all time.

Gene Vincent, known to teenagers in 1957 through his "Be Bop a Lula" (which he'd written with Sheriff Tex Davis) had been booked for one of Good's TV shows. His orgasmic record conjured up a picture of a real dagger-boy. Perhaps it was Sheriff Davis's calming influence or perhaps it was a bumpy plane trip—whatever the reason, Vincent emerged from his airliner at London airport wan and haggard but distinctly polite, even addressing Jack Good as "sir." Altogether he looked homey and crinkled. "This won't do at all," thought Jack. "My people won't like this!" Noticing that Vincent had an El Greco-ish look and walked with a slight limp, Good had a brainwave: *he would model Vincent into the RICHARD III OF ROCK!* A leather suit. Yes! High-heeled boots. Yes! A metal pendant. Yes! He remembered that once at Oxford he had played the part of the murderer Light-bourne in Marlowe's *Edward II* and had worn a black glove. So should Vincent.

Good put the costumed Vincent on the set and had him slink around. He and his wife attended a rock show in the Elephant and Castle area of London a few days later. The place was full of black leather and metal pendants. The rocker had arrived.

Jack Good, the rock Svengali, through the medium of television, had modeled the final version of the authentic rocker.

HOW I JOINED THE ROCKERS

Between 1957 and 1959 the rockers rocked around. Some formed groups, inspired by the tour of Buddy Holly and the Crickets (who appeared on television here). Some just jived in the aisles. Some mounted motorcycles (with sidecars for their birds) and roared over sweet ornamental gardens, reasonable bowls contests, and peaceful village greens where the only thing that was wrong was that everything was right.

While they were pissing over cinema balconies to the tune of "Giddy-Ap a Ding-Dong" I was at a fairly expensive, progressive public school in the heart of Dorset. For some reason or other this early, crude, non-progressive rock 'n' roll appealed to me enormously. I was the first boy to sneak Bill Haley's album into the school. At that time jazz was looked on as O.K. but rock was "common." Jazz came from folk roots, was the music of a charming but oppressed race, and was played in Britain by a delightful old-Etonian called Humphrey Lyttelton. My liking for Elvis, Haley, Vincent, was considered typical of an immature boy who, at fifteen, still read Kid Colt Action Comics.

Our small circle of rock-lovers had to rock after lights-out at low volume. "Burn that candle!" whispered Bill as the bass clickety-clicked, the sax belched and the off-beat thacked every so often. In the distance could be heard the gush of the house-master's bath tap mingling with the tinkle of his harpsichord as he tried out a new bit of Bach.

You really had to work hard as a middle-class rocker in those days. I made my own small contribution. One night I sneaked out and wrote ROCK N ROLL IS HERE TO STAY in the snow on the lawn in front of the main school building. Another time, our middle-class rocker gang grabbed bikes and pedaled furiously up hill and down dale (puffing illegally at Craven A cigarettes) to the local cinema in order to catch *The Tommy Steele Story*. All the town teds and rockers were there. Afterwards we watched them set up their guitar group in the Paradise Café and play "That'll Be the Day"—almost as good as Holly himself.

You really did have to fight for your rock. If you wanted to hear the stuff live you had to trail to some dark, dank underground club. In the Stone Age of Classic Rock there was no arty embrace from the quality Sunday papers like *The Observer,* no scholarly musical investigation from conservatory men. There were no pop *concerts.*

Instead there was Jerry Lee Lewis, sitting bolt upright at his grand piano, an imperious smile playing on his face. The scene was a London variety theatre. The time was just after it was announced that Lee Lewis was about to marry a thirteen-year-old girl. The audience was booing.

And there was the figure of screaming Little Richard, who once stopped his act to order a spotlight to stick on him and stop spotting elsewhere. "I'M THE GREATEST GREATEST STARRRR!!!"

By 1959 I had renounced hard rock. Perhaps it was the effect of too much reading about art and aesthetics. Or it may have been the effects of the daily cold baths (the school was "progressive"). I gave up the visceral world of the lower half of my body and joined my spotty, spectacled friends in listening silently to Dave Brubeck, the Modern Jazz Quartet and other chamberish jazz combinations.

Actually, hard rock had begun to fizzle out for some good reasons: the early wild men had sprung up spontaneously, usually in the deep South. The whole rock thing, which had just *happened, naturally* (there was folksy spirit about it all, from American Bandstand in the U.S.A. to Six-Five Special in the

U.K.), became mechanized by show biz. By 1960 the age of
Bobbies Vee and Vinton had set in and the teenagers were big
business. Self-conscious artiness (the discovery of a lower music
by higher "art music" specialists, browned off with twelve tone
and suchlike) was yet to come.

Jack Good fled to America and reappeared in 1964 with his
rocking Shindig TV show. The teddy boys grew up and joined
the army, or became clerks and got wives and children and all
that.

The age of the rockers was over, so it seemed.

By 1967 rock-pop had become an art form, something that
had happened to jazz, another kind of pop music that had begun
spontaneously. Jazz had been mechanized into swing. By the late
1940s it had lost its audience as it progressed into an esoteric
music called Bop. In an effort to return to its roots, a revivalist
jazz sprang up: in America the Lu Watters band played hot New
Orleans music; in England the George Webb band attempted the
same sort of sound.

I really thought something ought to be done when, in 1967,
my dull cousin, who'd always hitherto doted on Brahms and
Beethoven, started studying the San Francisco sound and writing
Dylan songs on his viola.

By chance, I heard that Fats Domino was to appear at London's Saville Theatre together with the Bee Gees and Gerry plus
his Pacemakers. What I found there was not only Fats Domino
but also hundreds of rockers, young and old, who had somehow
risen from the fastnesses of West country villages. Some had
aged: buttered hair receding into a hat of black spaghetti. Still,
they were rockers. The Bee Gees were given the bird and invited
to get back to Australia; Gerry and his Pacemakers to fucking
Liverpool. Answered Gerry, "Shut Yer Face!" When the comfy
Fats Domino came on, the rockers—as one man—charged to the
front of the stage and jived with each other to the strains of
"Blueberry Hill."

Fascinated, I followed the rockers to their next assembly. A
concert by Jerry Lee Lewis at Kempton Park Race Track deep in

World War One-style mud on a pouring wet night. This time I decided to see if I couldn't infiltrate their ranks. I approached a group of them who were throwing rotten pears at a quartet on stage dressed in Tibetan robes and known as the Ultramarine Branflakes. I mentioned that I had met Eddie Cochran's brother. They accepted me at once and introduced me to their leader, Breathless Dan of Epping Forest Road, a man of indeterminate age. As we joined in a chorus of "Get off the fucking stage you stupid gits" (addressed to the Pink Floyd, who had just started their first number), Breathless told me all about his particular chapter of the rockers. He boasted that he had the largest collection of early rock 78s in Britain, several strands of Charlie Gracie's hair, as well as one of Bill Haley's socks.

"You ought to meet the chief rocker—Lord Mauleverer," said Dan. "He's your class—you know, he talks posh and all that." He paused, his breath floating away into the cold night air. Suddenly he filled his lungs and cupping his horny hands to his face he yelled, "WE WANT JERRY LEE! WE WANT JERRY LEE!"

A few calls later Lee Lewis appeared, as gracious and noble as ever. At once he launched into "Sweet Little Sixteen" after explaining that it was written by "a very fine gentleman." Together, at the command, like a soccer team, the rockers and I rushed the stage. Pretty soon I found myself right inside the grand piano, looking out and into the eyes of Jerry Lee. He winked and pounded on. A little later I found myself off the stage and in the mud together with a tangle of rockers.

Several months later Breathless Dan managed to get me a meeting with Lord Mauleverer, at his house hidden in the depths of Somerset. I'd found out that Lord M. was an ex-public school man who had been expelled for shouting "Tutti Frutti" during prayers and had later fought for both sides in Vietnam. He greeted me with a firm, Roman handshake and I inspected his Panzer officer uniform. He offered me a Molotov cocktail (three parts scotch to one part cider), then waved a hand in the direction of a wall. There, in gilt frames, were oil paintings of Eddie Cochran and Buddy Holly. Also some banners: I remember that one read KEEP ROCK ROLLING and another, GIVE PEACE THE FINGER.

"What's next on your plan of campaign?" I asked.

"Well, next month we've a coach trip to the West End. We're taking three hundred members to *Hair* and we're really going to participate. You know how the cast is always going on about how the audience ought to get up off their arses and live a little life? How they invite you to jump on stage and do your thing? Well, we're going to take them at their fucking word! We're going to invade that stage and give all those weeds and drips a fucking good punch-up! Have another cocktail?"

I was able to tell Lord M. some news: that Jack Good was back and producing a new television show featuring Jerry Lee Lewis. It was to be called Innocence, Anarchy and Soul—Three Chapters from the History of Pop. I had written a rocker theme song specially for the occasion and would Lord M. like to organize several hundred rockers to come and sing it? "You bet!" he replied.

Unfortunately the show never went on the air because the technicians were ordered to strike right at the moment of shooting. Jack Good said that they'd do the whole show without cameras. Union officials protested but were pushed aside and soon Jerry Lee Lewis was standing on top of his white grand piano singing "Whole Lotta Shakin' Goin' On." Then Good leapt up and joined him. Breathless Dan, together with lieutenants Lame Larry and Fingers Frisby, led the rockers up to the piano and started the jiving. By now both Jack and Jerry Lee were acting huge chunks of *Othello*—for Jerry Lee had just starred in Jack's rock production of the play in Los Angeles. "Odds codpiece! What manner of man is this that holds his privates in parenthesis?" The rockers cheered. Lord M. gave three cheers for Jack Good. At eleven thirty we filed out back to motor bike and motor coach to return to the countryside. The ghosts of Eddie Cochran, Buddy Holly, Ritchie Valens, Big Bopper, Johnny Burnette smiled down a warmth on us from the rocker heaven.

ANTHEM OF THE ROCKERS

Heroes of the Rocker Pack

*Some say they come from Somerset and others
say from under a stone*

Hear the roar and rattle as the rockers ride and
    hear the hippies moan
They will trample all your roses with their boots
Use their daggers on your Nehru suits
Pass some water on your incense as well
And replace it with a healthy body smell
With leather clinging to them and sweat and
    blood and plenty of cock
They ask no questions, give no answers, sway to
    "Rock Around the Clock"

They cycle up to Margate and they burn a few
    things
Then they cycle back to Taunton singing "Shake
    That Thing!"
So tug your forelocks to the heroes of the Rocker
    Pack.

B. Pfohlman

SAM THE SHAM

Sam, what's new in your recording life?

Well Buddy, I've been working out with the blues. I have this great sound idea to make it communicate with people.

Isn't this a new bag for you?

Hell no! I've been working with the blues for years. Only before I didn't have the space to say it or perform it. The record company wanted something else. So when they're blowing smoke up your ass, you do as they say. Regardless of what they say.

You sound down about the industry. Isn't it a great scene?

Sure, it's a great scene. Only there is this one scum percent of people who make the business a bumkick. These are the people who trade in the "FLESH MARKET." They put every artist through such changes. They'll cater to an artist, play on his emotions, and then turn him against his own mother for their own personal monetary gains. They are always so kind while they rob you blind. When they get done with you, you can forget your pride—you can forget your money and you can forget who you were. Like, welcome to the living dead.

But doesn't every business need a boss man?

Usually it's a blood man in this business. If it wasn't for the artist there wouldn't be a product to sell. They don't care. I bet there is a car right now with a load of poor SOB's who drove two hundred miles from the last place they played, their minds turned around, their bodies filled with pills, trying to make their next gig. These great agents will send you to Bum Fuck, Egypt. But you don't mind cause you're still goggle-eyed about the gold watch they gave you. Then when the smoke settles and the air clears everyone else is fat except the artists. Look out suckers here comes the shaft. I guess when you come right down to it you have no one else but yourself to blame for getting involved and taking their happy horse-shit.

Sam, I can recall this scene of you throwing a facsimile of your turban out to your audience. Do you still do it?

This was something a manager thought up. To answer you: No, I don't do it anymore. In fact I don't even wear one anymore. When I think back it took me a long time to get rid of the fucking turban. I finally got rid of it in St. Louis and now I live in constant fear of someone finding it and returning it to me. Man, for the longest time I hated wearing that thing. People thought I was an Arab or something. The record companies do strange things like that. I can remember unknown American groups being booked as British rock groups only 'cause that was "IN" and made money. As soon as they were found out, they were tough out of luck, but their managers still made off with the coin.

Sam, you said earlier that you were heavy with the blues. What did you mean?

Buddy, I'll tell you; some people get their high smoking pot, others from drinking booze. All these people are looking for that great total feeling of doing their own thing. My mental high comes when I get a rig together and get it together tight. It's the only way you can get that sound of motion. The locked-in fuck rhythm of the blues. That is the sound I want to unleash on the world. When you get your shit together that good you can consider yourself a heavy in the field of blues.

Are you working with any other heavies at present?

I'm working with a good friend from South Texas, Andy King. Andy is an undiscovered heavy, but won't be unknown for long. We're putting a collection of sounds together right now, and they are so tight that their combined power will be able to move buildings. My new wave of musical sound will knock the slats loose in your cradle. . . .

T. Procter Lippincott

THE CULTURE VULTURES

Then it's time to go downtown
Where the agent man won't let you down
Sell your soul to the company
Who are waiting there
To sell plasticware
And in a week or two
If you make the charts
The girls will tear you apart.
　　　　—THE BYRDS

("So You Want to Be a Rock 'n' Roll Star")

We "freaks" rap a lot about the growing momentum of our groovy "alternate" subculture. The fact remains, nevertheless, that its driving force continues to be dampened by a fundamental conflict: the attempt to develop a truly human, revolutionary life style within the confines of an exploitative commercial system. Profit motive is robbing us of our thing, especially our music, which doesn't get better just because somebody makes money from it. Music is meant to be dug for its own sake; not traded and sold as a market commodity that's no good if it doesn't sell.

Beautiful music, I believe, can be described simply as that which grabs you where you *feel* it, drives you to your feet, takes you to new places . . . music that tells it like it is. For me, that used to be boogity-boogity-shoop[1] (strictly commerical exploitative in the worst way, and a teenage culture staple for many of us—remember those boppin' high school dances?), but it wasn't really ours. Then, in the early '60s, instead of just singing about how parents were such a drag and how teenage love tore us up,

---

[1] The black rhythm 'n' blues and country & western music of the '50s that found its own commercially through the fusion of the two in a form called "rockabilly" and exemplified first and most successfully by Elvis Presley beginning in 1956. :

we started getting into the *reasons*. This led many to dig on alternate life styles: civil rights and antiwar demonstrations and a music that became an integral part of it (urban folk); beads, dope and long hair to avoid the restraints of the business "culture" and the plastic career, and music to go with that (acid rock). The new music was organically related to styles that *threatened*. People began putting pieces together. In a certain way, with this movement and its subculture growing by leaps and sounds, the whole American Way of Life (death) appeared to be on the line.

While the content of rock may have revolutionary implications, however, money factors consistently work against this tendency. The calculated hype and image that enshroud an artist's real self (if successful) not only set him or her apart as something super, thus virtually forestalling the possibility of human relationships between performer and spectator (a dehumanizing situation for both parties), but it establishes a false basis for exchange of any kind. As an artist achieves fame and financial recognition, his isolation from those to whom he theoretically relates becomes fairly complete (in many cases, groupies and hangers-on are the only ones to whom traveling pop musicians have a chance to relate personally and, after all, does anyone seriously consider that "relating?").

Advertising and promotion give exposure and an air of the extraordinary to a particular artist or disc; in turn, the record itself enhances the power of other kinds of advertising on the Top 40 and "underground" FM radio stations. That is, in the same way that a luring female body may be used to sell a new Pontiac or some other fancy short (even though the woman has nothing to do with it), so may Top 40 record programming (or, in the case of magazines like *Esquire* or the now-defunct *Eye*, well-written reviews and Dylan fold-outs) give credence to ads for pimple cream, h.i.s. clothing, false eyelashes, or the U.S. Air Force. As a broadcasting personality told me, "No matter how hip a deejay may be to music, if he can't read commercials well enough to sell the products [in spite of what he personally may think of them], he might as well forget it." That's where it's at. So a good record (no matter what its content), if given adequate exposure, makes good money for big record companies as it provides an atmosphere of credibility around a whole host of unrelated products that, by association, are supposed to be just as hip.

It should be said that the music business, even more than most industries (because of the potential fast buck involved) makes much of its bread at the merciless expense of the musician and the consumer. The wildly unpredictable fate of the musician depends upon the promotion and exposure his record company chooses to give him and upon the consumers' response to it. The consumer, on the other hand, is supposed to function as much as possible as an unthinking entity which responds predictably to promotion of specific artists and specific music (thus ensuring maximum return on such investments). When the consumer fails to react positively to a particular expensive promo job, as was the case with the so-called Boston Sound (Bosstown)—a concept based solely on hype in the first place—it can really mess up quarterly profit reports. M-G-M suffered a relatively substantial setback in 1968 because it had decided to push hard with several of the Boston groups.

The fact that musicmaking is an increasingly lucrative business should surprise no one. According to George Albert, president and publisher of *Cash Box*, "The record business in 1968 . . . [surpassed] the $1 billion sales mark." This, as Albert pointed out, raises the stature of the industry to that of a true giant, a fact that has not gone unnoticed in the non-music business community. "When outside companies make acquisitions in this area," Albert went on to say in his magazine's July 5, 1969, issue, "it is frequently stated for public knowledge or at least understood that record and music units are regarded as possessing great growth-potential. There have been some undisputed instances where purchases of leading leisure-time entities have been made with a very direct eye on their music field affiliations." Even with this mixture of trade jargon and bad grammar, the point is clear: there's some hard coin being made by the music magnates.

The number of sides designated as Gold Records is another indicator of capital growth in the business. In 1967, there were 95 Gold Records (i.e., records with sales worth $1 million or more); 34 of these were singles, 61 were LPs. For 1968, the Record Industry Association of America (RIAA) reported a new all-time high: 120 Gold Records (45 singles, 75 LPs). And the market shows every sign of expanding. In fact, the *Wall Street Journal* reported (August 9, 1969) that "Record industry sales in the past several years have risen about 15% to 20% annually. Five years ago, Columbia Records, a 'complete label' offering everything from classical to pop, did about 15% of its business in rock. Today rock (using the term loosely) accounts for 60% or more of the vastly increased total."

With the advent of rock as financial king of music, the record business hasn't been the only important monetary avenue to open up wide. Rock concerts have become extremely big business; in spite of the increasing significance of the recording studio, personal performances are still the most essential ingredient for success. This means that the gamut of entertainment vehicles— small clubs (discothèques), theaters, stadiums and festivals, not to mention TV and film—are all in heavy use, with the whole circus of profit adventurists (including members of "organized crime"), in tow. And, in addition to regular coverage of rock music events by the expanding trade papers (*Billboard, Cash Box, Record World* and *Variety*), the underground press and even the straight press (right down to *Reader's Digest* and *Good Housekeeping*), a new kind of pseudo-underground journalism has evolved to produce such specialist music papers as *Rolling Stone* and a host of imitators (attendant with a similar national development in FM radio which deals with the same phenomena).

As the industry becomes truly giant sized, the big corporations jockey for an expanding role in the act. *The New York Times* reported (September 9, 1969) that since the Woodstock Festival in August, "Several large Establishment-oriented corporations and Wall Street investment firms are interested in cashing in on the youth market that Woodstock proved exists. These firms

are hiring highly paid 'youth consultants' to advise them on
forthcoming trends that percolate from the deepest underground
. . . to what John Morris, 30 [Woodstock's chief producer],
calls 'the silk-shirt hippie types from Forest Hills [a comfortable
New York City neighborhood] who do so much of the buying.' "[2]
A massive Youth Fair, held at the New York Coliseum in May of
this year and designed to capitalize on the rapidly expanding
youth market, had no "revolutionary" illusions about its undertaking. Featuring mod clothes, name rock bands and "young
ideas," the Fair refused to admit members of the underground
press because, as the producer told me coldly, "We don't need
your kind of coverage."

The three broadcasting networks, of course, have been heavily into music stuff for some time. CBS, for example, has at least
eleven labels in its Records Division (including Columbia Records, mentioned above). Fender guitars, basses and amplifiers
are part of Columbia's Musical Instruments Division; Columbia
also owns seven big radio stations (each with AM and FM) and
has 237 affiliated stations around the country. At the same time
that it records, distributes and profits from "our" music, it is
involved with multifarious operations around the world (about
sixty of CBS's eighty subsidiaries are foreign), many of which are
defense-related. In addition, by virtue of directors held in common, CBS can claim links with numerous multinational corporations, the Rockefeller Foundation, Atlantic Refining Corporation,
the Council on Foreign Relations, the CIA and so forth. An
exposition of such links as these helps dramatize the conflict of
interest between money and a revolutionary life style that I was
talking about earlier.

An increasing number of conglomerates (i.e., the super holding corporations that have been formed by mergers of large
corporations, creating monstrous entities that produce a wide
variety of unrelated products) are sticking their thumbs into the
music pie. One such conglomerate is the Transcontinental Invest-
ing Corporation (TIC), which has interests in jazz and rock-

[2] See September 9, 1969, *New York Times* article for some very lucid
quotes on the attitudes of the Woodstock promoters.

music production and distribution. In February of this year, TIC acquired Attarack, Seymour Heller Management, an important music outfit. One month later, it not only launched the Forward Record label, but it acquired Hurok Concerts Inc., the huge classical concern (interesting that a firm whose primary music interests have heretofore been in the pop field should buy out a classical music operation, instead of the other way around). According to the *Wall Street Journal*, TIC "owns Transcontinental Music Corp., a major wholesale merchandiser of phonograph records, tapes and recording accessories. It also owns several music and publishing concerns that produce contemporary music and *develop* groups performing the music in person, on records and in movies" (emphasis mine). In addition, TIC has considerable real estate holdings, a rubber company, the Hullabaloo complex (the dance centers and the magazine), Love's Enterprises, Inc., and a host of other diversified operations.

Some of the other conglomerates that are into music are: Transamerica, a $1.1 billion-a-year insurance, computer, airline and movie-distribution fat cat that also owns fourteen music publishing companies and, as part of Liberty/United Artists, Inc., at least ten record companies; Commonwealth United Corp., owner of Sunset International Petroleum, an insurance company and a travel agency; under its subsidiary, Commonwealth United Music, Inc., it owns at least eight music publishing companies, two recording studios, an independent production association, and the Seeburg Corp. (a Mafia outfit which manufactures juke boxes, phonographs, pianos, electric organs and vending equipment); Gulf & Western Industries, manufacturers and distributors of auto parts, producer of integrated zinc, owner of movie theaters, film companies (including Paramount Pictures), a realty corporation, an investment company, a bank, the South Puerto Rico Sugar Company (the major producer of sugar in the Dominican Republic, where they're also constructing a cement plant and a hotel) and the CATV franchises and operating system in nineteen cities and seven countries; Viewlex, Inc., largest company in the United States devoted exclusively to the design and manufacture of audio-visual equipment for industrial, commercial, education and defense projects, missile electronic control subsystems, etc., etc., owns the famous Bell Sound Studios (for recording, mastering and tape manufacture), some seven pressing and component plants, eight recording companies (including Kama Sutra and Buddah) and at least three music publishing companies; Metromedia, Inc., owns TV and radio stations (including the WNEW complex in New York), has contracts for metro transit advertising, produces TV programs, owns its own record company and six music publishing companies. There are at least five other significant conglomerates heavily involved in the music industry, to say nothing of the thousands of small independents who are somehow wound up in the same rat race. Since profit is what that race is all about, those who control these enterprises feed off of us by commercially, hermetically packaging and selling back our subculture to us at outrageous prices.

Not only have some "consumers" decided that no one has a right to demand big money for music which belongs to the people, but an increasing number of rock festival goers have begun to storm the bottlenecks where tickets are taken or they have torn down fences to provide free access for everybody. A free music for those who want to be free and who find obnoxious such things as "hip" gestapo who keep you cool at the Fillmore. Groovy . . . I mean the festival actions have started to put the music entrepreneurs uptight enough that their real heads come through. We must continue to wake up if our music is to be effectively reclaimed (and it will never be completely so, as long as capitalism defines our society). Other actions must be conceived that will send tremors through that corporate structure that makes commodities out of us and our music. Further, frameworks need to be established where bands relate regularly to their communities and vice versa: how better to combat the sterile idol idea that promoters count on so heavily?

As suggested earlier, musicians and consumers are separated unnaturally. (Society generally is organized to keep us apart, setting up false divisions between "religion," "work," "vacation," "love life," etc., and inducing us to compete by race, sex, jobs, income, and so forth; the music world, obviously, is no exception.) Owing to the nature of the system, only germinal rock groups manage to develop a truly organic relationship with their audience and then only until commercial hype separates them. The Jefferson Airplane and the Grateful Dead could claim such relationships with other residents of Haight-Ashbury in 1964; in Detroit, the MC5 were beginning to develop a powerful relationship with people until their manager John Sinclair was busted for marijuana last August. The ten-year rap John received at the hands of Michigan "lawnawdah" demoralized the group and those who actively related to it and its precepts.

There have also been times in New York, apparently, when this community idea almost functioned among jazz buffs—at the old Five Spot for example, and in certain small coffee houses. Music was cheap and real and a dynamic was created that elevated both performers and spectators. Interplay existed between the two for sustained periods of weeks or even months. As a first step towards revolutionary music, let's decentralize the music that we have, make it real on the local level.

A New York High School Student Union pamphlet distributed at a demonstration at the aforementioned Youth Fair in May (when the Berkeley People's Park actions were a national issue), summed up the hip culture scene this way:

> *We can have long hair and talk differently as long as we are part of the consumer society. We can even be stoned as long as we pay to hear concerts and buy their plastic psychedelic shit. The Berkeley people made their own music in their own outdoor concert hall. They took the ideas of our music seriously. They were building a revolutionary community—a threat to the Establishment. That's why the cops came, that's why the National Guard came, that's why shotguns were fired into the crowd, and that's why James Rector, 26 years old, is dead.*

We can't be free until everything is free, because money's what's used to control things. The money game even controls the Man. . . .[3] He tries to market the moon; he figures out ways to

[3] The Establishment, collectively described.

keep people working at jive jobs, making things nobody needs so they can afford to buy things nobody needs. While we sit around grooving, the rock moguls are cleaning up and using our bread to influence our heads and control the "stars" . . . and telling us that revolution means buying their stuff! If businessmen in beads and cops in bellbottoms (Woodstock Festival) is revolution, how come the war's still going on in Vietnam and the axe is coming down at home? If this is the Age of Aquarius, why do people get busted when they try living Real Lives? If this is It baby, why is it that the same corporations which are into robbing Latin America of minerals, oil and sugar and selling it back to them to "help them develop" are the same corporations which are packaging and selling our "revolution" back to us?

Dig it. Everybody look what's going down . . .

CHECK THE WIRING!

NICKY HOPKINS & JEFF BECK GROUP

Are we recording?

How loud does it record? Let me just sort of try it. A-A-A
(three notes sung). Is it going?

Yes.

A-A-A-A (four notes sung). Let's stop and play it back . . .
(In the background, *The Guiding Light* is on.)

HEY! You rat fuck!

Did you like playing at the Tea Party?

I like the Tea Party. There are a bunch of really filthy people
there that need a good wash. Ha.

HEY.

Why don't you do . . .

No, just rap kind of, because I'm not really that into the
things you people have been doing.

How did you people all get together?

I don't know. It wasn't all together anyway. It was sort of one
by one, wasn't it. Tony was the last to join, the drummer. It was
Ron before that and. . . .

TELEPHONE.

Could you put the phone back on the receiver for us please.

And check the wiring.

And check the wiring.

And check the wiring.

Were you all playing with groups before you got together?

Well, you ought to know.

How come you started playing in a group?

I don't know. I got fed up with doing session work. And I wanted to do a bit of traveling. See the States. Won't do it again. (?) You know, I wanted to do it. It was just a thing I wanted to do . . . Boston's neat and the west coast, but that's about it. I just don't like the rest of it but I wanted to see it. . . .

And how about you? What were you doing before?

Playing in a few bands.

What were *you* doing? He seems to be the noisy one.

Pass the ashtray. I sang with Julie Driscoll and Brian Auger.

Did Beck have an idea of the group he wanted to have when he left?

He had an idea. Rod. It was only him and Rod when I joined.

Were those two together when you joined?

Yeh. They used to hang about together and call each other nice names.

They had a selection of drummers. About four drummers in a week. This was about two years ago.

He had a selection of bass players. And guitar. Because I was on guitar at first.

Yeh, and there were two guitar players at first. Ron was on guitar. Superb.

Trouble was I used to shake all night.

Did you all play together on "Hi Ho Silver Lining?"

No.

Was Beck still with the Yardbirds?

The group wasn't really formed then.

No, I just did a session on it.

Beck was still with the Yardbirds at that time.

He had gotten thrown out. Incredible. Getting thrown out.

Has that been released over here?

I don't know. I have a single of it.

You've got a single?

But that was due to Mickey Most. You see, Mickey Most is very commercial-minded and when the band was first formed, we thought that was the only way to get it off the ground, by releasing a trashy record like that. It goes over in England. Well, England is very gullible to that sort of thing anyway.

It's not a bad record really. I heard it about three months ago, the first time I heard it since it was out and it didn't sound as bad as I would have imagined.

It's strange. The whole song is so trite sounding.

Well, Nicky likes that sort of thing. Haha.

No he doesn't. I do really. I've played. . . .

I've played really diabolical. . . .

There's some guy named Jack downstairs.

With guitars?

Maybe it's Jack Casady.

No, it's not Jack Casady.

Do you know Jack Casady?

No, I've never met him.

He's a really fine bass player.

I want a coke.

The nearest place to get coke is Harvard Square.

A drink of water.

Tommy's in the bathroom.

(TELEPHONE)

Jimmy Page made the same complaint about Mickey Most, about the *Little Games* album.

Mickey Most is just changing now. He's becoming more hip . . . packaged stuff. . . .

Just out of curiosity, how come you have him around?

I'm not sure. I've an idea we've been given him. . . . A contract that Jeff signed a long time ago and we just got him.

Do you play around Beck?

No, it's an interchanging thing. It just happens.

(TELEPHONE)

It's this guy on the phone, a piano player. He wants to jam after the show. We just don't know, man. Tell him we'll see after the show's finished. We'll probably be too shattered but we might do it.

Where's the light switch?

Your piano playing is a lot more subdued with Beck than it had been with the Kinks.

Yeh, I was noticing that last night.

I don't think that organ's as loud as a piano really. It comes from over in the corner.

(Phone.) Popular group.

The last time you were here, what kind of fuck-ups happened? About two months ago?

I don't know, it's very difficult to say. I don't know really. It wasn't really good.

Last night?

Better than I thought it would be.

The amplifiers aren't really. . . . They don't seem to have enough power. You had lack of power on yours, didn't you?

Yeh.

How do you people feel about talking about the group? What was wrong last night?

Nothing was wrong really. When you walk out on a gig like we did, you can't turn up and put them on cold. We thought they might give us a hard time. The audience. I think we all thought that, 'cause we didn't turn up for the last gig. When we changed the drummer; and the bass change. After we did the first number, it was all right.

What is it with the new drummer? What's his name?

Sid . . . Brian . . . Tony Newman.

TONY—it's OK, man.

(Maid interruption.)

Did you read the groupies issue of *Rolling Stone?*

No.

What's your reaction to the whole thing in general? The big thing like Jeff Beck being top-rated?

I don't know. A good issue, actually. Why doesn't *Fusion* do a thing about it?

Rolling Stone doubled their sales. The thing is they didn't do anything about the New York groupies. They're a different breed. Competition.

Do you find groupies hassling, fun?

Fun. Some of the New York girls are really very sweet. It's a sad story.

(TELEPHONE)

Did Cyril Davis ever make any records?

Yeh, good record.

What label?

I don't know. He's on Dot? I've got about four copies of it.

You can't get it here.

He's only recorded about four tracks. "Sweet Mary." "Country Line Special."

What kind of music is he playing?

Chicago blues before anybody else. Chicago blues is big in England.

Where did you pick up your style from? You sound a lot like Otis Spann except not as heavy. You ever listen to him?

Otis Spann, yeh. A long time ago. I haven't really listened to him lately. It's very weird, because it's like I'm back into a blues thing after being out of it.

It's really strange because he does studio work a lot and yet he's much more known in his own right.

Does anyone have an Otis Spann record called *Check the Wiring?*

What's this about Booker T breaking up?

I don't know. I hadn't even heard about it. That would be a shame.

Have you got our new album coming up?

I've heard it. Great album. The only thing I've heard is Nicky's piece. I really like that. When I first heard it, I was expecting Aretha Franklin to come in and start singing at some point, but she never did.

Haha.

Which keyboard instrument do you prefer playing?

Piano.

You do a lot of stuff on the harpsichord, don't you?

Yeh. Use it for recording sometimes.

What do you think of Americans?

They're usually nice, the ones you meet, but the ones you bump into. . . .

When you play for an audience here, do you get different vibes from them than you get from an English audience?

Yeh. Music lovers. . . . There's none of the reserve of English audiences. They don't even bother to clap. They wait for the guy next door to clap and he doesn't clap until you clap.

That's very strange.

Well, that's England. I've done it myself.

Is there a thing between you guys and Jeff? Jeff isn't here. Do you spend more time together without him for some reason?

Yeh . . . ????

Is that reflected on stage?

No. It's just the opposite on stage and that's where it counts.

Because there were times last night when you weren't together.

Last night? Yeh, things were falling apart. We were going on too long.

No, I don't think things were going on too long. They could have gone on longer, some of them. It stopped short before it had a chance to develop.

You know it.

He develops it the way he wants and that's it.

All the numbers don't perhaps sound together all the time because we're trying to get into something else to make the number a bit more interesting. That's the general idea.

That's a really heavy accent. Where do you come from?

Heavy London.

Do you like it here in Boston?

Yeh. It's a lot like England, really is.

Better than other parts of the U.S.?

San Francisco and Boston, but everybody says that. And that's it.

How about New York?

The St. Marks Hotel is about the only place we can stay and get away with murder. Rat-infested, New York.

What do you think of Dylan's new album?

I think it's great. When I first saw it, I thought it was Ramblin' Jack Elliott. I like him.

Where do you work out of?

What studios do you mean? Olympic.

Jimmy Miller.

How's he as a producer?

He did a good job on the Stones' album.

Are you going back to doing more old stuff like "Jailhouse Rock?"

I really dug that.

Yeh.

No, not really.

Well, it was just an idea that happened in the studio. Somebody said let's do it and we did it and it turned out good.

It wasn't planned?

It was just a jam on record, sort of.

It's not really a very serious LP coming out, is it?

No, you can either sit down and get a really good thing worked out or you can do the second best thing which is to make the best of it. Oh, it was done so fast though. We only had two weeks to do it and we only spent five days in the studio.

Do you essentially play around Beck when you start to do something?

Who comes up with the ideas?

Me.

What's the new Stones album like? You played on it, didn't you?

Yeh, it's an extension of *Beggars Banquet*.

An extension of Buggers Gringrut.

A long extension of the air raid shelter.

No exceptions!

PRESENT ARMS! CHECK THE WIRING!

We got that on tape. We've been trying to get that on tape for. . . .

Do the one with the queen.

STEADY AIM! CHECK THE WIRING!

Nicky, present arms out the window. CHECK THE WIRING.

Nicky, do you play on the *Buttons* album?

No, he was on the Chocolate Eclairs album.

No.

He just cut a record with the Rotten Bunions. They're an up and coming group.

Do you ever feel you're a r & r star? With fans, *et al.*?

No.

Never feel that way.

No.

Are you a r & r star?

Beck is, but he's just a guy who plays really good guitar.

Do people exhibit the same adulation in England?

People don't go crazy over Beck there, no.

How 'bout John Lennon?

Well, he deserves it.

John Lennon. Why?

What did you think of the Beatles when you played with them?

I don't know.

As musicians?

I think they're nothing spectacular, as musicians, strictly. I've always liked what they've done, though, arranging. It's always right.

The stupid pack. It's always running out.

How do you like American cigarettes?

I like these.

I really dig Deep Purple, the Nice.

I really like their sound but I don't dig the organist climbing over his instrument. But they're getting away with it.

They play a lot at Middle Earth.

We've played there. We were supposed to in January but Beck didn't show up.

You played with most of the hard rock groups?

Yeh.

Your sound is somewhat different from that. Your work for the Kinks is a much better, lighter sound, notably the difference between the earlier albums and *Face to Face*.

Of course, somebody's paying me.

Do you prefer doing hard rock, I mean the stuff you do for Beck is very different from your studio work.

Yeah, I know. It's a different thing.

You seem incredibly meditative and introspective.

Yeh. There's a lot going on in my head.

Are you staying with the group?

Yeh, I think so.

I had heard a rumor that you were leaving.

Oh, really? Who from?

Just from the trades, etc. What with all the other groups breaking up, you know, rumors fly.

Is touring with Beck easier than touring with Davis?

Oh, yeah. That was six years ago, anyway.

Stupid sign, it's been on the screen for about ten minutes. Interesting. It shuts down during the day. Still a damn sight better than our television. It's such a drag. I've still got some more Stones sessions to do.

How is working with them?

Very good. I'm looking forward to getting back.

They seem very relaxed. Like jamming.

Yeah.

Do they arrange their sound that way?

No, it's just trying out things.

Does Ian Stewart still play?

Yeah. He's done some work.

How 'bout Nietzsche?

I think Jack did one, Ian a couple, I did about three before I went away. There are about three more sessions.

Do you work a lot with the Beatles?

No, I just did that one single with them.

Has there ever been thought of your touring with the Stones?

Yeah, there's been thought but that's about all. I don't think we'll ever get together. It would be nice if we did. I don't know. Nobody knows what they're going to do.

There have been so many rumors about an impending tour.

Do you still work at all with the Kinks?

No!

That was such an abrupt answer.

Yeah, it was. I'm a bit uptight about that. I did about 70 percent keyboard work on the *Village Green* album and not only did they leave me off the credits on the thing, but they put Ray Davies down on keyboard.

Yeah, I noticed. It was strange.

I mean, what's that all about? I was so mad. I'm not biased. I mean, apart from that, I'm just not into the Kinks. They just don't mean anything to me whatsoever.

That's been one of their problems. They're a pretty good group.

Yeah, but I don't know. They're halfway between two things. Ray Davies is such a mixed-up person. He's unbelievable.

I just can't get over this city. Take a look outside that window. All you can see are trees with one or two houses. We were here in the autumn. The color of the leaves! Incredible coloring. Is this the nicest part of Boston?

Yeah. A lot of the city looks like around the Tea Party. Really ugly. The river's nice. Have you been down to it?

No, we drove past it.

Any final comments?

Yeah, Ronny's got a great parrot called Sadie and all it can say is "Fuck off." "Milk." "Motoring." "Bored!"

"Check the wiring!"

(As we left, the group was really getting into *Dark Shadows*.)

CALIF. ROCK BASH LEAVES
4 DEAD AND 2 BORN

Livermore, Calif., Dec. 7 (UPI)—The last of 300,000 young rock fans straggled out of debris-covered hills today after a free concert by the Rolling Stones which left four persons dead.

Some 2,500 persons, who camped overnight around bonfires in barren ranchland fifty miles southeast of San Francisco, hiked to cars parked as far as ten miles from the concert site.

Tons of empty wine bottles and other refuse were strewn on the hills around Altamont Speedway, a motorcycle and jalopy track which became the scene of the biggest one-day musical bash of all time.

Hundreds of abandoned cars—many of which ran out of gas or broke down during the six-hour traffic jam after the concert—dotted the area.

Sheriff's deputies and highway patrolmen investigated four deaths—a stabbing, a drowning and two lives lost in a traffic accident.

Two births also occurred during the day-long concert yesterday which drew crowds estimated at upwards of 300,000, despite less than twenty-four hours' notice as to the site.

A handful of incidents, most involving Hell's Angels motorcycle toughs, marred an otherwise peaceful exercise in togetherness of hippies, teenyboppers and other rock fans.

Detectives investigated reports that the stabbing death of Meredith Hunter, eighteen, of Berkeley, occurred after he pulled a gun during a scuffle with Hell's Angels. He died of knife wounds in the back and face.

Members of the motorcycle gang earlier clubbed five men while forcing their way onto the stage and were involved in several other incidents which prompted bands to stop playing and demand an end to the fighting.

An unidentified young man drowned in an irrigation ditch near the race track and two Berkeley men were killed when a car ran over them as they sat around a roadside campfire after the con-

cert. The driver fled on foot after killing Richard Salov, twenty-two, and Mark Feiger, nineteen, and seriously injuring another man and woman.

Volunteer doctors at four first-aid stations also treated hundreds for "bad trips" on drugs, including a youth who broke his pelvis after leaping forty feet off a freeway overpass.

Thousands got high on wine or drugs, which were openly peddled in the crowd. A handful of men and women danced naked in front of the bandstand.

George Paul Csicsery

ALTAMONT, CALIFORNIA, DECEMBER 6, 1969

In the beginning there was rock 'n' roll. The Beatles came and made it good with love and the bluebird of Paradise. But even while the children lifted their faces to the sun, Mick Jagger coiled himself around the tree of flesh, offering a sweet bite of chaos. Saturday, the children swallowed that bite, after chewing and tasting their alliance with evil for nearly a decade.

Until Saturday, evil was value-free, something to dig for its own sake. A lot of people who thought they were children of chaos dropped out of their sugar-coated camp trips Saturday to see the core of their religion at work.

Altamont, like the massacre of Song My, exploded the myth of innocence for a section of America. As the country grows more sophisticated, it learns to confront its own guilt.

The media projected WOODSTOCK. A great people event put on by the younger generation to celebrate its freedom. Traffic jams creating technological time-space motion transcending normal blurb time events. Birth, death, dope, violence, groovy teeny-boppers dancing—an instant consumer package of life. Look at all the hippies, America. They're grooving while the rest of you schmucks have to watch it on TV, because you're too uptight. The media needs hippies now more than ever, to show there is still someone in America who can dig on a scene.

But this time it didn't work. The helicopters could not feel that something more than a happening with three hundred thousand people was going on below. Altamont was America. Years of spreading dope, hair, music, and politics came together and reflected nothing less than the whole trip.

Those who expected the illusion of their own inherent goodness to last forever are still freaked. Others who pay less attention to the rhetoric of a cultural revolution say they had a good time. Putting it all together reads like America's pulse NOW. After all we not only make beautiful music, love, and beadwork; we pay our pigs to exterminate Black Panthers, we fry Vietnamese in their own homes, and we elect Spiro Agnew to govern our lives.

Altamont was a lesson in micro-society with no holds barred. Bringing a lot of people together used to be cool. Human Be-Ins, Woodstock, even a Hell's Angel funeral, were creative communal events because their center was everywhere. People would play together, performing, participating, sharing, and going home with a feeling that somehow the communal idea would replace the grim isolation wrought on us by a jealous competitive mother culture.

But at Altamont we were the mother culture. The locust generation come to consume crumbs from the hands of an entertainment industry we helped create. Our one-day micro-society was bound to the death-throes of capitalist greed. The freeway culture delivered the crowd, separate, self-contained in Methedrine isolation, to an event where they could not function as private individuals. The crowd came from a country where everything is done for you. Welfare state—relax, work, and pay your taxes. We'll take care of the war in Vietnam and the war at home.

Yeah, but nobody made sure the machine would function at Altamont. Three hundred thousand people sucked on a dry nipple because it was free. Everyone tried to get to the same place all by himself, and since everyone made it there was no pie. The pie was watching yourself at the spectacle, watching the spectacle watching you at the spectacle doing your own thing watching.

America at Altamont could only muster one common response. Everybody grooved on fear. One communal terror of fascist repression. The rest was all separate, people helping, people walking, people eating, people standing in line to shit. The revolutionaries were there too. Everybody related to people freaking out as well as the mother culture relates to Yippies. Here they were running through the crowd naked, stoned, trampling on our thinning privacy.

They expressed our own lack of control, our desire for space, for the freedom to live out our own body lives. But the crowd reacted with blind hatred, paranoia pressing them forward to get a better look at their own private crush on his satanic majesty.

But it wasn't all a freakout. Back up the slopes of Altamont Speedway, as in the secluded suburbs and woods of America, people kept to the illusions of better dope and more space. The loners, couples, and communes saw nothing, heard nothing and cared less about the crowded valley of fear. Most of them say they had a good time, but few escaped the heavy vibes from below.

Around the stage, at the epi-center, the Angels lost control. Their violence united the crowd in fear. Even people who had no fear of the Angels grew tense from a repressed feeling of panic that swirled around the stage. Mostly it was a fear of being trampled that was intensified by fights and people who did freak out. Since the Angels were the only group there who were to-gether enough to organize their violence they became a clear focus of crowd hatred. Thousands of times we've blamed pigs for less while holding the myth of right-wing Anarchist sacred. Marlon Brando, freewheelin' agent of chaos, another of Satur-day's toppled camp heroes.

The Angels protected Mick, their diabolic prince, well. He escaped without serious injury. Later on KSAN they too de-fended their actions on the grounds that their private property was violated. ". . . ain't nobody going to kick an Angel's bike and get away with it . . ." The official cover-up came Ronald Reagan style from the Stones' Manager Sam Cutler. When asked about the Angels' violence he answered ". . . regrettable, but if you're asking for a condemnation of the Angels . . ."

It was over. No explanation was needed, only a feeble plea

for someone in America to clean it up. The stirrings of a young but growing movement to salvage our environment. The job of cleaning up Altamont, or America, is still up for grabs. America wallows in the hope that someone, somewhere, can set it straight. Clearly nobody is in control. Not the Angels, not the people. Not Richard Nixon or his pigs. Nobody. America is up for grabs, as it sinks slowly into Methedrine suffocation with an occasional fascist kick to make her groan with satisfaction.

TO DREAM . . .

Love is but a song we sing
Here's the way we dance.

Music that can make half a million people dance!

A new Nation, a nation of children singing and dancing—for what else have we yearned all these years? A new nation, a no-nation—EARTH PEOPLES PARK.

The collective hallucinations of two generations of madmen. For this? To die in this . . . CITY? Of course not—the mushrooms are already breaking through the cement floor in the basement.

A nation of madmen and children—Earth Peoples Park.

"What if you could put a rainbow on a flagpole?"

Who said that? . . . who said that?

Can you remember the way they danced? Can you remember the way they sang? At Woodstock Nation . . . in Peoples Park? All of that to die defending a part of their city?

From Indian Rock you can look out across that terminal disease called "Civilization." From Indian Rock you can witness in horror the penultimate product of that dying civilization— THE CITY.

Do you live down there too? For what reason? Do you like the game of mutual cannibalism?

We can remember how to sing and dance. Is that political? If so, then call it the Politics of Joy, if so, call it the Revolution of Joy.

From Indian Rock, if you look hard enough you can see the germ of life that the million-year-old-death-kit has failed to destroy: Peoples Park . . . Woodstock Nation.

In whose national interest is it to keep the sun from shining? In whose interest is it to poison and putrefy the land and the sea? Are you a part of THAT nation?

Or are you part of a new nation, a no-nation. A nation where there is no "your space" and "my space," where there is no inner space and outer space—where there is only FREE SPACE.

The collective hallucinations of two generations of madmen and children—the Children of Alamogordo with only the Morning Star to light their way.

> *Here comes the Sun*
> *Here comes the Sun*
> *And I say*
> *It's all right*

A nation of children who remember their real heritage, who know that their heritage goes back further than the artificial geographical boundaries of nation-states.

A nation where the land is returned to its real owners—nobody-everybody.

And what if all the people who can still remember how to sing and dance come together in wholly communion.

MUSIC THAT WILL MAKE HALF A MILLION PEOPLE DANCE TOGETHER!

Couldn't it be used to take back the land from those who thought they could section off the seamless universe and claim a part of it as their own?

How can one man own another man?

How can one man own another's Time?

How can he own another's energy?

How can he OWN a piece of the sky, or the sea, or the earth.

Free space—a no-nation—Earth Peoples Park.

RENE DEBAUGE

MICHAEL ROSSMAN

MICHAEL ROSSMAN

ROY ARANELLA

CRAIG ANDERSON

EXCLUSIVE XXXX MANAGEMENT
WILLIAM MORRIS AGENCY, Inc.
NEW YORK CHICAGO LONDON HOLLYWOOD

IAN WHITCOMB

Robert Fitzpatrick Management
9000 Sunset Blvd., Los Angeles

ROY ARANELLA

ROY ARANELLA

ROY ARANELLA

SUBJECTS

You ask me to plow the ground.
Shall I take a knife and tear my mother's breast?
Then when I die
She will not take me to her bosom to rest.
You ask me to dig for stone.
Shall I dig under her skin for bones?
Then when I die
I cannot enter her body to be born again.
You ask me to cut grass and make hay
And sell it and be rich like the white man.
But how dare I cut off my mother's hair?
It is a bad law and my people cannot obey it.

— Nez Percé Smohalla, about 1870

They spent a million years developing the fine art of war and weaponry and they called it Civilization. And a million years making excuses for that civilization by calling it Culture.

Culture Vultures and nothing more. Have you had enough? Do we want to fight them for the world they've destroyed, or should we try again?

"We had to destroy it to save it."

Who said that? . . . who said that?

Could it be any plainer? Could it be any more absurd? To be normal requires a man to be stupid and vicious. Are you a citizen of THAT Nation? Or were you simply singing and dancing.

We told them about love . . . and they hated us for it.

We turned them on . . . and they passed laws against it.

We carried signs and protested . . . and they beat us and jailed us.

And then we told them we would defend ourselves . . . and they shot us down and declared war—AGAIN!

Are you ready to die for that piece of neon madness—is that your home?

Or are you ready to sing and dance in the creation of a new nation—a no-nation—a nation not of geographical boundaries, but of free spirits howling at the moon—Earth Peoples Park.

A tribal council of those madmen who know that civilization must destroy itself for the birth of the Aquarian Age.

Now, like no other time in history, can we see Black Elk's

vision as he stood beneath the rainbow entrance to the tepee. Now, as at no other time, can we hear the Grandfather's words so clearly:

"Take courage, younger brother. On earth a nation you shall make live, for yours shall be the power of the white giant's wing, the cleansing wind."

> *They are appearing,*
> *They are appearing,*
> *The thunder nation is appearing.*
> *They are appearing,*
> *They are appearing,*
> *The white geese nation is appearing.*

Danny Fields

WHO BRIDGES
THE GAP BETWEEN
THE RECORD EXECUTIVE
AND THE ROCK
MUSICIAN? I DO.

You're what's known in the business as a company freak. What does that mean?

Well, a kept hippie, mediating between the turtle-necked titans of the record industry and the unpunctual, crazy monsters called musicians. The titans supply his salary and expenses, but his heart is with the musicians, which makes schizophrenia a very possible occupational hazard. You've got to distinguish the company freak, whose presence is definitely felt, from the token house hippies that you find in book publishing, who have sideburns and go to lunch in real restaurants and mean very little in the corporate context.

Look, Columbia Records, which is the largest and most diversified label there is, claims that 60 percent of its sales are now coming from rock. This means that the record company, as a communications medium, is the only national mass medium dominated by the products of the alternate, or revolutionary, culture. There *are* media which are alternate in both form and content, like the underground press and the FM rock stations, but those are local or community media. The record industry is establishment in form, but anti-establishment in content. So now these executives have to deal with a new generation of money-making talents, with whom communication is often kind of difficult. Their artists are on the other side of the generation gap, and the company freak is someone who is supposed to provide the liaison factor between the company and its artists, and also between the company and the alternate media. No hip FM dj, for example, will have anything to do with the promotion sharpies in shiny suits—you don't get to their heads by slapping them on the back. And yet a record company has to reach these cats because they have a lot of influence on kids who buy records. Hence, the company freak.

I think Billy James was the first company freak, at Columbia. I went to see him in Hollywood after he'd left Columbia and had been propped up by Elektra in their plush little suite in the Sunset Vine Tower, and it was fantastic—what a setup. It was my first sight of a company freak, this charming, barefoot dynamo, running around the office, sitting on the floor, putting his feet up on the walls. And the room is full of kids coming in and out, hanging out, receiving solace, advice, encouragement. You know, you're paid by the record company to represent them to their artists, but the companies are really embracing a scorpion, because it's often impossible to justify the policies of the company to the artists; sometimes the artist is a little unreal in his demands or expectations, but I just think that in almost any dispute the artist has God on his side. So you take the bread and go ahead and tell the artist that the company is probably wrong, and that he must endure, and you'll see what you can do.

I shouldn't make it sound all so frustrating; it has compensations other than financial. I suppose as jobs go, these positions are among the great "glamour jobs" available to us now. It's a new category of glamour jobs. I had once planned to go into book or magazine publishing because it looked to me, as a collegiate English graduate, that those were the kicky jobs to have in New York. Television I always thought that you had to go to Television School for. It's good these jobs exist now because here I am, and here we are, and I'm one of many coming out of a disastrously inefficient and unreal educational system, and we don't even know all the groovy things we can do. We never heard of these jobs as possibilities. Whatever it is that's supposed to make you aware of all the professional possibilities before you're, say, twenty-three, isn't working.

But there have got to be company freaks, because as a generation we represent wealth and the necessity to distribute the existing wealth among ourselves. Distribution is a key concept, it is very much an aspect of rock, the distribution of the recorded product to a mass audience. And it's an aspect that the artist wants to see covered well in his behalf. He's got to have his music covered (he covers that himself); and his photographs and his equipment (now he has to go to other artists and to technicians); and his distribution (and now he has to go to a record company, the operations of which it is extremely hard for him to cover, i.e., control). So that rock has generated, in a sense, this person called a company freak, who acts as the artist's agent within the distributing mechanism. I'd rather see the company freak as someone the artist puts in the company—after all, his salary comes from money that the artist earns for the company. It's like when you're busted, the government wants your ass, but they have to get you a lawyer, who in turn is going to contest the disposition of your ass with the same bastards who hired him. Like it's the artist's right and his safeguard. Enough theory.

You brought several artists to Elektra. Is that part of the job?

Well, whatever you can do is part of the job. It's a role anyhow, not a job, and you invent it as you go along. Of course, the company would certainly like you to bring them artists; it's a benefit that they expect will accrue from your being on the scene, going to clubs, hanging out with musicians and writers. Naturally, when you find an artist and you take him from Potato Salad, Idaho, to the offices of a big New York record company, you want to guarantee that he has some protection from the sharks up there. And so I would actually sit in Jac Holzman's (he owns Elektra) office with my discovery and tell Jac to give more money to these people. Then later Jac would tell me, "You just stay out of that," and of course he was right. I was getting to be a bit much, and this led to my splitting from there.

But discovering talent was the best part of the gig. You're a New York talent scout, and you're giving the artists their Big Break, sending them first-class tickets to come to New York and we'll tell you how you're going to be famous and rich; you feel pretty good doing that, like an agent of the Medicis. Then it turns out you're a Judas leading the lambs to slaughter. It can make you very crazy.

Of the artists you brought to Elektra, David Peel seems the most personal discovery. Can you tell us how that happened?

This is a great show biz story: I had thought (and I think the thought was thought a little ahead of its time) about two years ago that it would be possible to make a record of drug songs and *call* them drug songs, in the sense that drinking songs used to be. Not psychedelic-metaphoric, but yo-ho-ho let's get high. And that it would be a kind of giggle to do that, and interesting to try and market it as a novelty. I had the concept, but the content of the album eluded me. I didn't want to write anything, because it would probably turn out clever and collegiate, and I didn't want it to be that. I'd given this idea to Holzman, and he said it was a good idea, but what do we put on the record? So it just sort of simmered. And then one day, March 31 of last year, the day that LBJ abdicated, I was walking through Washington Square, and there on the fountain is this incredible dynamic *freak* shouting, haranguing and singing, "I like marijuana, you like marijuana, we like marijuana too." And gathered around him, transfixed, is an audience of hippies, tourists, teenyboppers, little old Italian ladies from Sullivan Street. One old lady says to another, "He's very good this week."

I pick up on all these things, pick up on that between songs this kid could decide to shift physically or have a conference with his band, and the eyes of the audience are still on him. He could do that, he could keep the crowd between songs. And the songs, these were really the folk songs of the Lower East Side hippie ghetto, post-literate urban folk. Simple and funny and direct, street songs, a whole new thing. Richard Goldstein put David Peel down by accusing him of not being as literate as the Fugs.

What bullshit. The Fugs all have advanced degrees in literature, they're extremely educated and David Peel is not. So who cares what he isn't? What a poor approach to criticism when you can't figure out what something is, to talk about what it isn't, what a cop out.

David Peel grew up in Brooklyn and he heard about Greenwich Village when he was in the army in Alaska, playing his guitar and somebody said, "Hey, you ought to go to Greenwich Village and play your guitar." So when he got out he went to the Village instead of going back to Brooklyn.

Anyhow, there I was, discovering the content of my concept, and being knocked out by David's showmanship. I mean, he was so good. I started getting paranoid, and I thought, Uh oh, these aren't just bystanders in the crowd, I'll bet they're agents from William Morris and the Grossman office and Warner Brothers Records. You know, it's New York and the kid's so talented, they must be waiting to snap him up. I didn't know that he'd been there every Sunday for a year. I used to hang out in the Square, but who hangs out there any more. So I stood there all afternoon waiting for him to finish, and I edged towards the front of the crowd of "agents and promoters" and it was really getting cold and damp and the chick I was with said we should go and get coffee and come back. And I said, "Are you kidding, someone will snap him up, we gotta wait, gotta beat out all these other scouts in getting to him." Then he finished and put down his guitar and everyone applauded and walked away, so I went up to him and said How do you do, I'm from Elektra Records, blah blah blah. I felt kind of corny doing it, I always do, but he was knocked out too, so we went to Max's and had steak and champagne. Later he told me that people were always coming up to him with their business cards and he would say thank you and never call them because he didn't trust the way they looked, and he dug that I didn't even have a card with me and I looked sort of grubby but could sign for steak and champagne dinners.

So then I got Peter Siegel interested in David—Peter is a very groovy producer at Elektra—and we recorded David live in Washington Square, which was a first. I got very excited about the record, but then at one point this important Elektra executive says to me, "Why are you making such a fuss about it, this album isn't going to sell more than five thousand copies." (I got the title, *Have a Marijuana,* from *Time* magazine. They had sent a reporter to cover the Yip-In at Grand Central Station that turned into a police riot, and David was there singing "Mari-marijuana, mari-marijuana," which is the chorus, and the *Time* reporter heard it wrong, and wrote, "The Yippies stormed into Grand Central Station singing Have a Marijuana." That just jumped off the page at me, and I said there's the title.)

Five thousand copies, projected sales, and I thought, omigod, what a terrible way to go into something like this. So it's not rock or snazzy bullshit blues or glamorous, but it's unique, and it's funny, and everyone can sing along with it, so why not market it as a novelty and shoot for one hundred thousand records. Elektra told me not to be silly. It's sold fifty thousand as of now, but I'm the company freak and what do I know about selling records?

But you know, it's a great job when you can go around finding artists in Washington Square, it's like a 1940s movie now. You know, the bands and their girls and the bus breaks down in northern Vermont and they hock their instruments and they're looking for their special sound, all those things. It's the same story, it's like being in it.

You found David in Washington Square. What do you think of the rock scene in New York?

There are only two significant people presenting important live music continually, Bill Graham and Steve Paul. I don't think what either of them is doing is ideal, but they have to be considered. Do you remember what Graham did in San Francisco? He was brilliant, look at the posters—the local groups got billing over national groups then, the Airplane did, and Big Brother, and the Dead. Graham made them stars in San Francisco, he really helped invent a scene out there. But he comes to New York as a capitalist—not into making a strong local scene, but into having an uptown rock palace starring hot national recording acts in the middle of the Lower East Side. It's quite a different thing. Now he points to bringing B.B. King to a white audience, making Richie Havens a star. He says, look, these cats were neglected until they played the Fillmore and then they got stories in *Time* and *Newsweek* because they appeared at the Fillmore. Now, for Graham to cite those people, and I have every respect for their talent, is almost like identifying with another generation. So he's brought back the living dead, what about the living living? So Graham is into a big-time scene now, and he's not going to make any more history doing this, just money.

Steve Paul I think is fantastic. I don't think the Scene is fantastic, like physically it's a mess, but everyone has played there when they were starting, and all the superstars hang out there, and thank God for it, alas. But that isn't why I think Steve is fantastic, I mean I think he's greater than anything he's done yet, he's got one of the great brains in this universe, his thoughts, his raps, his words, are dazzling. He's so good that there aren't too many people capable of appreciating how good he is. You know he's invented this albino blues guitarist named Johnny Winter, who's a very excellent blues guitarist if that's what you're into, but Steve is really the star, a much bigger star than Johnny and someday the world will know that. But the New York rock scene . . . I don't know. New York is too busy being nationally significant to have a local scene, maybe that's it. It's too bad. There was the Group Image, that was great, and before that the Velvet Underground and the Plastic Inevitable. That was the first group I was a fan of, long before I was in the business, when I was editing college textbooks.

Nico was with the Velvet Underground then, wasn't she? Is that when you met her?

No, it was before that, in the days when I used to give big parties at home. I had scheduled one for Thanksgiving weekend in 1963, Friday, November 27, and then there was the shit in Dallas and I wasn't sure what to do, but I decided to have the party—everyone needed a party then—and it was just incredible.

Everyone said it was one of the most beautiful parties they'd ever seen in New York, wonderful, beautiful people.

And then in the middle of the evening the door opened and Nico came in, dressed in tattered Levis and a tattered Levi jacket. She came in with two men, a Chilean count and a false English dandy, and the room of beautiful people just turned and stared. She walked over to the table on which there was a punch bowl and dipped the ladle in and threw her head back and poured the punch perfectly from about a *foot* over her head into her mouth without spilling a drop. Show stopper. That's how I met Nico, she crashed my party, the chick from *La Dolce Vita*. She had just come to New York, and then she and the Warhols picked up on each other, and she began to sing with the Velvet Underground. There were hassles between her and the band, but I think that was a golden age in music, it's there on their first album.

So then she went out on her own and got a gig at the Scene. Steve Paul did beautiful ads, the moon goddess in a sacred service of mystical chants, and all that, he really did it up. Chic crowd turned up at Nico's opening, and there was only an organ onstage, and she sat down at it and there was one spotlight on her. It was like a child discovering a musical instrument for the first time. She would just press one note and bend her ear towards the keyboard and listen to it, and press it again and again, and then another note, and she'd listen to that. And this was in front of this reverent opening-night audience, which didn't know what to make of it, not at all. She did this for half an hour, then she tried a few combinations of notes and got into that.

Meanwhile people were starting to file out quietly, except for about twelve people including me who were just mesmerized by the whole performance, and she finally sang two chants and that was it. And we all sort of noticed each other because the room was empty. Twelve people, all male, just transfixed, and it was over and it was one of the most beautiful things I'd ever seen. Not the kind of thing you could do at the Fillmore, but there's a quality of magic in it, in everything she does, I guess. I'd like to put on a whole show based on magic with Nico as mistress of ceremonies, and a super cast, like Bishop Pike's son, if we could get him.

I introduced Jim Morrison to her—I was very officious then—I had been backstage with the Doors in the San Francisco Fillmore and I was kind of appalled at the quality of the groupies hanging onto Morrison. Universal band pigs. So, as his press agent, I was concerned about his burgeoning image, and when I ran into him a week later in L.A. I thought wouldn't it be nice to try and elevate his taste in females. It was presumptuous of me, but I thought it would be interesting to see what happened. Nico was staying at the famous rock castle in the Hollywood Hills, and I brought Morrison up there to meet her. Edie Sedgwick was staying there too, and Dino Valente, and me, quite a cast.

Morrison and Nico had this wondrously strange affair, which consisted of the two of them standing in adjacent stone doorways of this false castle, and staring at the floor in front of them, or staring at the same spot on the floor, I guess communicating via reflections off the stone. An entire afternoon and evening passed, and all they did was shift doorways and start staring at the floor again. The whole thing had a sort of weird ending, but I don't think I'll go into that.

Nico's a very bright girl, she's no dumb blonde, and it just takes about two and one-half minutes of talking to her to know that if you've had any doubts about it. They wanted to photograph her for *Cinema* magazine, and she wanted Jim to pose with her, and I asked her if she and Morrison were going to do anything cinematic together, you know I'm trying to think like the cat who's going to have to write the caption in *Cinema* magazine. I asked if he was going to make a movie with her in it, or if she was going to make a movie with him in it, like what? And she said, "Oh, why do you need that? Why can it not just be two beautiful people together?" And of course she was right, in fact I copped the idea and later took it to *Eye* magazine, and told them they should do a series on beautiful couples and wouldn't Nico and Morrison be great for a start. So they thought it was groovy, and started to set it up—Nico and Jim would be dressed in black leather and photographed at the Cloisters, something predictable like that.

But Morrison refused to do it, and he was angered and he said don't ever do that without asking me about it first. He was really pissed at me, and Nico was hurt that he didn't want to pose with her, *Eye* magazine was baffled, and I was slightly embarrassed. But you just don't tell him what to do. He may understand and may do it one day, or he may not ever do it, but he's never going to say thank you for telling me what to do. Not that he's uncooperative or arbitrary, he just insists on doing everything on terms that only he can define, and don't you dare step in there. And he said that someday he would do a movie and Nico would be in it, but he wasn't going to have his picture taken with her for *Eye* magazine.

I was the Doors' first New York press agent, in the fall of '66 when they were here to play Ondine's. The day after I heard them the first time I ran over to Elektra and introduced myself as the person doing the Doors press; their L.A. press agent was a friend of mine and had asked me to do what I could for them their first time in New York. The reason I ran was to tell Elektra to release "Light My Fire" as a single.

Well, they said it was too long, and they had another single ready for release, and it wasn't until eight months later that they did it and the rest is history. And Jac Holzman remembered that I was the first person outside the company to tell them that "Light My Fire" was a hit song. But they waited until the first single bombed and four hundred dj's told them to get "Light My Fire" off the album and cut it to single length.

I also told them to release "Both Sides Now" as a single, but they said it was too soft and wouldn't make it, and then they released it almost a year later, and it was a gold record, and it made Judy into a million selling artist, brought her to a whole new commercial level.

You're a literary culture dropout, aren't you? Wasn't your first job at a magazine?

Yeah, I've dropped out of a few things, starting with Harvard Law School, then NYU graduate school, then I took all these toy jobs, getting into publishing from the bottom, so I sold books at

Doubleday's and worked for *Liquor Store Magazine* (really), then I was writing college ponies, you know, great novels in twenty-five words or less, and the history of the world on the head of a pin, and all the famous people who ever lived all in one book. I had a good time with that one, I gave Marilyn Monroe about twice as much space as James Monroe and things like that.

Then there was this ad in *The New York Times* help wanted, about an expanding teen magazine seeks editor-writer, some magazine experience and knowledge of pop scene. So I wrote this far-out letter, not at all like the kind you're supposed to write to prospective employers. I wrote about the pursuit of truth and beauty and the exciting possibilities for a magazine, and I gave them all these story ideas. I thought when the ad said, "pop scene" that it meant the pop art crowd, like Andy and Edie, and those were the people I was hanging out with then, so I just dropped a lot of names from that crowd. I didn't know he meant the pop *music* scene, but when I went for an interview I covered that over and came on real bright and enthusiastic, and got the job over literally three hundred applicants. It was this teenage service magazine named *Datebook,* the publisher was named Unger. He wanted to go from articles on how to get along with your new stepmother and my profitable summer working in a leper colony into a teenybopper fan magazine, because he had done some Beatles coverage and there was big reader response to that, and he'd heard that *16* had a circulation of a million, so what he really wanted was for me to do an imitation of *16*.

This is a hangup all these publishers have, and it is possible to cop a successful formula and survive, but I couldn't get into that. I mean, only Gloria Stavers can do *16*, you know, she's brilliant and that's one of the great magazines, only the semi-hip put it down and only the semi-human (i.e., publishers) care so little about history and their own dignity that they can get into imitating something that already is up there. Well, Unger wasn't that terrible, I did convince him to do a controversy issue, for the cover of which I selected a quote from a John Lennon interview which read, "I don't know which will go first, rock and roll or

Christianity." Remember that? But by the time the furor broke, I'd been fired. I wouldn't do anything on the Dave Clark 5, I just wanted to do stories on the Byrds and Cass Elliot and the Velvet Underground and Bob Dylan, none of which were very potent in influencing magazine sales.

My brother in Berkeley sent me the first single of the Jefferson Airplane, and I flipped and made them my first New Group to Watch—it was the first thing about them in a national magazine. I had the first real interviews with McGuinn, and the first interview with Peter Townshend in any American magazine. I found him at a party for Herman's Hermits, it was his first time in America, he was here to negotiate some business, and somebody dragged him to this enormous party at the Hotel Americana. He was very pissed off that the Hermits were collecting their eightieth gold record, while nothing of the Who had broken here. I'd been reading about them in the English rock press and I'd been fascinated with them. I was walking out with Linda Eastman— we were sort of a writer-photographer team—and there was Townshend, sitting alone at a table, and I said, psst, Linda, look who, and she said it's Townshend! and started snapping that Nikon, and I went over to him and got my interview.

I met Linda Eastman and Richard Goldstein and Gloria Stavers all the same day, at the now legendary Rolling Stones boat ride and press conference. Gloria and I missed the boat, and when she saw me there, looking out down the Hudson and crying, man she was *furious*. They'd told her she would be the only representative from any teen magazine, and there was me from *Datebook*—I had wormed an invitation from the Stones office—and she just muttered something like, well so much for the Stones, and called a cab and split.

But I really wanted something on them, they've always been my number-one fave rave group, I guess, so I waited for the boat to return, and there she was, she'd just taken her first photographs. Her brother had brought her a camera from Japan, and she learned that if you point it at someone beautiful and press a button you get a beautiful picture. But she's very special, you know, she has this quality I find in Libra ladies—Nico, Gloria

Stavers, Genie the Tailor who I am going to miss a whole lot—
men have a tendency to dance for them, to perform, to please
them. And the pictures she got that day—there were the other
pictures, the official pictures of the Stones taken by some professional news photographer, and then there were Linda's pictures.
The Stones were *doing* things, striking poses, being arrogant and
beautiful and fantastic and sexy. They did it, they danced for her
camera, and she always had this quality. She took the best
portraits of beautiful people of anyone. The publicity group shots
she did were okay, and that's most of her stuff that's been published, but her portfolio of close-ups was just astonishing. It
could have been printed just the way she had it set up to take
around with her to show people, and it would make the most
beautiful book of all time.

**While you're into talking about great ladies, what about Judy Collins.
She was a reigning superstar at Elektra before you got there. How did
you relate to her?**

I'll tell you how Judy became my muse. You've hired as a
publicist, you're the company freak, and as much as you can
invent your own role, you're still working for the stable of artists
on the label. So there was Judy Collins, and I'd always thought
she made lovely records, but she hadn't been terribly important
to me. So I had to figure out how best to serve Judy Collins, how
to effect some kind of involvement with her, because you can
only want for your artists what they want for themselves. Unless
you understand that, you're not going to be working successfully
with them. I needed an attitude toward her; I had to invent my
own feelings about her, so that then I could in my public context
as her publicist have something to communicate. Well she helped
me do it in this way that proved to me that she was very special
and magical.

What happened was, it was Newport, two years ago, and it
was the first time I'd ever really met her. I was up there on behalf
of Elektra and she was performing at the Folk Festival. Well it
was late at night, we were staying at the Viking where everyone
stays, and I had taken acid and somehow found myself sitting in

a chair in the corner of her room. And there were some friends of
hers crashed on the bed, and she and Leonard Cohen were sitting there giggling and saying lovely things to each other—they
have a whole private thing they get into when they're together,
it's quite extraordinary—and I was nervous because I was tripping heavily and I didn't know them very well, and I didn't want
to blow my cool.

Leonard took his guitar and taught her this song he'd just
written, "Hey, That's No Way to Say Good-bye," and she took
out her guitar and picked up on it, and they sang it together. The
whole night it seemed, they just sang that song over and over and
they became like all the lovers that ever were and all the beautiful people who ever sang together. Then, they'd finished singing,
and Judy was just sort of picking her guitar, and I was going
through this bit of acid agitation, the point where you want to
assert your ego and be part of the other people. And just then
Judy put down her guitar and looked at me and held her hand
out and said, "Come, I want to show you the sunrise from the
cliffs." She'd just responded to this inner urgent need, just like
that. Because she's Taurus, she's the Earth Mother, she's there to
respond to the needs of the people she's with. And they took me
out and propped me up in her car and we went out to the cliffs,
Judy and Leonard and I, and we saw the sunrise.

The next week it was all reinforced when I went out to the
castle in L.A. to stay with Nico, and there was no radio there, no
TV, no phone, no electronic device in the house, and I was
desperate for some music. There was a closet with a sign on the
door that said "stereophonic equipment," and I opened it and it
was empty, just some shelves and loose wires. The only thing in
the closet was a picture of Judy Collins, so I took it over to one of
the grand pianos in the living room and put it up on the music
stand.

Now I'd never played the piano in my life—I've been very self-
conscious about actually making music because my father played
a lot of instruments and made me uptight about it, but I started
to play first with one finger, then with all the fingers on one hand,
then with both hands, and then I just started to *fly*, and people
came out on the balcony and said, hey, I didn't know you played

the piano . . . I was doing this incredible thing with Judy's picture on the music stand. The only time I played an instrument before or since, so it was like Judy was telling me something. Then after that, I could be her press agent, not that I could go around telling this insane story to editors, you know, they'd think I was completely bats, but it gave me the equipment I needed to present her. I knew who she was. Things happen in funny ways.

Do company freaks ever deal in hypes?

Well, to me the word hype is simply synonymous with lots of publicity. So there's two kinds of hypes, the real one where the publicity is merited, and the bad hype, where the publicity is out of proportion to the merit of whatever is being publicized. Good hypes are great, once you get past the counter-hype. Bad hypes are dangerous. Look, if you know enough influential people in the media and people who make opinion and they owe you favors or you've scored brownie points with them, you could conceivably convince them to give you space on something that isn't worth it. But anything like that which is done for the wrong reasons is going to set off a chain of ironies that continues for ever and ever. And I've seen that and I've seen myself get hyped, and have gotten into perpetrating a hype, and when it starts to fall apart, it really starts to fall all over you. You can go out for something you don't believe in and get your seven pages in *Life,* but it doesn't mean a thing if the artist isn't going to come and vindicate you. It doesn't mean a thing to the artist, and you'll have trouble being believed next time around.

You were very involved with the MC5, and many people thought that their publicity was a hype.

Sure, but it's a good hype. Listen, that's the best goddamn band in the world. Nothing less than a hype would suit them. They're so good that people refuse to believe what they read and it all sounds like too much, like it's made up. Well it *is* too much, and they are so extraordinary that they come off sounding like a press agent's fantasy, but it's no fantasy. You'll see that. What I did, right after I saw them in Detroit and got them to Elektra, was to bring Jon Landau out there to see them, because I knew that they were what he'd always been looking for, the definitive hard rock band.

Now I didn't expect Landau to write anything, I didn't ask him to. But he's like a critic's critic, I'd say he's the single most influential person in America on the rock scene, so what happened was that when I brought Goldstein out there, I had Landau back. Goldstein listens to Landau, and sometimes he listens to me, but I'm a press agent and I'm still suspect. And Goldstein was a little terrified, but Landau cooled him out, and said, look man, *that* is rock and roll, and Richard said yeah, he knew, but it was terrifying, all those kids waving their arms, and the volume, and the energy. But Landau said again, look, man, that's rock, and Richard went back to New York and wrote a piece in the *Voice* and a piece in the *Times*, both great. He knew what it was all about, he just didn't like it, but Landau made him see that it didn't matter if he liked it, it just mattered what was happening in that room when the MC5 played, and Goldstein wrote these beautiful, accurate, superbly comprehending stories, and he never got to saying whether or not he liked the music, which I don't think he did.

Then Landau was talking to the people at *Rolling Stone,* and he talked about the Five, and they had a story on them and decided to make it the cover story and run it for six pages. Before their record even came out, they had been the most publicized group in the history of American rock, but it's real, they're the best. The prejudice against them comes from the literate literary crowd; the best reviews of their music are in the high school underground papers, 'cause those are the kids who know what it's supposed to be and what rock is about.

Why, then, did you leave Elektra?

It's very complex. There are certain artists with whom I'm very involved, and I can be most effective outside the record company working in their behalf. You know Elektra has a very groovy roster, and it's supposed to be very hip, but I think that the days of a record company exerting *any* artistic control over its artists are numbered. Record companies will function best simply as distributors of complete artistic packages. It's like what happened in the movies. In the old days the studios had a corporate identity, and something of a creative stamp was put on all their products. Now the big studios are just distributors for the products of production companies.

And I don't know what the role of company freaks will be in the future. I think we'll start seeing freak companies. 'Cause now the freaks are really ineffectual, you know. That means they can't sign checks. Money's such a dumb thing to get hung up on. It's another commodity you deal in: vibrations, applause, good photographs, and all. One tries to have an adequate and sufficient flow of all those things, and money is another thing. That's where I come to differ with the people who play money games at the corporations; to them it's an end, to me it's another manifestation of something happening. If what you've got is good and you're doing it well, there will be money, as there will be press and applause. Seen that way, it has a more organic connection with everything that's happening and everything is so much easier, if only those bastards would realize that. They hang you up for pennies.

I learned how to negotiate a contract when I took the Five to Atlantic. I had never been able to talk money, but I had to do it, so I learned all the figures and percentages and I went in there and talked money with Jerry Wexler and Mike Mayer, maybe the two shrewdest businessmen in the industry, and I came out with a good contract. So let this be a lesson to all freaks, that if you have to talk about it, and you know how to, then it's another area that you've got covered. And I think it's an area that the revolution must have covered. Right now I'm pretty busy with the lousy Repression, it's so real, so operative . . . it's a full-time thing, countering the repression. Kokaine Kharma was dropped from WFMU, and that's supposed to be the hippest radio station in the New York area, and that show was probably the best, liveliest, freshest, hippest show in American radio, with Bob Rudnick and Dennis Frawley. The MC5 is fired by Elektra, which is the hippest record company, and the Smothers Brothers are fired off the hippest network, and Columbia records is dropping its ads in the underground press. The hard rain is falling, it's falling right now.

Jon Wiener

WOODSTOCK REVISITED

Remember Woodstock? Remember how the radical press attacked this biggest rock festival in the history of the world
(450,000 people) because it was a business that was going to
make a profit of $1 million by selling us our own music?
Remember how so many kids came they couldn't collect tickets,
and a quarter of a million people got in for free? And remember
how the promoters announced that they *lost* $1 million, and how
everyone called that a victory for the people?

Well, the promoters made plenty of money, it turns out;
exactly how much is difficult to say. Their wailing "we lost a
million" was part of a clever and, up to now, successful attempt
to fool the public and undermine the radicals' attack on their
operation. The true story has been uncovered by the show-biz
newspaper, *Variety*.

The Woodstock promoters—Joel Roseman, John Roberts, Michael Lang and Artie Kornfeld—claimed to be $1.3 million in
debt at the end of the festival. Then they started trying to buy
each other out, and it was reported that Albert Grossman,
manager of Dylan, Janis Joplin, and The Band, among others,
was offering $1 million for one-fourth of the business. Albert
Grossman is the most successful money-maker in rock music; he
doesn't make mistakes. Why, *Variety* asked, would Grossman
offer $1 million to acquire a debt of $1.3 million?

The answer was that there was no debt, that the promoters' report of their expenses was filled with lies.

The promoters sold $1.4 million in mail-order tickets; they claim that their expenses were $2.7 million. They say they spent $600,000 on emergency helicopters, food and medicine, which makes them seem pretty generous.

But their eight helicopters cost $500 an hour; for three ten-hour days, that's only $120,000, which leaves $480,000 for food and medicine. And half the helicopters were hired beforehand to ferry the performers around; this raises the emergency food and medicine cost to $550,000. But, as everyone who was there has testified, virtually the only source of food and medicine was the Hog Farm. The promoters' claimed emergency costs were a half-million-dollar lie.

They claim they paid the talent $250,000. But simply adding up what they say they paid the individual acts gives the figure $150,000. Some had argued that "the performers don't make the money on these things"; Woodstock's list of who got what disproves that idea, and provides a financial ranking of the popularity of the various rock groups.

(The most expensive group was the Jimi Hendrix Experience —they took home $18,000 for their set. Next was Blood, Sweat and Tears—$15,000. Creedence Clearwater Revival and Joan Baez got $10,000 each; The Band, Jefferson Airplane, and Janis Joplin got $7,500 each.

From there on down, the list reads: Sly and the Family Stone, $7,000; Canned Heat, $6,500; The Who, $6,250; Richie Havens, 6,000; Arlo Guthrie, $5,000; Crosby, Stills, Nash and Young, $5,000; Ravi Shankar, $4,500; Johnny Winter, $3,750; Ten Years After, $3,250; Country Joe, $2,500; the Grateful Dead, $2,500; and down through other groups to Quill, $375.)

Woodstock claims production costs exclusive of talent were $2.25 million. The Isle of Wight festival cost $50,000 to produce, which is probably closer to the true figure for Woodstock.

There are two particularly interesting figures in Woodstock's budget: $16,000 to charter a plane for the Hog Farm, and $10,000 for "Yippie Headquarters." The policing and relief work done by these two groups were cheap considering the services they provided for the promoters.

The final unreported source of income for Woodstock is the royalties from the feature-length film *Woodstock*, which will open across the nation at Christmas time. Warner's, according to *Variety*, is certain it will be their biggest money-maker of the season.

All of this adds up to what many had suspected all along: the Woodstock rock festival was not a victory for "the people," it was a victory for the businessman-promoters, men who make a profit by exploiting youth culture.

The stars of rock have helped perpetuate business dominance of pop music, turning their music into a commodity to be sold to whoever has the money—at the same time that these same stars claim to be part of a political movement that opposes exploitation. Joan Baez insisted at her last New York concert that no one be allowed in for less than two dollars—if you want to hear her sing about not paying her income taxes because they go for war, you have to pay for it. And Dylan, who was crucial to the recent development of the protest song, demanded $85,000 for his Isle of Wight appearance—which turned out to be more than $7,000 a song.

We don't need any more multi-day rock festivals with expensive tickets—"festivals of love" that turn out to be festivals of profit for the promoters; instead, we need free concerts, and a lot of them—free music in all the parks every week. Contributions of low-priced admissions could cover the expenses of the bands— they have to eat too. But the junior assistant west coast promo man and his profit-minded counterparts across the country have got to go.

J. *Lawrence*

EXPLICATING THE BEATLES

LONDON, Oct. 6 (Special)—The Beatles have seized control of the British Government, dissolving the Cabinet and Parliament, retiring the P.M., and relegating the Queen to the vice-presidency of their New South Wales fan club chapter.

Word has leaked out that George Harrison (whom many observers call "the quiet, sneaky one") was the mastermind of the plot. A top-secret dossier, released this morning by Scotland Yard, contains evidence that Harrison was the agent of an international conspiracy involving an unknown number of persons and said to possibly include the Smothers Brothers, Ethel Kennedy and the Man from UNCLE.

Informed sources inside the Beatles intelligence complex and 256-track recording studio have reported that the four leaders have already begun work in their chosen and/or assigned posts:

Harrison: Minister of the Interior (Consciousness)
Lennon: Roving Ambassador to the Universe (and ice-cream vendor)
McCartney: Executive dilettante
Starkey: Director of Undersea Operations
produced by George Martin

When asked for an official statement on the takeover, an Apple spokesman said a complete report would soon be forthcoming.
(*Ed. Note: Three days later an album called ABBEY ROAD was released.*)

Here come big Injun,
He got plenty laundry,
he know jabberwockey,
he dig walking chicken,
he chew rockaberry,
he see brother down in the east:
Got to be a scrapper-giggle-put down a thief.

Here Come(s) the Sun (King George):

Doot'n'doo-doo
Oh Boy! Oh Boy!
Here it comes:
So warm/friendly/intimate:
acoustic guitar fingerpick—
capo makes crystal steel harpischord
on seventh fret
in D chords.

Sun (2-3) Sun (2-3) Sun (2-3)
Here it comes:
Red-orange, red-orange, red-orange,
Yellow-orange;
Moog (da-da), Moog (da-da), Moog (da-da)
Here it comes:
painting/sweeping/strokes/across
brighter and brighter
bolder and bolder
(six in all).

Doot'n'doo-doo
Here come(s) the Sun (King George):
old hair and shoe
(does it really matter if they're brown?).

Light comes from within (here it comes):
Are you coming, lil darlin'?
To prove thy innocence (be not guilty)
and teach us how to die
(please, we have waited three long years).
No longer a northerner alone/ sing and smile
No more to weep for all, No more too much
Too cold and too long
Tomorrow.
Will we ever know?
No more.

But it's all right, it's all right.
Sun, here it comes, and
i could come too;
i am happy for you Harrisong.

PROGRAM NEWS FROM BGA-TV

The B.G.A. television network proudly announces a new weekly series, a situation fantasy titled "Maxwell's Silver Hammer."

The hero is an eccentric technological maverick named Maxwell Edison, a self-styled vigilante who occasionally drops out of medical school in the manner of a Jekyll-Hyde. Maxwell vicariously runs amok with his co-star, a jovial and energetic Silver Hammer that is played by Peter Sellers.

Program sponsors and producers, who last year gave us the popular "Bungalow Bill" (which is still running well abroad), have here employed the same proven formula—namely that as violence increases so do ratings.

The following are capsule descriptions of three upcoming episodes:

1) A lonely female student of the occult gets whacked on.
2) A reprimanding female teacher of the school of discipline gets whacked on.
3) A stern old justice of the peace gets whacked on.

As you can plainly see, all the shows have a common theme expressed in a wide variety of story situations.

What makes the series so unique is its characters: Maxwell is a flamboyant and thoroughly professional breed of TV hero, and his hammer bangs and clangs on the head of each victim until both of them are SURE THAT HE OR SHE IS DEAD. And with each killing, Max (backed by a groovy mod vocal group) sings the show's catchy themesong (which will soon be released as a single).

Related promotional tie-ins will include Maxwell's Silver Hammer sweatshirts, lunchboxes, dolls and full-color bubble gum cards showing the most exciting scenes from each show. Beatle George Harrison is expected to show up in a number of cameo roles, playing a retired guru, an itinerant magician and a Moog synthesizer.

The show was originally scheduled to be a children's cartoon program, but the genius of the producers fashioned it into prime-time adult entertainment. To insure a firm grasp on the over-forty audience (they ain't heads, Jack), vintage music of the 1920s and '30s will be a major part of the sound track. Watch for it soon on your local station.

I

More than for any other musical event, the release of a new Beatles album serves as the occasion for launching numerous and verbose critical dissertations—not on the album itself, but on the Beatles and Dylan (Dylan?) and the total state of the art. The event triggers loose all the thoughts that have been stored up since . . .

II

Before one can speak, write, or even think about the Beatles, one must decide whether they are to be viewed as artists or entertainers. As artists . . .

III

Just as with each new Beatle release of the last few years, many people don't seem to know what they think about it. They seem to clamor to be told not only WHY they like it (as they probably do), but even WHETHER they like it. If you need to be told whether or not you do or should like *Abbey Road,* then . . .

IV

And in the end, perhaps the only validity this writer can evoke is that *Abbey Road* is to be listened to rather than talked about, enjoyed rather than understood, appreciated rather than . . .

V

Although it has been most frequently compared with *Revolver,* *Abbey Road* can be more closely related to three other albums:

a) Individually, the songs are a direct extension of *The Beatles* (with "Mustard" and "Pam" being actual leftovers from those sessions).

b) As a whole, the album recalls the structure of *Magical Mystery Tour* in that it seems to be two distinct parts, Side Two being *Abbey Road* (a cohesive if contrived *Pepper*-like trip), while Side One is merely a collection of unrelated singles (even if all six do not get released in that form).

VI

Just as they have done so often in the past, on *Abbey Road* the Beatles are putting us on. The Beatles have always been putting us on. Compared to the way Dylan has put us on, however . . .

VII

(put-ons & cop-outs)

Anyone who raves about the Beatles being put-ons commits the ultimate cop-out. For to dismiss what one can neither understand nor appreciate is the epitome of lameness. We must look beyond their . . .

VIII

What makes the Beatles great is their affinity with the roots of Western folk music. For all their explorations into new genres of rock and pop, they maintain a down-home simplicity as their musical framework. As Stalin (or Lenin (Lennon?)) is said to have told the composers of his day: "Give us tunes ve can vistle." He would have loved the Beatles.

IX

While we all waited for the coming of *Abbey Road* we created our own fantasies of what it would be like. It has turned out to be just what we expected—but with more surprises than we could ever imagine. Who among us was prepared for . . .

X

(before the fact-positive)

"Mmm, I will play it safe and say that it's goddam great. I will lay on lavish praise. I will be nebulous (an indication of my own inner confusion and uncertainty) but I will above all be positive. I will be hailed as a seer for recognizing true art and beauty. And after all, isn't that what the Beatles produce by definition."

XI

(before the fact-negative)

"Mmm, sooner or later the Beatles are bound to fall—if not into obscurity at least into disfavor. So for me it may as well be now. I will jump on them, slash, pan, badmouth and denounce. I hope for history to prove me right when the Beatles are revealed as cheap tricksters. Besides, I am sure to gain notoriety for myself for putting them down. (Isn't that how Mr. Goldstein achieved his infamous posture—with his anti-*Pepper* thing?)"

XII

So Fuck you, Nik Cohn.

The Theory of Beatle Recognition

At last a conclusive and proven formula for recognizing which Beatle sings (and therefore wrote) a given song: First, listen carefully for who it sounds like. Mmm, it's not Paul. But then, it doesn't sound like John either. It's obviously not Ringo and it couldn't be George.

Therefore it must be Paul.

Sandy Perlman

SAUCER LANDS IN VIRGINIA

Obviously Jimi Hendrix has to be one of the most significant burlesque acts in years. Yet what exactly are we supposed to make of his masturbatory behavior at Monterey? Behavior highlighted when he (regarded by R. Meltzer as clearly the best-dressed man in the place) and Noel Redding both played guitar with their teeth, thus probably performing rock's first public double-tonguing. And (to continue in this vein) could it have been a less-than-sinister coincidence that the initials of the Army nerve gas BZ—whence STP was allegedly (but falsely) derived—are exactly the same as the last two initials of WBZ, a Boston rock station? Or what about the fact that the Doors hadn't even read *The Doors of Perception?* And these are certainly not the least problematical or coincidental things to be thought of.

Once Thomas Pynchon said—in the Fausto's Confessions section of *V.*—that this was "life's single lesson: that there is more accident to it than a man can ever admit to in a lifetime and stay sane." And later something very odd would even prove him right. Whoever does *Time* Magazine's radio ads lifted a tiny section of their favorable review of *V.* and, making as if they hadn't cared for the book, used it to prove that *Time* would even tell you about bad and difficult modern fiction. But maybe that's only because the ad guys don't read the magazine. Only because the ad guys had accidentally stumbled on the right wrong thing to say about the right book. A coincidence, that's all.

On the inside cover of the Mothers' *Absolutely Free* it says, "Kill Ugly Radio." And if you listen to—I guess—Pretty Radio, you can sometimes hear Frank Zappa carrying on about the Top 40. But that isn't being grateful. R. Meltzer's statement that "[At the same time rock has transcended any difficulties encountered in the sociology of knowledge.] Because it is so wantonly eclectic, any moment's linear connections can bear contradictory relationships to those of the next without difficulty"—which became the by-now-overly-familiar commonplace about rock contextualizing everything—must have issued from the education he received at the radio. And even today you can hear everything from Frank Sinatra to Nancy Sinatra on the radio. And that is a big spread. When all sorts of things are played, then even more things become plausible as rock, and the field of contextualization expands. Which is one reason why even the Mothers are plausible and money-makers. The mere universal overexposure which constitutes the Top 40 is a catalyst for the contextualization of anything at all. This means that untold millions will listen to one or another form of anything. The Top 40 made Zappa possible, and not only for his material. That's how the dialectic works today.

Universal conceptualization is complemented by a sort of universalized relationship. This Top 40 does strange things to you. A few years ago—to pick an overly blatant example—you could have heard "The Lion Sleeps Tonight," a version of the South African pop song "Wimoweh" about a native hero who would awaken to liberate his people. It was sung by the Tokens, four nice boys from Lincoln High in Brooklyn (Sandy Koufax's school), and since it was a hit it was often followed by the latest bad news from South Africa. Today some are impressed by "Light My Fire" following the adventures of H. Rap Brown (who was recently photographed with Nina Simone so this isn't just whimsy). And with things like that going on it becomes easy to accept the notion that perhaps things are related to one another. But not logically. Rather the relationship appears "strictly coincidental." The Top 40 is by nature a plethora and when the plethora principle strikes again it proves only that overexposure makes things plausible. Therefore, although there is no apparent logical connection, the coincidental relationship of rock to everything else becomes all too clear. As does the significance of BZ and WBZ. Coincidence seems at the heart of a great world system, as overexposure ("News every half hour, bulletins when they are received!") makes possible such eclectic variants as the early Tokens, the late Beatles, the Big Bopper, Paul Simon, Bobby Purify and Joan Baez.

And yet, amid all that the Top 40 has done, certain themes begin to stand out. These themes reveal a certain longing. And after we realize just how plausible the omnipresence of what appear to be merely coincidental (It's just an accident!) relationships can make everything, we can then realize that certain themes appearing in certain songs by certain groups are related (not merely coincidental) even to current events, even to H. Rap Brown, even to—strange to say—science fiction.

Consider these: The Byrds, The Velvet Underground, The Mothers of Invention and Love. Not a random choice among them. Because they are all groups with their own great world systems. I mean each group has its own comprehensive way of doing things, of looking at and organizing them. Often all we can recognize are the final results—this or that song—and in so doing we forget that this or that implicates some comprehensive view behind it. Not that everybody has a great world system. Not everybody is a philosopher. But for those who do, it can determine such diverse matters as album covers, wardrobe, haircuts, half-time banter, appearance of the instruments, group athletics, etc.

The Byrds have a great world system which works through a constant form making all sorts of potentially eclectic material—Dylan, Joan Baez folk, Gene Clark's stuff, science fiction and so forth—come out very mysterious and awe-inspiring. The Byrds form enchants its material. Systematically.

Then there is The Velvet Underground, named after a book on perversions in the suburbs. Their album cover doesn't make them look very healthy at all. Why it even features a pink peelable banana ("painting by Andy Warhol"). And all that wasn't just teasing either. With The Velvet Underground the pussyfooting has stopped. They do songs like "Venus in Furs" (now a movie), "Heroin," "The Black Angel's Death Song." That shows us what their world view is like. When the Stones did their first nihilist album (*December's Children*) you could have missed it without the album cover's help. You might have thought it merely beautiful. But the world system of the Velvets—rooted in sex, violence, disorder, perversion and stuff like that—is far too obvious. These guys are so serious that they have a coherent position.

The Mothers of Invention are—like Jimi Hendrix—a highly significant burlesque act. The Mothers will always give you a good clean tit show (one critic regards the prunes of "Call Any Vegetable" as "complex sexual symbols"), complete with social criticism. They are funny. And they are even supposed to be so. You are supposed to laugh. There isn't supposed to be any ambiguity about it. The Mothers' destructive humor—there are those who would call it nihilist—is much too blatant to avoid. This world system humorously arranges things through exaggeration and juxtaposition. Just another perfect way of looking and displaying.

As for Love, on the *Da Capo* album they employ exaggeration and juxtaposition to systematically render everything just silly. The principal devices are Arthur Lee's voice ("Revelation," "7 and 7 Is," "Stephanie Knows Who," "She Comes in Colors") and certain referential elements (merry-go-round music in "Que Vida!," bits of the Stones' "Going Home" in "Revelation"). Often they will put things together that just don't fit. But no one laughs. Either because there's no joke or the joke is much too exhaustive. For example, somebody has noticed that on "Revelation" we have Arthur Lee (a spade) imitating Mick Jagger imitating Ray Charles and some other spades. Now be that as it may, it all goes to prove that you can even make a system out of things that don't fit together. And, anyway, Arthur Lee was imitating Mick Jagger's "Going Home" and maybe he was just incongruously closing the circle. A revelation, see. You find whatever significance in things that you can make up about them.

But all of these are really instances of the taste for order. Even the nihilistic stuff. That certain longing they reveal is a longing for order. Actually it gets harder and harder to imagine something nihilistic. I mean, what would it be like? If you do songs about perversion, drugs and popular ideas about disorder, then you are summoning up an alternative, that which you happen to find tasty. And tastes change. And then what you have found tasty may even become generally palatable. And then what? Rock's great world systems are sets of alternative arrangements—or at least visions—of the world. Idealized arrangements, according to the tastes of whoever made them. They are sort of perfect—because they don't matter. Irrelevancy can always set you free and guarantee your privacy. Despite the fact that rock is big business, why should anybody care about what goes on? Unless you were really smart you would have to toil at making it as important as something else: politics, say. That people do care is, then, very nice. Simple altruism probably. But most who care are still on the outside. And those on the inside, the ones who make the rock, don't care enough. That audience of theirs is so young, so impressionable, and yet they'll say anything at all. Simple irresponsibility probably. Or maybe they're self-consciously irrelevant.

Which finally brings us back to both H. Rap Brown and science fiction. When H. Rap Brown, following Stokely Carmichael (who went to the *Bronx High School of Science!*), cried Honky too much for his own good, he obviously showed himself to be only an artist and not yet a politician. Politicians being artists (of a sort) who have (somehow) gone all too relevant. This irrelevancy made him famous. And it came from his irresponsible audiences. Like artists for many thousands of years, he had summoned an alternative world. He was on to another great world system. Which is to say that, like those old-time artists (even the Greeks did it), he was doing science fiction.

To do science fiction is not necessarily to be mysterious or obviously strange or scary or even to invoke lots of gadgets. Rather the important thing is to arrange things according to what is merely tasty. That is, to let the imagination be irresponsible.

With H. Rap Brown things become scary because there was an unusual coincidence of the irrelevant production of an irresponsible imagination and people who even wanted to do all those things H. Rap Brown talked about. Things which remained "socially" irrelevant, out of place.

To be tasty is very important. And the longing for science fiction is all over the place—but it's not universal. There are some people who don't care to summon all those alternatives. You can pass from that longing to something else. Or perhaps never even experience it. The Byrds have made four beautiful albums about the way the earth turns, all dominated by a very enchanting form. And the Rolling Stones have passed from the ideal attitude of being really mean and nasty, found on their first two albums, to that authentic—and sadly weary—nihilism of *December's Children* (where they hardly bothered to pose) to *Between the Buttons* where they view everything with equal disinterest, where they do pose, where (i.e., the album cover) they look bored and knocked out, where their pose is for merely technical reasons. And where they manage to break through to a contradictory and aggressive nihilism. A nihilism preserved by the lack of a point of view and such dualisms as "Ruby Tuesday" and "Let's Spend the Night Together." Which really must have given Ed Sullivan the heebie-jeebies. Because how can you throw some guys off who are sincere enough to do "Ruby Tuesday"?

And then the Beatles. The great blues guitarist Don Nielson once said that in comparison to the Stones, they turned out music that was "only pretty." And they have been unusually bland. Except for a few pieces (for example, George and his ragas) they have steered clear of other worlds. Of course they do serious stuff ("Eleanor Rigby" has been recognized as serious by such as Richie Havens, Joan Baez, Johnny Mathis and the Vanilla Fudge), but all those themes—love, necrophilia ("Baby's in Black"), *The Book of the Dead*—have long been rendered far too ordinary by overuse (the plethora again) on the part of everyone in the world. At last *Sgt. Pepper's* came along. Quite spectacular in every possible way, coming as it does in an expensive fold-out jacket, it has any sort of song at all, it could even be taken as a contradictory whole if you cared to do so and it is, I think, a really odd case: one of the most spectacular and big budget (it cost more than *Between the Buttons*) idealizations of the bland ever made. Certainly the attitude was cynical—maybe even bored—but the bland is so undemanding that here we have an idealization which does not call forth another world. The Beatles have matched the Stones. Both have made it to cynical detachment. (Oh boy.) So *Sgt. Pepper's* is here. It's much too contradictory to be easily criticized, it can only be expected to be saying something, but not nearly so pretty as they've done it in the past and it's not an alternative to anything. In other words, "our sweet boys" have become nihilists. And bypassed science fiction.

ENGLISH HEAVIES

THE MOTHER COUNTRY'S 25 BEST

It all started when radio station guys were willing to go overboard over the whole early English thing. There were nine Beatle songs on the top ten (plus "Hello Dolly"), they played Searchers flip sides and Herman album cuts: fans were ready for the biggest big plethora so far, they were hungry for totality, albums were finally nearly the whole show, bigger than singles, bigger than radio, almost as big as life because they were almost as big. Before England there were Ventures albums and jazz albums and show albums and Atlantic albums (which had good covers) and oldies anthologies. With England, rock becomes a list of long novels.

1. The Zombies. Well before one fact and in the middle of another the Zombies were Doors keyboard and mere mystery and Beach Boys vocals and lyrical mereness, and now everybody knows that the Doors are just the Beach Boys anyway. Therefore, something-or-other. Where'd the Zombies get it all from? Must be from Hank Marvin & the Shadows or the Swallows or some other pack of English prehistorics, since there's no clue in all of Beatle-era recorddom. Therefore, seemingly original (if that matters).

2. Odessey and Oracle (Zombies). "Care of Cell 44" had Mc-Cartney bass plus Ringo drums plus enough other giveaways to indicate that the boys had finally picked up enough influences-in-the-air to become the link between the Beatles and the Doors that no archeologist will ever give a dang about unless he does. This album was a breath of fresh air when it appeared and it still is, as you can use the cover as a fan.

3. *The Early Zombies.*   Another one and it contains their never-played-in-New York (only in Connecticut) awe-packed single "Whenever You're Ready" and the mellow (not the original) version of "She's Not There" with a longer break in the middle and "Leave Me Be" (flip side of "Tell Her No"), the heart of jelly equivalent of "Heart of Stone."

4. *Piper at the Gates of Dawn*   (Pink Floyd). Nothing if not the very big-big-biggest psychedelic overstatement of them all at exactly the moment when the biggest overstatement was possible and expected and ignored. So heavily English that even the Dave Clark Five is in the stew.

5. *Blowin' My Mind*   (Van Morrison). The biggest original move made by England was geographical (it was not the U.S.A., it was somewhere else, a place to come from and seem strange in coming from). Van Morrison wasn't even from England (he's a Belfast guy), and with this album he wasn't even in Them, another possible claim to fame. Okay, so he's a homeless weirdo who can sing about the horror of the home in "T.B. Sheets" ("The cool room Lord is a fool's room"). And he's a vocal weirdo who can (in any given stretch of lyrics) transcend even the gratuitous mere weirdness of Jagger (uh-huh).

6. *The Fortunes.*   "You've Got Your Troubles, I've Got Mine" preceded the Association by who knows how many years. But preceding always came easy to English rock. And English muzak and easy-listening too. Even if you throw history into the sea, the Fortunes are no turkeys. They're one of the best one-and-a-half hit limey groups of all.

7. *The Ivy League.*   A Beatle imitator's Beatle imitator, the Ivy League struck during the summer of *Help!* with "Tossing and Turning," not to be confused with Bobby Lewis's winner of the same name and never confused with it except in retrospect.

"What you gonna do tonight, nobody to hold you tight, are you lonely?" was even typographically altered to "nobody to hold you thigh" by *Hit Parader* as a sign of how over-under-overzealous the times were.

8. *Meet the Searchers.* You met them with "Needles and Pins" but then you really got to know them with "Ain't That Just Like Me," the transition from nursery rhyme to sexual oblivion within one short cut. That was the summation of the opposite direction of the evolution of many later guys' content. As well as the harbinger of longer cuts ('cause they were so much fun to begin with).

9. *Tyrannosaurus Rex.* With Donovan, the Englishman's enunciation of the English language returned to Hermione Gingold and the Galloping Gourmet. Tyrannosaurus Rex, operating with an even more ostentatious grocery list of conventional mere metaphors than that of Donovan, turns the trick vocally by doing the words as if they were Polish or Hiberno-Northumbrian or something like that or something backwards or something. The road to "Surfer Bird" from within.

10. *Moody Blues #1.* Why not? It's the only Moody Blues album with "Go Now" on it, and after all "Go Now" was the hit thought of as no more than mere hit until the word got out that it was English and, hence, the starting point of an album (yup) by a suddenly relevant group with a suddenly not-so-dumb name, derived from (where else but) the great American blues catacomb. Unlike the Zombies, who were small enough to merit an archeological assortment album of minor singles, the Moody Blues reemerged as big time so they did more albums of original stuff, leaving only singles to tell the tale. And most of the singles aren't on this album, a masterpiece of inclusion/exclusion.

11. *Wild Thing* (Troggs). The Righteous Brothers were an early attempt, but they were too close to it. Only the twice-removed-at-least English could pull off overstatement and authenticity transcendence of this calibre.

12. *Animal Tracks.* Whether Eric Burdon's self-pollution inauthenticity cycle was conscious or not at the very beginning, "The

Story of Bo Diddley" sort of lends credence to the theory that at least he didn't care what they thought of him doing their stuff. So why'd he waste his time caring about it himself? Who cares, Eric is nobody's fool.

13. *Bread and Butter* (New Beats). When they did the hit single by the very same name they were heralded as English (good enough for you, good enough for me). When the single led to an album, the urge for liner note accuracy prevailed (too bad): they were not English at all, they were from Nashville (if you can believe that). So What?

14. *Friday on My Mind* (Easy-beats). So what if they're Australian? It all sounds the same, right? Precursor to the Bee Gees' really big splash similarity-to-any-specific-element-in-the-British-Empire (and the Beatles in particular). And this very album contains an even better version of "River Deep, Mountain High" than Eric Burdon's!

15. *My Generation* (Who). Good production jobs were the ruination of the Who, who sound best with the absence of clarity and distinctness. You've gotta go all the way back to the beginning to get it, back when "The Kids Are Alright" was a dead ringer for a Beatles plagiarism move.

16. *Something Else by the Kinks.* Proclaimed a mere bubble gum creep (whatever that could mean) by the English fans these days, Ray Davies here demonstrates all that could conceivably mean inside a context where it can be fully appreciated. If you're an American or something like that, you're a lucky resident of the major international receptacle.

17. *12 by 5* (Rolling Stones). Their first album was a dilly. Their second broke even more ground for them, laying to rest (with "Under the Boardwalk" and "Grown Up All Wrong") any misapprehensions fostered by the first one about how serious they happened to be.

18. *Tobacco Road* (Nashville Teens). More totally acceptable unabashed Americana, another name for easily disguised easy plagiarism at a distance, which is really what made it so palatable.

19. *Little Bird* (Marianne Faithfull). The Isle of Wight Festival revealed exactly how much all those dumb Englishmen were hot for folk swill. Tom Paxton was the big hit. Well they were always looking jealously for a Joan Baez of their very own, and Marianne should have been more than enough, but that was her problem: she looked much too good and she wasn't nearly pretentious enough with her voice, so she never became the official folk pig that Mary Hopkin ended up as. Shucks.

20. *Eire Apparent.* Well, um, uh, Jimi Hendrix produced it and guess what: there isn't a trace of a melody anywhere on the album (that's a lie but wouldn't it be great if it were true?): too much!

21. *Led Zeppelin.* Something the Yardbirds could never do was have four people produce arbitrary palatable topical noise on the spot with other than nostalgic import. Huh? And Cream was musical excess and who ever wanted music? And Jeff Beck is just a crooner who can't sing, and you know. And the Yardbirds, when they were down to four guys, were just a limp rehash of what used to be with five. Which leaves only Led Zeppelin. Good news.

22. *Best of the Beatles.* Everybody owns and knows all about all mere Beatle albums, so they need no further mention. But *Best of the Beatles,* taken off the market during Xmas rush as a merely sneaky sales gimmick, is one you've never heard, no doubt. See if you can find a copy. Excellent tubs work (no joke).

23. *The Move.* Copy the American stuff in the beginning, forget about it for a while, then copy it again after it's become irrelevant. That's the John Lennon dull peace-creep move. But sometimes going back to the American content for the nth time actually works. The Move, who weren't around at the dawn of Anglo-American rock history anyway, pick their shots pretty well for a nineteenth-generation quasi-copy band: "Hey Grandma," Byrds stuff, Coasters stuff, even Van Dyke Parks stuff. Great monism from across the sea. And what's best, it's never been released on this continent.

24. *Greatest Hits, Vol. 2* (Herman's Hermits). With all this interest in the Hollies nowadays (Graham Nash's fault), it might as well be brought out in the open what the Hollies had going for them: five or six pretty little nuggets over the years. Herman's songs were prettier, more nugget-like, and there were at least ten or fifteen of them that amounted to more than a hill of beans. And once (on a Leonard Bernstein reevaluate rock and roll TV special) Herman and Graham himself suggested that Donovan could save the world. So distinctions need not apply, but if you want 'em take Herman of course.

25. *Little Children* (Billy J. Kramer & the Dakotas). An early holdout from obscurity, Billy J. was on the Ed Sullivan Show long before the Rolling Stones. Who can ever forget the way he flailed around? And he left a recorded legacy behind him. Not that bad either.

Gary Allen

THAT MUSIC:
There's More to It Than Meets the Ear

All across America parents are throwing up their hands in exasperation and despair—the universal complaint being that they are unable to communicate with their teenage sons and daughters. One reason they are finding it so difficult to get through to the "turned-on" generation is that today's young people so often have a blaring transistor radio plugged into one of their ears. Such electronic paraphernalia seems, alas, to have become a part of the teenage anatomy. No wonder our teeny-boppers appear so vacuous—they are in shell-shock from having turned in the local rock-music stations blasting out the latest revolutionary horrors on the "Top Forty."

While the youngsters groove on the cool sounds, parents avoid such rock music—considering it a cacophony of piercing sounds, and screeching, garbled voices, guaranteed to send any-one over thirty scrambling for the Excedrin. Besides, the lyrics often feature words and references no more meaningful to the Geritol set than a lecture on Homer in Swahili. Should they "tune in" and listen, however, parents might learn why the generation gap is fast becoming an unbridgeable canyon.

Rock music, universally in high regard among a whole gen-eration of adolescents, has somehow evolved as one of the major influences on our children—and, through them, on our nation's future. Rock singers are in constant communication with our teenagers—promoting attitudes and ideas which, if they were aware of the message, would blow the minds of most parents. The adulation by young people of rock bands and singers has reached fanaticism, and is fed by a bevy of magazines aimed at teenagers which cover the lives, promote the attitudes, and sell the radical political views of the new "gods" in hoary detail.

Mere goldfish swallowing?

Hardly.

Turn on your radio, tune in a rock station, and listen to The Beatles' new hit about how great it is to be out of America and "Back In The U.S.S.R." Pretty crimson propaganda to be coming from Capitol Records, isn't it? Still, if that little ditty leaves you "uptight," and you vent your displeasure about it to your local mod squad, a dime will get you a dollar that the song will be defended and your complaints made the object of ridicule. That's the degeneration gap, Baby, and it's no accident. Paul Cantor, of the wildly popular acid-rock group called The Jefferson Airplane,* admitted recently on the Les Crane television show that the new rock music is *intended* to broaden the generation gap, alienate parents from their children, and prepare young people for revolution. Clarifying this, the "underground" *San Francisco Express Times* carried in its issue for November 13, 1968, a "White Panther Manifesto" which declared:

> *With our music and our economic genius we plunder the un-suspecting straight world for money and the means to carry out our program and revolutionize its children at the same time. And with our entrance in the straight media we have demonstrated to the hunkeys that anything they do to f*** with us we will expose to their children. You don't need to get rid of all the hunkeys, you just rob them of their replacements and let the breed atrophy and die out, with its heirs cheering triumphantly all around it.†*

* The Jefferson Airplane takes you on a "trip," *i.e.,* it simulates a drug experience.
† Editor of the *Express Times* is Marvin Garson, one of the originals from the Free Speech Movement at Berkeley. Marvin is married to Barbara Garson, author of a scabrous play called *MacBird!*—the story of a small town boy who made good by murdering his way to the Presidency.

Of course, "Liberals" become giddy sniffing the fumes of such glue. *McCalls* magazine, for example, enthused in its issue of November, 1967:

> *Pop is music to be alive by, right now. It's music to make the mind and/or the body dance. It's the cutting edge of today's youth culture, the beat of the Sixties, the new language of the contemporary state of mind. It contains freedom, participation, energy, love, sexuality, honesty and rebellion. It scorns convention, pretense, sentimentality and false patriotism.* *

The *Saturday Review* (of Leftwing Literature) registered even more moisture over the new revolutionary music in its issue of August 26, 1967:

> *Music and songs are the new youth's primary tools and means of expression. . . . The drive is away from a general sense of hypocrisy in diverse areas of life—a separation from older values. Existing circumstances are source material for comment. The threat of the Bomb and fighting unnecessary wars to stalemate, keeping us constantly on the precipice of disaster, fan the flames.*

Of course, the announcements of the Far Left that music is being used as a powerful political weapon hardly amount to the revelation of a new concept. The culturally sagacious have for centuries recognized that as music can be used to produce a powerful effect on the emotions, it can be a powerful propaganda agent.

Music is both an art and a science. Eugene Helms noted in the *Scientific American* of December 1967:

> *What is seldom appreciated, even in the musical world, is that the roots of the relation between music and mathematics stem*

---

* *McCalls* is owned by Hunt Foods (no connection with H. L. Hunt) which recently bought a vast store of vegetable oil from the Soviet Union. The magazine came out editorially, in its issue of July 1968, for World Government. President of Hunt Foods is Leftist Norton Simon, a member of the Board of Regents of the University of California who has consistently supported appeasement of revolution on California's campuses.

deep into antiquity. The roots of these relationships were under-stood by the Chaldeans, the Egyptians, the Babylonians and the Chinese. The rules of harmonic proportions were worked out by Pythagoras.

And it was Pythagoras who first noted that music was an exact science which could be used to produce profound and disturbing atonal effects. Plato went farther in *The Republic* and warned that "the introduction of a new kind of music must be shunned as imperiling the whole State; since styles of music are never disturbed without affecting the most important political institutions." Emil Neuman, in his *History of Music,* summarizes Plato's ideas concerning music this way: "He insisted it was the paramount duty of the Legislature to suppress all music of an effeminate and lascivious character, and to encourage only that which was pure and dignified. . . ." Many philosophers have shared this opinion. Henry David Thoreau prophesied in *Walden,* more than a hundred years before The Beatles made their first record: "Even music may be intoxicating. Such apparently slight causes destroyed Greece and Rome, and will destroy England and America."

When words are combined with music the emotional and political effect may be heightened. As Andrew Fletcher observed:

> *I knew a very wise man who believed that if a man were per-mitted to make all the ballads, he need not care who should make the laws of a nation. And we find that most of the ancient legislators thought they could not well reform the manners of any city with-out the help of a lyric and sometimes of a dramatic poet.*

One would have to be naïve in the extreme to think that the Communists, master propagandists that they are, could ignore a field with so much influence as music. They haven't. Lenin, speaking to the Third All-Russian Congress of the Young Communist League on October 2, 1920, informed the assembled young Comrades that they must "rework culture"—that only by so doing could they hope to build "a proletarian [Communist] culture." A part of that "reworking" was the subversion of music.

By 1929 the Russian Association of Proletarian Musicians had been formed. Its purpose, according to Nicholas Slonimsky in *Music Since 1900,* was the "extension of the proletarian Communist influence to the musical masses, reeducation and reorganization of these masses in order to direct their work and creative talents toward . . . ultimate victory of the proletariat as builder of Communist society."

Sidney Finkelstein, described by the House Committee on Un-American Activities as "the cultural spokesman for the Communist Conspiracy" in the United States, made Lenin's "rework culture" speech the theme of his book, *How Music Expresses Ideas.* Finkelstein called for breaking down the barrier between classical music and "popular" music. Realizing that the proper sort of music could be used to sell a revolutionary message in the same manner that a singing commercial sells soap, Finkelstein called for the replacement of classic symphonic music by revolutionary music with a jungle beat.

The Communists have made extensive use of such music in America, where they were early successful in the field of folk music. Such talented Communists as Pete Seeger, Leadbelly, Malvina Reynolds, and Woody Guthrie, popularized songs of class warfare and subversion for millions. Now, the New Left crowd has taken folk music, combined it with rock and roll, and turned it into folk-rock—with revolutionaries like Phil Ochs and Bobby Dylan projecting the philosophy and songs of Communist Woody Guthrie into the protest music of the Sixties.

Writing in the Communist *Mainstream,* Comrade Ochs has noted: "I have run across some people who seem to consider Guthrie solely a writer of great camp songs. They cannot fathom or don't want to fathom the political significance of a great part of his work." We should certainly not have too difficult a time "fathoming" the significance of *Ochs's* work. One of his latest albums features poetry by Mao Tse-tung on the back cover.

Phil Ochs's newest hit is called "Rhythms of Revolution" (*Only the dead are forgiven as they crumbled inside the rhythms of revolution*). He is, however, more famous for "I Ain't Marchin'

Anymore" (*Call it "Peace" or call it "Treason," Call it "Love" or call it "Reason," But I ain't marchin' anymore*), and the "Draft Dodger Rag" (*If you ever get a war without blood and gore, Well, I'll be the first to go*).

Antiwar songs, aimed at helping to defeat our men fighting and dying in Vietnam, are Comrade Ochs's bag. Declaring "The Vietcong are right . . . We should support Ho chi Minh," he has created such popular horrors as: "White Boots Marchin' In A Yellow Land" (*We're fighting in a war we lost before the war began. We're the white boots marchin' in a yellow land*); and, "Cops [Soldiers] Of The World" (*We've rammed-in your harbor and tied to your port, and our pistols are hungry and our tempers are short. So bring your daughters around to the fort, 'Cause we're the cops of the world*); and, "The War Is Over" (*Serve your country in her suicide; Find a flag so you can wave good-bye. But, just before the end, even treason might be worth a try . . .*). As Phil's songs all follow the same theme on the Vietnam War, they are obviously very big with that great poet, Chairman Mao. Unfortunately, they are now also very big with America's teenagers.

While Phil Ochs specializes in the mad-dog approach, Bob Dylan is smoother and even more influential. *Look* magazine has said of the latter that "Dylan is unchallenged as the teen and college crowd's Absolute Hipster, their own 'hung up' idol, the singing analyst of a jingle-jangle reality that makes more sense to them than any square, whitewashed American dream."* *Look* also tells us that Dylan's heroes are "Woody Guthrie, Leadbelly, and Pete Seeger." The *Look* editors, of course, forgot to mention that Dylan's trinity of favorites are all Communists.

The Establishment's other mass slicks have gotten into the act of promoting Dylan. *Life* calls him "a major poet of his generation," and the *Saturday Evening Post* says that he is "probably the most influential voice in contemporary music." Even two

---

* This about a creature who told another national magazine: "I want my woman dirty, looking as though I'd just found her in some alley. Dirt is very attractive. It triggers animal emotion. I want dirty long hair hanging all over the place." Bobby's thousands of fans among adolescent females no doubt took notice.

years ago it was estimated that over ten million Dylan records had been sold.

What were the songs which made this crimson troll the "spokesman for his generation"? One of his first hits was "Masters Of War," an attack on general officers and those who manufacture our nation's defense equipment. Even more potent was "Blowin' In The Wind" (*How many times must the cannon balls fly, Before they're forever banned . . . ? How many years can some people exist, Before they're allowed to be free? Yes, 'n how many times can a man turn his head, Pretending he just doesn't see? The answer my friend is blowin' in the wind. The answer is blowin' in the wind*). The latter song became an unofficial anthem of the Communists' "Peace" Movement, and the answer that was blowin' in the wind was Revolution and support of the Vietcong. Fifty-eight different versions of this tune have now been recorded.

Since the revolutionary Bob Dylan is the "certified spokesman" for his generation, it is not surprising that his "The Times They Are A-Changin'" has become a sort of theme song on the road to the generation gap.

> *And the first one now*
> *Will later be last,*
> *For the times they are a-changin'.*

No wonder the Communists' *People's World* and *The Worker* and *The Guardian* have called Dylan "America's greatest poet," and the Communist Party has given him a "Tom Paine" Award, and published one of his "poems" in a revolutionary anthology. He has, after all, become the most successful proponent of the new class war: Youth versus Age. Of course, Dylan has become a millionaire while singing about the poor overthrowing the rich ("the first one now will later be last").

Bob began at the top, with Columbia records, where the godfather of his career was one John Hammond, an extreme Leftist who just happens to have regularly stumbled into a number of officially cited Communist Fronts. Yes, Dylan got off to a flying start, thanks to Hammond and an expensive Establish-

ment promotion job. Promoter Hammond, who has been affiliated with the Communists' notorious Highlander Center, also
served as the producer of Communist Pete Seeger's albums.

Isn't it a small world!

Since it is now against the law of the land to discriminate
because of sex, I am required to mention at least one of the
female revolutionary singers—someone like Judy Collins. Miss
Collins was named as a member of the Communist DuBois Clubs
at a special workshop on the arts during the D.B.C.'s summer
1966 convention. An activist in "Civil Rights" and "Peace"
demonstrations, Judy sings one of the most violent of the hard-
core songs, called "Marat/Sade"—a popular contemporary shriek
about the glories of the French Revolution. The content of the
lyrics makes it obvious that it is a call for a repetition within our
own country of that bloody Revolution. Part of this one goes as
follows:

> *String up every aristocrat,*
> *Jail all the priests and let them live on their fat . . .*
> *Down with the ruling class,*
> *Throw all the generals out on their a**;*
> *Why do they have the power?*
>
> *Why do they have the friends at the top?*
> *We've got nothing, always had nothing,*
> *Living in holes, dying in holes;*
> *Holes in our bellies and holes in our clothes.*
>
> *Marat, we are poor and the poor stay poor;*
> *Marat, don't make us wait anymore.*
> *We want our rights and we want them now,*
> *And we don't care how,*
> *We want our revolution now.*

As the pop cycle has evolved from folk-rock to the hippie-
oriented *acid-rock,* the theme of revolution has evolved with it
and is now accompanied by the piercing twang of amplified electric guitars. To start the new year right "The Lovin' Spoonful,"* a

* A spoon is used to cook heroin or to mix amphetamines with water
before "shooting" them into the vein.

group heard thousands of times a day on rock radio across the nation, has released an album entitled *Revolution '69*. The lyrics to the title song are reprinted on the back of the album lest anyone miss them in the din of the screaming electrified instruments. Some go as follows:

> *Let's hang together then good friends,*
> *or you know we'll hang alone;*
> *And the hawks that fly will tear your eyes*
> *and rip the skin clean off your bones.*
> *I'm afraid to die, but I'm a man inside,*
> *and I need the Revolution.*

While revolution* is a favorite theme of the rock-music groups, it is by no means the only one. The theme most often heard, outside the wide range of songs which deal with boy-girl love, is that of *drugs*. Drug lyrics are a mystery to most adults because of the Aesopian language used by the singers. Teenagers have always seemed to have a code language all their own, and no adult can hope to understand the lyrics on the "Top Forty" unless he is familiar with that jargon. The current adolescent vernacular, however, is simply incredible. Only if you have served time in a state penitentiary, or been a prostitute or a junky, would you fail to need an interpreter. For, alas, it is just such an underworld which is the source of most of the current hippie language.†

Youngsters pick up the meaning of the argot through disc jockeys, conversation with their peers, and the teenage and

---

* Other contemporary popular songs having to do with revolution include: "My Back Pages," The Byrds; "Chimes of Freedom" and "My Generation," The Who; "The Cities Are Burning," Frederick Douglass Kirkpatrick; "War Blues," Ronnie Petersen; "Burn, Baby, Burn," Bill Frederick; "Hell No I Ain't Gonna Go!," Matthew Jones and Elaine Laron; "My Country, 'Tis of Thy People You're Dying," Buffie Saint-Marie; "The Time Will Come," Elaine White; "Sounds of War," Ricardo Gautreau; "I've Got to Have Peace on My Mind," The Outlaw Blues Band; "There's a War On," The Rainbow Press; "Street Fighting Man," The Rolling Stones; and, "Ballad of Ho chi Minh," Ewan MacCall.

† Those interested in an instant Berlitz-style course in the hippy idiom may wish to study the *Hippy Glossary* prepared by Ken Granger. It is available for fifteen cents from T.A.C.T., P.O. Box 8352, San Marino, California 91108.

"underground" newspapers and magazines. The hippie vocabulary allows verbal communication in code and separates those who are hip from the squares. Our teenagers, not wanting to feel isolated from their fellows, pick up and use the hip vocabulary. The result is more generation gaposis between parents and their children: Youth versus Age.

As New York music critic Richard Goldstein has observed: "Rock lyricists today try to invest their slang with a depth of ambiguity that allows the words to be heard equally well on all levels right down to the [revolutionary] underground. No one doubts that the purpose of so-called psychedelic rock is to reconstruct an actual drug experience." That is why it is often called "acid-rock." *Acid* is slang for LSD. By making the lyrics deliberately ambiguous and couching references to drugs in code and double-entendres, it is generally possible for the musicians and the radio stations to avoid complaints from irate parents. The evil, they piously maintain, is in the ear of the listener.

When Gordon McLendon, owner of thirteen radio stations, tried a while back to eliminate the playing of the drug-cult music on his network he was subjected to national ridicule (including a blast from *Newsweek*, which has often run articles downgrading the harmful effects of marijuana). McLendon nonetheless had the courage to object to the "songs that glorified dope addiction . . . ," and raised the question nationally. Bill Young, program director at Mr. McLendon's radio station KILT in Houston, remarked: "The hippies know what they are saying on these records, but old John Q. Public doesn't. We're tired of them putting it over on John Q."

The intent of the lyrics of acid-rock is carefully obscure— often bathed in the mysticism associated with Zen, Hinduism, and other Eastern religions which have been affected by the followers of the drug culture. Few of the young people understand all of the lyrics to the songs played on the rock stations, of course. Indeed, some of the lyrics are so obscure as to defy interpretation by anyone this side of the Himalayas.

One can conjecture that many of these songs are written under the influence of drugs, as has admittedly been done on a number of occasions by The Beatles.* The carefully coded promotion of narcotics in The Jefferson Airplane's "White Rabbit" is all too typical:

> *One pill makes you larger, and one pill*
> *makes you smaller,†*
> *And the ones that mother gives you*
> *don't do anything at all.*
> *Go ask Alice when she's ten feet tall,*
> *And if you go chasing rabbits, and you*
> *know you're going to fall,*
> *Tell'em a hooka-smoking caterpillar***
> *has given you the call. . . .*
> *Feed your head, feed your head.‡*

The Beatles are still the Number One pop group. According to their authorized biography, by Hunter Davies, they started using drugs at the beginning of their career together. They have during the past two years popularized many songs which have been interpreted by young people as dealing with drugs. For example, "Lucy In The Sky With Diamonds" is advertised on posters with the letters *L,S,D* underlined. While The Beatles have dismissed charges that the song deals with drugs, teenagers who buy the record know better—claiming that the lyrics don't make sense unless one interprets the imagery as a "trip" on LSD.+

---

* See Hunter Davies, *The Beatles*, Page 268.
† The pill that makes you larger is an amphetamine or "upper" (a stimulant), and the pill that makes you smaller is a barbiturate or "downer" (a depressant).
** Marijuana is sometimes smoked through a water pipe.
‡ Drug users refer to taking drugs as "feeding your head."
+ A "trip" to your local record shop will reveal that there are now literally hundreds of songs designed to be interpreted by those who speak the language as promoting the use of drugs. A sample includes: "Colored Rain" (Methedrine), The Wichita Falls; "Mary Jane" (marijuana), Willie and the Rubber Band; "Jumpin' Jack Flash" (when Methedrine, taken intravenously, hits the brain it is known as a "flash"); "Lady Jane" (marijuana), "You Turn Me On," "Eight Miles High," and "You've Got Me High"—all by The Rolling Stones; "Rainy Day Woman" (a marijuana cigarette), and "Mr. Tambourine Man" (drug peddler), Bob Dylan; "Mainline Prosperity Blues" ("mainlining" is

"Yellow Submarine" has been one of The Beatles' biggest hits and has been called by *National Review* "a beautiful children's song." Those who are a little more hip than the crew at Buckley Review know that in drug terminology a "yellow jacket" is a submarine-shaped barbiturate, seconal, or "downer" (a "downer" submerges you). Among other Beatle songs generally interpreted as referring to drugs are "Norwegian Wood" (British teenagers' term for marijuana), "Strawberry Fields Forever" (marijuana is often planted in strawberry fields, in order to avoid detection, because the plants are similar in appearance), and "Magical Mystery Tour" (*Roll up, roll up* [*your sleeve*] *for the mystery tour. . . . The Magical Mystery Tour is waiting to take you away*), and "A Day In The Life" (*I'd love to turn you on*).

The music reviewer for *Holiday* magazine in its issue for October of 1966 deals with whether all of these lyrics promoting use of narcotics have been sneaked on to the records because those in the business are naïve:

> *Is it possible that record producers have been fooled by the jargon of the songs—have put out such discs not knowing what they mean? It is unlikely because it is impossible to be in the music business long without seeing pot smoked. The terminology of narcotics is widely known and understood in the industry, both*

───────────────

shooting drugs directly into the vein), Richard Fariña; "Puff The Magic Dragon" (smoke marijuana) by Peter, Paul, and Mary; "You Turn Me On" by Ian Whitcomb; "Yellow Balloon" (drugs are often carried in a balloon so that they may be swallowed and later retrieved in the event of imminent arrest) by The Yellow Balloon; "Up, Up And Away" (which sold 875,000 copies, won a Grammie Award, and was adopted by Trans World Airlines as its theme song) by the Fifth Dimension; "Along Came Mary" (marijuana) by The Association; "Bend Me, Shape Me" by The American Breed; "Acapulco Gold" (a particularly fine grade of marijuana) by The Rainy Daze; "Get On Up" by The Esquires; "Full Measure" by the Lovin' Spoonful; "Express to Your Head," Soul Survivors; "I Had Too Much To Dream," The Electric Prunes; "Faster Than The Speed [Methedrine] Of Life," "Magic Carpet Ride" by Steppenwolf; "Journey To The Center Of The Mind," Amboy Dukes; "Connection" (drug peddler), "She's A Rainbow" (Rainbows are nembutals or seconals), "2000 Light Years From Here" by The Rolling Stones; "Merry-Go-Round," The Youngbloods; "Rose Colored Glasses," Lothar and The Hand People; and, "Buy For Me The Rain" (Methedrine) by The Nitty Gritty Dirt Band.

*by artists, recorders and producers. Some publishers shrug off the
drug songs by saying, "These songs are a reflection of our times,"
ignoring the fact that 12-year-olds are listening to them. In songs
meant for children of 12 or even younger they proclaim that it is
wise and hip and inside to dissolve your responsibilities and problems of a difficult world into the mists of marijuana, LSD or heroin.*

No, Virginia, it is not an accident that a generation of young
Americans is being pushed toward drugs.

A third major category of songs (beside drugs and revolution) has to do with glorifying sexual union between teenagers.
Just as the songs of revolution have served to mentally condition
many young people to accept the ravings of the New Left, and
the myriad drug songs are doubtless a factor in the skyrocketing
use of narcotics by teenagers, so the open exhortations to indulge
in illicit sex acts are also a factor in the demoralization of youth—
helping to produce unprecedented numbers of illegitimate children and an unparalleled rise in venereal disease among teenagers.

As with the drug songs, some of the sex songs are blatant, but
most are couched in ambiguous double-entendres. Music critic
Richard Goldstein puts it this way: "Rock and roll has always
been raunchy. That's what it's all about. It's got a special code
and a lot of kids understand it. It's made for that purpose."

Many would dismiss the importance of sneaking raw lyrics
into popular songs on the basis that it has been going on for
years. Admittedly it has, but fifteen years ago songs like "Work
With Me Annie" and "Light My Fire" were heard on "rhythm
and blues" stations by a comparatively small number of young
people, most of them over sixteen. Today, however, the audience
is at least fifty times as large, with children as young as eight
becoming regular listeners. Today some $60 million worth of
such recordings are sold yearly—with the biggest group of
purchasers being girls from nine to thirteen years of age.

With this enormous audience of highly impressionable young
people, it is not surprising that the Far Left has been so successful in selling the line of a number of contemporary songs directly

promoting alienation between young people and their parents. This theme, as I have noted, is often found woven through the lyrics of songs about drugs and revolution. Some come right out and urge teens to run away from home to join the New Left. The Beatles' hit "She's Leaving Home" (*She is having fun; Fun is the one thing that money can't buy; Something inside that was always denied for so many years. Bye-Bye! She's leaving home. Bye-Bye.*) may have been instrumental in causing many a young-ster to run away to the hells of Hippieland.

But, for sheer gall and a solid one-two punch, you can't beat Scott McKenzie's "What's The Difference," with "San Francisco" on the flip side. These tunes were at the top of the hit parade last year for nearly six months. One side tells the young person to run away, and the other side tells him where to go.

Other examples of generation-gap music are those songs which depict adults, particularly businessmen, as shallow hypo-crites. Probably the most vicious in this category is Ray Stevens' "Mr. Businessman," which contains the following lyrics:

> *Itemize the things you covet as you*
> *squander through your life,*
> *Bigger cars, bigger houses, term*
> *insurance for your wife.*
> *Tuesday evenings with your harlot, and on*
> *Wednesday it's your charlatan analyst,*
> *He's high up on your list. . . .*

While the lyrics of these songs speak for themselves, the music is at least as important as the words. Practically anyone can deduce the significance of the lyrics, while only those trained in music will understand the significance of the contemporary use of rhythms.

Cheetah, one of the burgeoning magazines aimed at teen-agers, quotes a New York musician as noting: "If the establish-ment knew what today's popular music really is saying, not what the words are saying, but what the music itself is saying, then they wouldn't just turn thumbs down on it. They'd ban it, they'd smash all the records, and they'd arrest anyone who tried to play it."

Frank Zappa, leader of a rock group called Mothers of Invention, adds: "The loud sounds and bright lights of today are tremendous indoctrination tools. Is it possible to modify the human chemical structure with the right combination of frequencies? . . . If the right kind of beat makes you tap your foot, what kind of beat makes you curl your fist and strike?" Zappa, whose group has recorded some lollapaloozas in the fields of sex, drugs, and revolution, knows what he is talking about. Despite the mangy beard, long hair, and hippie costume, Frank has a Master's Degree in music.

Possibly the country's Number One expert on musical subversion is Joseph Crow of Seattle, who lectures extensively on the subject. Dr. Crow, who now operates a custom jewelry business and is an Associate Professor of Sociology at Pacific Western College, was a professional trumpet player for fifteen years—during which he did a stint with the famous Stan Kenton Band. He also studied music composition at the University of Washington and the Westlake College of Modern Music in Hollywood. Professor Crow explained it to me this way:

> *The harmonic and rhythmic fabrics of rock music are critically important. Only someone trained in music can fully comprehend the import of this music, but it is not necessary to understand the intricacies of music to understand what is being done with it. You can understand the impact of television without completely comprehending the laws of physics involved.*

In relating his education in music to what is going on today, Professor Crow says: "When I was studying composition we learned almost mathematically to utilize orchestration, sound, and timbre to really give foundation to a concept. You can write music to tell a story with it. Ferde Grofé's "Grand Canyon Suite" is a beautiful example. With rock music they are using a musical and lyrical formula for selling ideas. With the right musical background the lyrics take on more profound meaning."

The changes in rhythm and other musical techniques used to sell attitudes and concepts are not unrelated to brainwashing. As Dr. Crow informs us:

> *Many of Pavlov's experiments were conducted with a metronome to research the effects of rhythms as a conditioning agent. His famous experiment done with lights, controlling the salivating of a dog, was repeated with metronomes. A dog was conditioned only to eat his food when the metronome was playing at 60 beats per minute, and not to eat his food when the metronome was set for 120 beats per minute. By switching back and forth, or playing both rhythms simultaneously, an artificial neurosis was created.*
>
> *By changing the rhythm within a musical piece you can have a strong impact on the listener and the subliminal effect is to push the "message" much more strongly. Some people actually have a physiological response when, for instance, a beat is switched from three-four time to five-four time. Pop music now does this type of poly-rhythms all the time, because it accentuates the message. We were taught never to do this in music school, but we were not trying to use music for mind conditioning.*

As has been noted again and again by scientists and psychologists, the use of a rhythmic beat is also related to hypnotism. "All you have to do is attend a rock dance and watch the people to observe that they are in an almost hypnotic trance while the music is playing," notes Dr. Crow. He continues, "A young person may hear the same song hundreds of times. As Madison Avenue has proved, that constant repetition sells products. Repetition is the basis of hypnosis. When a person is under hypnosis, or something approaching it, he is highly suggestible. This means that the message contained in the lyrics is recorded deep in the listener's subconscious mind. He may not even be aware of it. If I asked you to write down the words to 'Little Brown Jug' you probably couldn't do it; but if I played the music you could recall the words. Everything you hear is stored in the memory banks inside your brain and may be brought out under proper stimulus—which is why this music is dangerous whether the young person fully understands the words or not."

Music can stimulate the emotions and penetrate the mind in ways that seem incredible. Famous composer-conductor Dimitri Tiomkin puts it this way:

> *The fact that music can both excite and incite has been known from time immemorial. That was perhaps its chief function in prehistory, and it remains so in the primitive societies which still exist in the far reaches of the world. In civilized countries, music became more and more a means of communicating pleasurable emotions, not creating havoc.*
>
> *Now, in our popular music, at least, we seem to be reverting to savagery. And the most dramatic indication of this is the number of occasions in recent years when so-called concerts of rock 'n' roll have erupted into riots.*
>
> *Those riots, however, are only the obvious manifestations of what I mean. More to the point is the fact that youngsters who listen constantly to this sort of sound are thrust into turmoil. They are no longer relaxed, normal kids.*
>
> *They will tell you they get a "charge" out of rock 'n' roll. So do the kids who smoke marijuana and shoot H [heroin].*

Professor Crow believes that without question the most important group now setting the trends in pop music is The Beatles. They began with standard Elvis Presley-style rock and roll and evolved into presenting drug and other message-lyrics in a highly sophisticated way. The Beatles have even changed their appearance, from smiling mop-tops to serious, bearded, and mustachioed hippies. They deny that they have used drugs since adopting Buddhism, but Beatle John Lennon was recently arrested along with his mistress, Japanese film star Yoko Ono, for possession of marijuana.

The song at the top of the hit parade as this is written is The Beatles' "Hey Jude," which is widely interpreted as being a song about Methedrine (*The minute you let her under your skin, then you begin to make it better . . . So let it out and let it in . . .* The song reaches crescendo with great screaming as the drug produces a "flash"). On the flip side of the single is a little ditty called "Revolution," which has been widely misinterpreted—and nowhere more grossly than by the *National Review Bulletin* of November 12, 1968:

> *The International Communist enterprise may at last have met its match: The Beatles. Radical sorts anxious to preempt the Beatles' creative and immensely popular music for the Left have found little or nothing in it to comfort them over the years.* *

The *coup de grace,* according to the swingers at *National Review,* is that "Revolution" puts down the Maoists. In this one, of course, The Beatles are simply telling the Maoists that Fabian gradualism is working, and that the Maoists might blow it all by getting the public excited before things are ready for "Revolution." The song makes it perfectly clear that The Beatles are on the side of, and working for, "Revolution"—and that their war is going to be successful (*it's gonna be alright*). In short, "Revolution" takes the Moscow line against Trotskyites and the Progressive Labor Party, based on Lenin's *Leftwing Extremism: An Infantile Disorder.*

The new Beatles album, containing "Revolution" and "Back In The U.S.S.R.," is according to a Capitol Records spokesman "the fastest selling record in the history of the record industry." No wonder the Communists have had some very good things to say about The Beatles, who rated a feature article in Volume 1, Number 1, of *Insurgent*—the Communist DuBois Clubs' official magazine. It was there that Communist Carl Bloice wrote: "If we are to be partisans of our generation in this chaotic world we can only cheer four guys from Liverpool who made it to the top and made so many of us feel more alive in the process."

Among themselves, the young Reds tell it like it is. After attending a workshop on the arts conducted by *Insurgent's* managing editor Celia Rosebury, Chicago Police Department undercover operative David Gumaer reported to his superiors:

> *It was mentioned that the reason the Beatles and other folk-rock groups received such success in the music field was because*

---

* Will someone please play "Back In The U.S.S.R." for the Billyboppers?

they were backed by the Entertainment Section of the Communist Party, and that music was a weapon used to win children and young adults to Marxism. It was also stated that Paul McCartney of the Beatles was a member of the Young Communist League.

McCartney is credited with being the co-author along with Lennon of both "Revolution" and "Back In The U.S.S.R." Professor Crow told me, however, that he has serious doubts that The Beatles really do write all their own songs, as is claimed. Speaking frankly, he explained:

Some of the newer Beatles songs are the same simple types they were doing four years ago, but other songs are of a very high quality and show an acute awareness of the principles of rhythm and brainwashing. Neither Lennon nor McCartney were world-beaters in school, nor have they had technical training in music. For them to have written some of their songs is like someone who has not had physics or math inventing the A-bomb. It's possible, but not very probable. Because of its technical excellence it is possible that this music is put together by behavioral scientists in some "think tank."

I know from personal experience that it takes a great deal of time to create complicated music and lyrics, and I don't know when The Beatles would have the time to put this kind of stuff together. They are always on tour, vacationing, or making a movie. The puppy-love songs go together pretty rapidly, but not the kind of intricate songs they have been coming out with lately.

Another important point concerning The Beatles, according to Crow, is the technical excellence they have developed and the phenomenal care taken in the production of their records. He notes:

In the last two years The Beatles and many other groups have evolved from being technically awful to being very good. It has been published that they spent $50,000 on engineering for the Sgt. Pepper's album alone. That's a lot of bread. Most people wouldn't have been able to tell the difference if they had spent

*half that much, but someone feels that it is important to have the
message presented perfectly.*

*The Beatles are no longer just four kids thumping away on their
instruments. In "Eleanor Rigby" (which is about the death of the
Church) they used a string quartet; and, on their newer records, a
120-piece band.*

*The high quality of their recent recording almost scientifically
creates a mood for them to push home the message in their songs.
I have no idea whether The Beatles know what they are doing or
whether they are being used by some enormously sophisticated
people, but it really doesn't make any difference. It's results that
count, and The Beatles are the leading pied pipers creating
promiscuity, an epidemic of drugs, youth class-consciousness, and
an atmosphere for social revolution. What The Beatles begin is
imitated, and often expanded upon, by literally hundreds of other
groups who in turn reach tens of millions of young people.*

Clearly, the generation gap has now been magnified and
distorted into class warfare in the Marxist mould. Youth versus
Age, along with Black versus White, has largely superseded
Labor versus Management as the premier target of Leftist propaganda.

It would be ludicrous to contend that Communists, Fabian
socialists, or Establishment *Insiders* (who manipulate the aforementioned groups) invented the tensions between parent and
teenage offspring. Such pressures have always existed. But much
of what we call the generation gap *has* been manufactured in an
attempt to exploit natural problems. Today, it is considered "hip"
for a young person to be disillusioned, lost, confused, and bitter.
There have always been such disturbed teenagers, but never
before have the Establishment media extolled them and cast such
outcasts as models to be imitated. Never before has the Establishment sought to make idols of the pathetic worst of a whole
generation.

Music is now the primary weapon used to make the perverse
seem glamorous, exciting, and appealing. Music is used to ridicule religion, morality, patriotism, and productivity—while glorifying drugs, destruction, revolution, and sexual promiscuity.

Youth believes it is rebelling against the Establishment. Yet the Establishment owns and operates the radio and TV stations, the mass magazines and the record companies that have made rock music and its performing artists into a powerful force in American life. Without the Establishment media, the Beatles would still be twanging away in some dingy Liverpool cellar, and their hundreds of imitators would be students, workers, or legitimate artists.

Without the Establishment's mass media, LSD would be just three random letters in the alphabet to most people, and marijuana would be a problem confined to jazz musicians and criminals instead of a national campus fad. Does it not seem strange that the same Establishment which has used the mass media to ridicule and denigrate the anti-Communist movement should open its door to those who think they are the Establishment's enemy?

It is the major Establishment record companies which have merchandised acid-rock music to millions of teenagers.* And, it is the full-page ads from these recording giants which keep many of the so-called "underground" newspapers financially solvent. It is now usual to find squeezed between the pornography, drug pushing, and shouts for revolution found in the "undergrounders" the full-page spreads purchased by Capitol Records, M-G-M, R.C.A. Victor (the holding company for N.B.C.), Columbia Records (owned by C.B.S.), and A.B.C. records (owned by the American Broadcasting Company). These vicious anti-American "underground" newspapers, in short, are financed by the Establishment they claim to be attacking. And, they are so financed to sell the music of illicit sex, drugs, and revolution.

Our teenagers would do well to ask why the Establishment would finance those claiming to seek its own demise?—unless what is happening is all part of a single revolutionary thrust, of which America's youth is to be the ultimate victim.

---

* While some of the rock groups appear on lesser labels, many of the smaller recording companies are subsidiaries of the major recording firms.

A. Martynova

BEATLES AS CINDERELLA:
A Soviet Fairy Tale

The following essay first appeared on December 3rd, under the title "A Fairy Tale About a Present-Day 'Cinderella'," in the Russian publication Sovetskaya Kultura, a daily paper published by the Ministry of Culture of the Soviet Union and the Central Committee of Professional Cultural Workers.

The four "Cinderellas" are George Harrison, Paul McCartney, John Lennon and Ringo Starr. After the stunning success of their first songs they traveled all over the hemisphere, released mountains of records and drove crowds of teenagers out of their minds; they brought to life hundreds of similar ensembles, earned millions of dollars, and returned home to Great Britain where the Queen received and congratulated them. Tears of adoration appeared in the eyes of millions of admirers—it is, after all, moving to see such simple and pleasant fellows get such high honors; it's as if they had rewarded you also. And so you sit by the TV or listen to records:

"Yesterday, all my troubles were so far away . . . O, I remember yesterday . . ."

You're at peace in your soul—they say that the English treasury's been enriched, but now you have heroes that aren't imaginary, ones who're always with you. Especially if you're not inclined toward reading, and if you don't trust all that abstruse gibberish "which is written only to confuse normal people." It's immensely more interesting to hear something new about one's idols—who got married, how many rooms there are in his apartment, and how that scandal in New York will end where John expressed himself so unfortunately about Jesus Christ.

The Philistine must have his idols to worship. He lives their lives as if they were his own.

The first English tour was successful. True, cries and sighs were not yet audible. Then, however, the Beatles released their fourth record, "She Loves You." With it began the general rage for the style of "yeah-yeah." Around that time the Beatles began to let their hair grow; in addition, they started dressing in a way that took into account that they should resemble no one. The people of Liverpool wondered at them but also began to let their hair grow, thereby upholding the prestige of their fellow townsmen. Then came the day when the Beatles were no longer simply an interesting musical ensemble, but "sensation number one" on the pages of the foremost London papers. On October 13, 1963, they performed at the Palladium in London. On the following day all the papers came out with headlines and photos. These weren't critical reviews, but a chronicle of events: police, victims, and flight by way of the back exit. Beatlemania had begun.

First-hand reports, covers of magazines with circulation in the millions, and mountains of souvenirs, shirts, suspenders, lighters —the market began to work for the Beatles, fanning the flame of Beatlemania. And, according to the steel logic of economics, the Beatles began to work for the market. Both sides were winners. Who, then, was on the losing side at that time? During the first stage in this escalation of success, it seemed that no one was.

Aside from unfortunate parents, perhaps, these spiritual tragedies bothered no one. They were played out in the young hearts of girls who had become victims of their "first love"—an emotion deeply false, but nevertheless in no way less intense than real feeling. For the first time in their lives the girls loved for real . . . imagined heroes, to be sure, but at the same time, not ones thought up by themselves. They were ready for everything for

the sake of their love. Thousands of crazed teenagers stupefied
by the unceasing "yeah-yeah" rushed toward their idols with the
despair of the condemned.

Only sometime later sociologists busied themselves with this
problem, and it came to the surface that idol-worship is not
merely a "disease of an age" but that it is a direct result of the
spiritual, but more exactly, spiritless atmosphere of bourgeois
society in which youth seeks out its "gods" in order to protest
against the canonized "gods." It appeared that Power, Money,
Career, and Well-being no longer instilled children, even of
bourgeois families, with great respect. Furthermore, they rejected
these values and sought their own.

It is not accidental that in the beginning of the Sixties young
people tossed about the expression "don't trust anyone older than
thirty!" Upon consideration, it's not as eccentric as it appears at
first glance—not to trust anyone when you're sixteen is not only
difficult, but even unnatural. Is it possible that children simply
stopped loving their parents and became egoists before their
time? As is well known, each family has its black sheep, but in
recent years in America and Europe there have been far too
many families that have given rise to "black sheep" who have
become vagabonds, criminals, dope addicts, so that it has become necessary to sound the alarm.

The phenomenon of youth abandoning the bourgeois family
is spreading so rapidly and unpredictably, and at times takes on
such ugly forms, that its essence becomes obscured. Beatlemania
and after that "mods," "rockers," "hippies," "yippies," "diggers,"
and "vagamps" [?]—what a number of incredible movements
and anti-movements have sprung up during some ten years in the
life of one society . . . When they first appeared they brought
on condescending laughter: when one's young, one's green;
they'll get over sowing their wild oats! Later people began to
observe more closely and became alarmed.

Beatlemania was one of the symptoms. Kindled by this society with the help of the radio, movies, TV and the press,
Beatlemania mangled spirits while "grownups" looked on in
bewilderment. As soon as the Beatles reached the height of their
success, that is, when they were transformed from "Cinderellas"

into idols, the fairy tale, as one is wont to say, comes to an end. Even if they sing about "love which is not for sale" or compose romantic ballads or shout "yeah-yeah"—it no longer matters, for now everything will be swallowed up just the same. It wasn't only the songs written by the Beatles that stopped belonging to them, but they themselves—after all, they also had their own lives—became the property of show business. Everything flowed together into the sea of Beatlemania; in fact, now the music was of lesser interest than they themselves. The Beatles willy-nilly had to keep up the created legend.

Therefore they publicly had to tell which girls they were spending their free time with, and, in addition to that, whether or not they were planning to get married (at this point the pictures of their sweethearts were printed in the magazines). Each step had to be carefully thought out, because they no longer had the right to live simply "like everybody." Moreover, they became fabulously rich—indeed, every feminine tear turned into a dollar. Brian Epstein and some others involved with their affairs got rich. Around 1966 not only popular magazines, but also the *Wall Street Journal*, which caters mainly to businessmen, started printing items about the Beatles.

Here the incomprehensible happened—Brian Epstein died under mysterious circumstances resembling suicide. Nevertheless, the Beatles stopped performing. They gave their last performance in San Francisco in August, 1966. George Harrison and his wife left for India to study Buddhism under Maharishi-yoga; John Lennon took on another role in a film. Non-drinkers, the Beatles took up drugs, in part, LSD, which according to the convictions of "the connoisseurs" opened up "a new, unfathomable reality." Newspapers began to talk about the group breaking up and about the end of such an incredible career.

Conversing with the Beatles, Hunter Davies noticed that they're confused, that they're looking for something, what that is they themselves can't understand, but basically they're looking for themselves. For they haven't had time to think, it turned out that they simply didn't have sufficient elementary knowledge to understand and appraise what was going on. Confusion led to despair—at one time the Beatles planned to renounce everything and to go off to an uninhabited island, but then they abandoned this idea which wouldn't have been so easy to realize.

Then a new idea was born, more acceptable to the society in which they live: the creation of their own stock company—"Apple." This also is an "island" of a sort, but one with a solid economic foundation. The shareholders have already gotten down to business—they have monopoly rights on any performance of their compositions. Moreover, fans recording their music are obliged to pay a fee to the company, Apple. The Beatles no longer perform for the public; everything that's done by them is recorded in a studio equipped with the most modern equipment, only on records and only for enormous sums of money.

Thus the Beatles have become businessmen. This activity now takes up the greater part of their time. True, records of their new songs from time to time appear on the market, and even with quite a bit of commotion. For instance, take the last record, *Two Virgins*. It went like hot cakes, and here's why: on the cover there was a photograph of John Lennon with his new girlfriend, Yoko Ono—both nude. Again there were headlines in the newspapers, again a "sensation." You can't get away from it. Without arousing the interest of the public, both Apple and the songs, however they were intended, won't last long.

It turns out that there's very little of the fantastic in the fairy tale but more and more numbers and calculations. True, some good songs remain, but they're not the ones that the young people sing when they go out into the streets to protest the war, violence and legalized slavery. They sing the songs of civil fortitude composed by Bob Dylan, Pete Seeger, Joan Baez, and others, ones who are truly popular youth singers. Their success, by the way, was in no way affected by Beatlemania. The Beatles have always been proud of their being apolitical and of their non-participation in the governmental machine. They invited one into the world of love, nature and pure feelings, in short, into another world, one separated from the surrounding one. Yet they didn't find such a world, even with the help of narcotics. Instead, they became the property of another world—of pop-art, the market, and business.

Robert Somma

THE BOSTON SOUND
REVISITED

If Boston and M-G-M were dead and buried, this article would be nothing more than an autopsy of a disinterment. But I've no desire to play doctor or rob graves and I don't groove on the odor of decay. Even more to the point, though the landscape is littered with bodies, there isn't really a corpse. Boston and M-G-M, with arms linked and usually in step, marched through a rock music campaign during the past two years and they both show the wounds. It seems to me that they're sufficiently healed not to give much pain when you touch—still, they're serious enough to leave scars.

The losses in morale and money which Boston music and M-G-M record company incurred during 1968 are reasonably well-known within the record industry, to managers and promoters, to reviewers, publishers and producers, and even by those who have only a passing interest in marketing matters, the general public. Despite the complexity of detail and the extent of the damage to reputations and to purses, the major facts of the experience are simple and easy to digest. There were, clearly, miscalculations. and misjudgments made in advertising and promotion departments and among bands. There is an understandable reluctance on the part of some of the people involved to discuss explicitly the moments of decision and commitment. I have no interest in relegating responsibility and only an indirect one in assessing it.

There is, to be sure, blame available, but if it helps to pin it on record company executives, group managers, and ad agencies, I'm not completely convinced that it would be useful to do so. I *am* interested in the chronology of events and in the nature of the circumstances which made it possible for both Boston and M-G-M to suffer such large losses in capital, prestige and confidence in so short a period of time.

Numerous personalities play leading roles in the drama: managers, promotion representatives, agents, editors and writers, top-level executives, low-level hangers-on, producers and musicians. Anyone approaching the Boston Sound, its pre-promotion musicians and deejays and its post-promotion apologists needs to have a flair for the coherent and the fair. *Every* side of the story has its explanation, its impulse, its logic. Opposed views on the matter are held and it's easy to see why they can coexist. Ray Riepen, who owns the Boston Tea Party, was actively involved in the presentation of the Boston groups. His estimate of the experience?—"Tragic—it set back Boston music two years." Dick Summer, then WBZ's deejay, moved from Boston to New York in the wake of the deflation, then back to Boston to WMEX. He has a different view: "The Boston groups reached a large audience. I'm a deejay and I'm supposed to help develop local talent. I'm not ashamed of having had anything to do with it." Summer, like Riepen in his hall, played an important role in presenting the Boston groups on the air. The prime movers in the Boston Sound are still around, if not in precisely the same capacity: Riepen's interests have expanded; Summer is a program director; Alan Lorber continues to produce in New York; Ray Paret still operates Amphion in Boston; Harvey Cowan and Lennie Scheer still work for M-G-M; *Newsweek* magazine, last time I looked, still publishes.

In the end, it's a matter of evaluating the known facts and drawing a conclusion which those facts could support. I believe the report which follows is a fair and comprehensive account of my efforts at unraveling a real event in the record industry, not to prove I could perform a resurrection, but with the conviction that my conclusions are evident and sound enough to warrant attention. The only advantage I have over the parties involved is my admission that, as in everything else, there is no one opinion or interpretation which binds all the various participants. Perhaps not even mine.

To begin in the most general way, the groups which had most to gain and most to lose during the winter of 1968 were Ultimate Spinach, Orpheus, and the Beacon Street Union. At the other end of the see-saw sat M-G-M records, a company which, even in mid-67 had a reputation for density and inflexibility at the corporate level. And midway between record company and rock groups were the notable and, it seems, essential middlemen—the managers and the producers.

Especially the producers. They had something the managers and the groups required before they could even begin to think in terms of commercial success, particularly recording success— contacts, experience, leverage within the industry based upon a demonstrated ability to achieve sales.

The group which made the largest gain in financial terms, that is, in record sales, was Ultimate Spinach, and it is for this reason that theirs is perhaps the most bitter experience. It was certainly the most extreme. Before the summer of 1967 they were just another rat in the race toward recognition in the rock market, with no national identity, no recorded material, no definite direction and lots of competition. One year later, they were booked into major cities across the country, and had sold a million dollars worth of records. They had been praised and analyzed, puffed up and put down in trade journals, national magazines, rock publications and the *Wall Street Journal*. They were mentioned in the same paragraph and on the same terms with the Beatles, the Rolling Stones, and the Jefferson Airplane (by Nat Hentoff, in *Jazz and Pop*). They were hailed, typically, in *Time* magazine as the "Jolly Green Giant of pop." It would be inaccurate to say that a completely undeserved success had been thrust upon them—but it's damn sure they had reached first base without much panting and without having hit the ball out of the infield.

One year after all that, and Ultimate Spinach no longer exists, except on a few poorly moving lps in the catalogue of a record company in trouble. No one will, or can, say whether it was in the stars or in them, but Ultimate Spinach and M-G-M, like the scientists in the opinion of Oppenheimer, know guilt.

During the summer of 1967 the music scene in Boston was healthy, if not especially central to the rock movement, whose focus had shifted dramatically to San Francisco. Out West, the Monterey Pop Festival, the attention of national magazines, the allegiance and optimism of a new generation, all contributed to an excitement and an intensity of activity in rock which would make 1968 the year of commercial ascendancy for the groups which had developed and grown there. Back East, New York had neglected or smothered its own groups, as New York seems to think necessary, thus surrendering whatever claim it might have had on the record industry as a fertile ground for new and active talent. The bands and the personalities were elsewhere, the direction was West and the distance was several thousand miles.

Cambridge (with *its* large concentration of students), was a huge market as well as a natural source of musicians, writers, agents, businessmen and fans. The folk movement had its heart there, if not its commercial mind, and the college community actively supported and contributed to the folk scene. The AM stations, WBZ in particular, weren't starving, though they simply had no Boston groups to promote. The entire city was geared for coffee houses, acoustic guitars, meaningful lyrics and a cerebral response to music. Attempts were made, not unsuccessful and not without reason, to attract rock groups, both at the Unicorn and at the Boston Tea Party. In July of 1967, Boston was ripe for a home-grown product to emerge and prepared to give such a group grass-roots support. But for that to happen, the city and the group had to rely on forces which stood outside of the city and which, in some ways, had other interests at heart than Boston's best.

It is important to realize that in the summer of 1967 more than one independent producer or fledgling manager must have made the manifest judgment that the East Coast could, if the right procedure were followed, duplicate the success of San Francisco. It was a commercial decision, and a sound one, based on a defensible estimate of market direction and available talent, for some producer or record company to tap the resources in the Boston area. The groups were forming, making the largely imitative moves toward the market. And young, market-oriented dudes in the record industry were well aware of the possibilities.

Alan Lorber was certainly interested in Boston as a source of commercial talent and his interest coincided with the evolution of a group called, first, the Underground Cinema, then Ultimate Spinach. This group was brought to Lorber's attention by Amphion, the management agency of Ray Paret and David Jenks. Paret signed a contract with Lorber, who, as an independent producer, had made a reputation and sales of $32 million and who had established a working relationship with M-G-M.

Lorber had carefully formulated his approach to the new market by releasing to the trade journals, on September 23, 1967, his plans for the development of the Boston scene. His reading of the market was, on a certain commercial level, a fair enough estimate of the then-current trends and tastes. At any rate, there seems, in retrospect, to have been a definite stir in the commercial waters:

> *Lorber feels that Boston will be more successful as a talent center than San Francisco has been. He feels that there was only a moderate talent situation in San Francisco which was backed and forced by strong commercial interests.*
> (Record World—Sept. 23, 1967)

It is pertinent to note here that Lorber attributes at least part of the ultimate failure of his enterprise in Boston to a reluctance on the part of local interests to support their own groups.

Lorber's procedure with "fresh talent" involved signing a group to his production company, producing tapes which would be sold under contractual agreement to M-G-M for promotion and distribution. This type of arrangement is known in the industry and can serve the interests of all parties, depending, of course, upon the specific terms of the agreement. M-G-M was committed to function in areas for which, presumably, it was well qualified, i.e., selling records. Lorber knew, from his singles experience, the ropes of production. In effect, the music of the group and the group itself were in the hands of a combination of interests, primarily Lorber, who would pass the product on to M-G-M. The implication in this is *not* that there is something unprofessional or unfair in the operation of either the record company or the producer, but, rather, that the commercial destiny of the group passed, under such an agreement, out of its control. In many cases, this is a fortunate thing. For Ultimate Spinach, the happiness was short-lived. By October of 1967 Lorber had completed taping with Ultimate Spinach and a release date was scheduled for the end of the year. In the interim Orpheus (a still-operative band) had signed a similar contract with Lorber, while Wes Farrell had found the Beacon Street Union. The commercial interests, which had at first just sniffed around, were now well into the hunt.

Here it's perhaps important to give some idea of the executive state of affairs at M-G-M. The record division of the parent company was in the hands of older men, individuals who, over the years, had committed the label to certain artists and groups. These last were a costly investment for the company. M-G-M channeled large sums of money into producing, advertising and promoting artists whose market value had crested by the mid-sixties. The Boston Sound promised a financial return which could help offset the losses which had become almost institutional within the label. Hence M-G-M approached the coming scene with enthusiasm. A decision was made, at a high corporate level, to commit the label to an advertising and promotional push. It appears, again *after* the fact, that it was, shall we say, *indelicate* and *imprudent* to place the groups under a single logo. Lorber even now contends, for his own reasons, that it was a natural thing to do, given the type of competitive marketing within the industry and the image-lusting mind of the audience. In this, Lorber finds support in the opinion of Dick Summer, who states with emphasis that "the promotion was a *good* idea, it was natural to try to reach the largest possible audience at that level." At best, the Boston Sound set up the groups and the label for a put-down. Thus, while it is undeniable that the producers of the Boston albums had an ear for the commercial sound, other factors came to dominate, factors not unprecedented though obviously unforeseen.

The first Ultimate Spinach album was to be released in December of 1967. But the release was delayed. M-G-M was preparing a promotion campaign for all three of its groups, which included trade ads for "the sound heard round the world—the best of the Boston Sound." Even prior to the Boss-town piece in *Newsweek,* M-G-M had planned a series of "press parties" for the three groups. Ultimate Spinach had several in its honor, in New York, on the West Coast, and at points in between. Beacon Street Union and Orpheus participated in similar ventures at the Scene and the Bitter End in New York. Ultimate Spinach was booked for a mid-January tour of the West Coast, and M-G-M continued to hold off on the lp release. After a farewell at the Boston Tea Party, the group went West, where they were met with an at first receptive audience. During the tour an event occurred which assured that the audience would turn against them and which must be viewed as one of the major steps in a long line of fateful, perhaps well-intentioned but finally unfortunate, if not disastrous communications movements.

During the last week in January the groups and the city stood poised on the verge of a rapid trip up and down the ladder of commercial success. Hopefully, the Boston groups would inject vitality into a pallid rock label, enhance an East Coast music scene and stimulate a lively cash flow toward the principal figures. On January 28, 1968, *Newsweek* magazine published its piece on the "Boss-town Sound." Lorber states that neither he nor M-G-M was approached by the researchers or reporters from the magazine. I'm not convinced either of them would have balked at the tone and substance of the article, which was, in effect, a lame piece of unsolicited ad copy. It was also a loaded piece of reporting, laced with quotes from clubowners, managers, and musicians. The statements sounded synthetic and the conclusions were generally useless:

from one Radcliffe girl:

> . . . *They're Thomas Wolfe in sound, with words that make you gloomy but always gladder.*

and:

> *However diverse, the Boston groups are held together by their general folk orientation, their subdued, artful electronic sound, an insistence on clear, understandable lyrics, the spice of dissonance and the infusion of classical textures.*

The point, of course, isn't that the *Newsweek* report was a piece of artless trash, but that it seemed to have originated with the producer and the record company and the groups. The misapprehensions and absurd precious-pop style weren't so indigestible as they were suspiciously similar to the worst promotional ploys in the business.

The response to the combination of national phrase-making in *Newsweek* and the intense promotional activity of M-G-M was complicated at the time, but predictable. The Boston groups found themselves the recipients of heavy record sales (75,000 in three weeks for Ultimate Spinach) and bookings, along with the testy and defensive disdain of the younger critics who knew a dog when it barked. The net result of the press exposure, both in the form of articles and reviews as well as ads, was similar to a balloon, filled with air, untied and let loose from the hand of a child—an upward thrust and a long fall to earth.

The exposure was quite massive and comprehensive. After *Newsweek* had keyed the audience-sensitive media to the topic, the press converged and like a huge vacuum cleaner sucked the Boston Sound into its machinery, ingested it into its belly, there to be roughage for an acidulous process whose known end is part nourishment and part waste matter. From February to July of 1968, everyone who wrote on any subject even remotely concerned with popular culture did his or her thing on either the

Boston Sound or one of its representative groups. Feedback was inevitable. It wasn't just *Newsweek,* but *Vogue,* the *Village Voice, Time, Rolling Stone, Jazz and Pop*—you consciously marched back and forth across the spectrum of clout in American publishing if you simply set down the whistle-stops where Boston's Sound made its printed appearances.

Three articles are vitally important, especially if one takes the most reasonable view of the incipient move toward the audience being made by the Boston talent, viz., that it didn't seem likely for any one of the groups to have reached a stage of development, whether as performers or as recording artists, which could justify the attention or overcome the hype.

The *Newsweek* piece, ill-advised, insidious, perhaps not even well-intentioned, put the groups right up there, grabbed the market by the earlobe and said "listen." The effect of this was, at best, negative—it reduced the stature, the promise, the qualities of the Boston talent to a conglomerate "sound" your parents would belch over, in between coffee, *Time,* and the TV. But the *real* audience, the one with the cash and an ear for the music, the one which responded to *every* flicker on the communications board, was hyped to the groups and came to them in an unnatural, forced manner and at an inopportune time. They were put on to them by one of the publications irrevocably identified with a different generation, and for all that under-twenty-fivers read *Newsweek,* they don't quite *believe* everything they find there. They took the groups home on record to see whether it was the real thing.

From that point on, nothing particularly unanticipated happened. The guarantee of initially large sales was in, and the sales sheets would come *after* the audience had radically changed its direction. A kid who bought *The Eyes of the Beacon Street Union* in March would be an entry on a summer account-sheet, but, by then, would have turned his thumb down. The prosperity, in other words, was false. And if the audience was (and is) a demanding one, even as to *how* it wishes to be manipulated and exploited, its critics were in a position to put those demands in an articulate, no-bullshit way. Two articles reflect the division in market between the establishment reading of a trend and the more accurate and up-to-date rejection of it—one in the *Wall Street Journal* and one in *Rolling Stone.*

Jon Landau, by early 1968, had already begun to establish himself as a sort of dean of rock critics. Even he was unaware, at that point, of the immense influence he possessed as resident arbiter of *Rolling Stone.* Landau had written direct, generally excellent pieces in *Crawdaddy,* knew about rock as a musician and as a critic, and had been around the Boston scene as long as there had been one. He seemed the perfect writer to review and evaluate the Boston Sound, the most appropriate index of its validity and its worth. Coincidental with Landau's emerging status was the rise of *Rolling Stone* and the equally emergent resentment of the West Coast and of the San Francisco area for the East. Cultural chauvinism is nothing new, but as *Rolling Stone* overtook the audience which had become dissatisfied with or alienated from *Crawdaddy* (whose offices at the time were right on 6th Avenue off West 4th Street and, later on, on Canal Street—nothing more East than New York) the West Coast began to resent the implication that San Francisco was, at the beginning of 1968, musically barren or that Boston had taken up the baton and was circling the track, heading the field and about to take over commercial supremacy from the West.

Landau's piece on the Boston Sound was a nail in the coffin, if we can agree that the *Newsweek* article, for all its obvious publicity value, had already put on the lid. He expressed every fear and suspicion the rock audience had for the Boston-based groups, most especially as they had been presented in *Newsweek:*

> *The side of Boston that is reaching the national audience with the first three of the albums is inextricably bound to an extremely heavy promotion by M-G-M and the question should really be whether or not there is anything lying beneath the hype.*

Landau confirmed, both implicitly in his tone and explicitly in his evaluations ("pretentious," "derivative," "extremely pretentious, angry and self-righteous," "boring") most of the suspicions, almost by rote and in a deliberate and balanced way. He saw merit in certain of the groups or in certain aspects of a single group, and his evaluations were accurate in terms of what the groups had produced and released. But from a commercial point of view, it was a real down. He did mingle his own tastes and inclinations with his judgment of the Boston Sound, but for all that one could dispute the peripheral details of the Boston scene or blame him for neglecting to calculate the long-range effect of his article, he was right. The Boston Sound was a creation of a publication and of a promotion department and as such was neither justified by the records of the groups nor particularly sought by the groups themselves. Implicit in its growth was the death of the bands and when, later on, money and the audience had dried up, the arguments would center on one or another individual or event as blameworthy.

Still, for all that the game was decidedly over, there were plenty of moves and many months left. Exposure in large-circulation publications and the consequent one-shot record sales brought intense market activity for the groups, as performers and as a recording band. Bookings were set up and the groups hoped that the sales fervor would carry over from their first to their second lp.

For Ultimate Spinach, the testimony of this activity came in May of 1968, not even a year after they had made their initial contract with Lorber. The *Wall Street Journal,* locus for prudent, topical and well-written articles on matters interesting to anyone even remotely identifiable as a consumer, carried a front-page essay by a staff reporter on the topic *Selling a New Sound.* If ever an autopsy was performed on a live one, this was it. No aspect of the group's success was overlooked, not even the fragility of the entire trip:

> *The Ultimate Spinach, four boys and a girl, is one of hundreds of professional rock groups trying to make it. Most won't. Bad music will wreck some. Bad management will finish others. High living will be the downfall of some.*

Background information on rock, on its commercial realities, its internal organization, its market sensitivity was cited. The Ultimate Spinach was analyzed primarily in terms of a group moving against this background. Much of the detail put down in the article wasn't all that new and gave off an odor of the half-baked ("It is music for collegians and drop-outs and others of the Now Generation, those in the know explain"). Its quotes, like those in *Newsweek*, seemed selected more for their entertainment value than for their fidelity to reality—at least, one *hopes* that to have been the case:

Mort Nasatir, then head of M-G-M's record division:

> *Some of this music is so intellectual that it is a little like the poet T. S. Eliot with his seven layers of ambiguity in each line.*

Ian Bruce-Douglas, Ultimate Spinach leader:

> *We try in our music to get across the idea one should be free and not bound by anything.*

Rick Sklar, program director at WABC:

> *Often this kind of music runs on and on . . . It's designed to simulate an LSD trip.*

On the whole, the *Wall Street Journal* article was an exceptional piece of reporting, given the context and location of its appearance. It certainly indicated, however long after the fact, the impact of rock on the commercial apparatus. It even suggested, however faint-heartedly, something which, out on the street, was a known fact: Ultimate Spinach had not quite made it.

One of the peripheral phenomena of the trip to this point was the active proliferation of Boston groups and their signings with major record companies: Eden's Children (ABC) and Earth Opera (Elektra) were the most attractively packaged. If anyone, either within the groups or within the record companies, suspected that a comedown (or better, a bring-down) was in order, no one actually let on. Articles in the trades as late as July of 1968 continued to extol the success of the Boston Sound. The reverberations of Landau's "no," which only echoed as much as it keyed the audience, didn't seem to have quite penetrated the companies.

At this point specific problems began to exert internal pressure. Ultimate Spinach, in particular, experienced, in the midst of its commercial success and press attention, personal difficulties native to the rock business. It seems clear enough now, even to the individuals directly involved, that Ultimate Spinach could not cut its bookings. They simply could not play up to the hype or the expectations of the press and the audience. That failure, coupled with the undercurrent negative response, killed off the band. Lorber, with some reason, points out that the band found itself in a position which demanded a personal and a professional maturity which were not quite there. And while some bands are given enough time to work out the various problems of their profession and their own lives and ambitions, the instant and overexposure denied such time to Ultimate Spinach. They were brought along much too fast and could not perform the difficult self-braking required by the commercial pressures, all of which pushed them more and more quickly.

It was only natural, considering the presentation of Boston talent in press and in promotion, that failure at the top would drag down the other bands and cause the "scene" to collapse. In some ways, it had been a gamble similar to our national politics —whether wisely or not, various groups were tied to a party line and when the head of the ticket could no longer command enough votes, the public rejection, fair or not, was comprehensive and across the board. The groups were locked in—they could no more dissociate themselves from the logo than they could persuade the large national audience of their individual identities. The pressures over which they had no control and which had tried to operate in their interests only turned on them in the end. The groups continued to record and to perform, of course, but as a long-term commercial venture, the Boston Sound had been rejected. When it was proved that a backlash works in music as it does in politics, the success and the demand withered, and with that the enthusiasm and optimism for a Boston scene.

❖ ❖ ❖

At M-G-M the experience looked, from the outside, like an unmitigated disaster. It's most fair, though, to point out that M-G-M records did not lose the 3 or 4 million dollars it's said to have lost in 1968 *because* of the Boston groups, and it certainly didn't lose that much *on* them. A source close to the operation estimates, with some authority, that M-G-M lost in the vicinity of $100,000 on the Boston Sound. M-G-M's record division troubles predated 1968 and have already been suggested in this article.

In any case M-G-M did lose money in its record division and even more through its parent company's movie interests. The executive decisions which aided and abetted the Boston Sound only reflected, particularly in the eyes of the public and the parent company, the susceptibility to miscalculation on the executive level of the record division. The Boston Sound was simply the most aggravated and latest case in point. For this reason M-G-M suffered through a period of great tension and even greater ambiguity and lack of direction during 1968 and 1969. With the departure of Mort Nasatir as president of the record division, there was a void filled, temporarily, by, first, Arnold Maxim, and then Sol Lesser, neither of whom was expected to act as more than interim appointee. Early this year, when matters were particularly acute and before any real commitment to a tangible change in attitude and approach was evident, a source at M-G-M described the effect of the Boston Sound on the executive level with this comment: "They're all sitting around, waiting for the axe to fall—would *you* feel much like talking about it?"

These circumstances didn't breed confidence or goodwill, not to mention job security or public trust. Thus, even if Boston didn't cost M-G-M much money as a direct investment, it did help to exaggerate or pinpoint already existing difficulties within the record company. It's too easy to hang the rap on Lorber for pushing a scene and a group to commercial success prematurely; or on M-G-M for lusting after a piece of the market; or on writers and editors for hyping a sound in a thoughtless way.

Certainly the Boston experience didn't help M-G-M solve its problems but it did occasion a large-scale assessment of company policies and practices and understandably led to realignments and replacements in personnel. More than anything else, though, it implicated the record company in an unsuccessful promotional ploy and it did not help to inspire respect among new talents or to make the label attractive to the market. Still, good did come out of it. With a new president, a more tactful advertising head and a sea of commercial hazards carefully charted, the label is at least prepared to market the groups it still has and the ones it can attract in a more credible way.

As a scene, Boston may or may not exist, although I doubt it ever could in the simplistic way understood by national publications and promo men. All the assumptions made by the press and the producers are true enough—there are clubs, there's talent, there are interested commercial heads. Dick Summer, for one, remains convinced that Boston is fertile ground for new groups, given the proper handling: "Now we've *still* got a huge untapped source of talent in Boston and I'd like to attempt to put it back into the spotlight." But whether Boston could ever support a scene, either in the clubs or on the air, depends upon your definition of the term and, in any case, is a moot point at the moment.

The effect of the experience with the commercial realities of producing and marketing on the three bands most involved is mixed: Ultimate Spinach, to put it briefly, blew it, and even if it had plenty of encouragement to do so, the group must surely regret, with the sense of an opportunity lost, the circumstances and the failures of the past twenty months. Beacon Street Union has settled back into local band status, playing high-school gyms, probably discouraged enough to sense the unlikelihood of recovering the original impetus. Orpheus has survived, seems to have matured, and continues to play and to record. In the end, for whatever it's worth, they responded best to the restraint and guidance Lorber seems interested in providing.

Plainly, there are lessons here, for the audience as well as its closely watching media-men. And if the individuals involved don't need to be reminded, others could with profit make their own observations. M-G-M tied itself to a process of promotion which was inappropriate and untimely. The groups were placed before the public and on the market prematurely, before they were personally and professionally ready to deliver. The bands didn't demonstrate an understanding of the demands and consequences of success. It's not impossible to put a group in front of the public, but management and marketers should place more faith in the rule of thumb that at some point in the evening, when the glasses are empty and the lights are out, and all that remains is you and the lady you've been courting, you've got to come across.

Bobby Abrams

BUCKSKIN COMES TO
THE HAIGHT

Okay, yeah, right, San Francisco had some rock groups. A Cid Symphony, Ace of Cups, Advance Token, Africa Creeps Up and Up, All-men Joy, All Night Apothecary, Amplified Ohm, Ancestral Spirits, Angels Own Social Grace and Deliverance Band, Anonymous Artists of America, Asmadius, Aum, Ball, Ball Point Banana, Baltimore Steam Packet, Bearing Strait, Beau Brummels, Berkeley Philharmonic, Bethlehem Exit, Big Brother and the Holding Company, Big Foot, Black Arm Band, Black Shit Puppy Farm, Blue Cheer, Blue Crumb Truck Factory, Blue House Basement, Blue Light District, Bronze Hog, Buffington Rhodes, Caspar Flats Jug Band, Celestial Hysteria, Charlatans, Chelsea Sidecar, Cherry People, Chocolate Watchband, CIA, Cleanliness and Godliness Skiffle Band, Cleveland Wrecking Company, Clover, Cold Blood, Collage, Colossal Pomegranate, Colours, Complex Network, Curley Cook's Hurdy Gurdy Band, Country Joe and the Fish, Country Weather, the Crabs, Crazy Horse, Creedence Clearwater Revival, Crome Syrcus, Crusader Rabbit, Crystal Sea Rock Band, Crystal Syphon Daemon, Daisy Overkill, Dancing Food and Entertainment, Dandelion Wine, Day Blindness, Deepwater Toad, Denver Overland Pony Express, Devil's Kitchen, Diesel Ducks, Direct Descendants, Drongos, E Types, Earth Mother, East Bay Mud, Edsel Buggy, Elgin Marble, Emerald Tablet, and Emergency Crew.

And there were more even. Endells, Butch Engle and the Styx, Entrophy, Evergreen Tangerine, Euphoria, Everpresent Fullness, Everything Is Everything, Exiles, Family Cow, Father Grumble, Fifty-Foot Hose, Final Solution, Finger of Scorn, Flamin Groovies, Flowers of Evil, Fourth Way, Fox, Freudian Slips, Friendly Strangers, Frosted Suede, Frumious Bandersnatch, G String Quartet, Gentle Dance, Gentleman's Band, Gladstones, Glass Mountain, Glass Thunder, Godd, Golden Toad, Golliwogs, Gordian Knot, Gossamer Kyte, Gotham City Crime Fighters, Granny Goose and the Soul Chips, Grass Roots, Grateful Dead, Great Pumpkin, Great Society, Green Medicine Jug Band, Gypsy Wizards Band, Harbinger Complex, Harper's Bizarre, Hastings Street Opera, Haymarket Riot, Heather Stone, Heavenly Blues Band, Heavy Bear, Hedds, Dan Hicks and his Hot Licks, Hmmm, Hobbitts, Hofman's Bicycle, Hour Glass, Dr. Humbead's New Tranquility String Band and Medicine Show, Immaculate Contraption, Incredible Justice League, Indian Head Band, Infinity, Initial Shock, Instant Action Jug Band, Iris, Jade Muse, Jaywalkers, Jazz Dome Scandal, Jefferson Airplane, Jook Savages, José's Appliances, Joy of Cooking, Judge Crater's Memorial Blues Band, Just 5, Lamb, Land of Milk and Honey, Last Mile, Lazarus, Liberty Street, Lightning Rod and Circuit Breakers, Lincoln Zephyr, Liquid Blues Band, Little Andre and the Five Dear Hearts, Little Miss Cornshucks and the Loose Troupe, Littlejohn Blues Band, Loading Zone, Mad River, Magnesium Water Lily, Mama Clover and the Rising Spirit, Mark of Kings, Martha's Laundry, Marvin Gardens, Maybe Tomorrow, Melting Pot, Meridian West, Midnight Movers, Steve Miller Blues Band, Mobus Lues Band, Moby Grape, Mojo Men, Morning and Evening, Morning Glory, Mother Earth, Mother Macree's Uptown Jug Stompers, Motor, Mount Rushmore, Mourning After, Mourning Reign, Mysore Sugoundhi Dhoop Factory, Mystic Knights of the Sea, Nepenthe, New Delhi River Band, Nimitz Freeway, Oklahoma Riverbottom Band, Old Davis, Old Gray Zipper, Only Alternative and his Other Possibilities, Ophelia's Death, Orange Jug Co., Orion, Orkustra, and Orphan Egg.

Lots others. Overbrook Express, Oxford Circle, Pacific Flash, William Penn and His Pals, Permanent Change, Petrus, pH Factor Jug Band, Phanganang, Phoenix, Pink Chablis, Psycle, Pipe Joint Compound, Pure Funk, Purple Earthquake, Pye- wacket, Quarter Dozen String Band, Quicksilver Messenger Ser- vice, Rain, Recurring Love Habit, Red Mountain, Rejoice, Remaining Few, Rock Shop, Rose, Rush, Sable, Salvation, San Andreas Fault, San Francisco Yeast Band, San Geet, Sanpaku, Santana, Sensory Task, Serpent Power, Shiva's Headband, Short Yellow, Silver Blimp, Skins, Slippery Gulch Band, Sly and the Family Stone, Smoke, Snuh, Sons of Champlain, Sopwith Camel, and Sounds of Picardy.

And still can we list. South Bay Experimental Flash, Spring Fever, Steve Lock Front, Strawberry Window, Stuart Little, Styx River Ferry, Sundown Collection, Sunshine, Sweet Smoke, TCB's, Third Half, 39 Homer Lane, Thorstein Veblen Blues Band, Threshold, Time, Time Being, Tiny Hearing Aid Com- pany, Tongue and Groove, Towaway Zone, Transatlantic Chicken Wicken No. 5, Trolls, True Blue Facts, Truman Coyote, Uncut Balloon, Universal Panacea, Vacant Lot, Vejtables, Venus Flytrap, Wakefield Loop, Warlocks, Melvin Q. Watchpocket, Wedge, Weeds, Weird Herald, Peter Wheat and the Bread Men, Whispering Shadows, White Lightning, Whytehaven, Wild Honey, Womb, Yellow Brick Road, and You. There were prob- ably more too except that I never heard them and we all know about falling trees in the forest.

Bernice, Iowa, had its rock groups too. A Cide Burn, Andy's Gang, Big Dick and the Masterbeaters, Diz Busters, Do Wah Diddy Motherfuckers, Electric Windmill, Four Skins, Exposed Rod, Gay People, General Mills, Intergalactic Warp, Lobsters, Los Callientos, Mack Truck, New Town Symphony, Orange Bar- rels, Paper Slips, Personnel Varies, Phall River, Pillbox, the Proghits, Pubes, Purpinkled Venus, Rip Off, the Shitkickers, South Bend Silver, Snow, Straight Machine, Timespiece, Tongue, Tree Stumps, Twenty-four Hour Dial, and Uranus and the Four Moons.

Okay so what. I'll tell you so what. There are a lot of similarities. Both had a mess of groups, some good, others not. What did happen in the golden city was a sigma move, summation of many divergent hypes. I mean can you imagine anyone singing "I left miiee hearttt in Bernice?" But there were those reference tongue moves. The great Clark Gable flick got it going. Now admit it, you really wanted to be there as you heard Gable and Jeannette MacDonald belt out "Saan Fraancisko . . ." And then Tony Bennett. He may have left it at the bank, but it was effective foreshadowing for what came later. For the young folk, Richie Havens came out of Bedford-Stuyvesant singing "Walking with my baby . . . ," the unofficial City College anthem. He was so soulful, so emoting, that all one could imagine was being down by that bay. The Youngbloods finished you off with "Grizzly Bear" or "Solid Gone" or whatever they called that old blues tune and it was almost all over.

Edgar Cayce had told of doom predicted between 1958 and 1998 for California (including San Francisco despite its pleas for cultural exclusion) by riven earth. This due to loss of spirituality via materialistic inverse proportion. A rerun of the Atlantis myth, as all life is a rerun. Praise be to Vico and summer TV.

San Francisco in 1965 was merely a city. Ecology to the dogs, the beats had been beat for a while and Carol Doda was the country's foremost expert on silicone. Even the shoeshines were topless. It was looking as if S.F.'s wad had been shot. This all was the beginning of the foolishness in the golden city by the bay. Love is a many splintered thing. L.A. with its smog and freeways was lightyears ahead. McGuinn, the ego, was adding layers of McLuhan even while McGuinn, the ego projection, sang folksongs in Berkeley coffeehouses under the alias Bob Dylan.

San Francisco pre-1904 was a town. The northernmost part of *El Camino Real,* it was the only civilized city in the West. Dancehall culture with lots of violence. More even than Saturday morning television. A curiosity for Easterners. And oh yes, oh my god the dance-hall girls of easy virtue, the real sights of any city.

San Francisco, Bob Somma to the contrary, may be the only city to live in. It's boring when compared to New York, but not when contrasted with Bernice. The air is relatively clean, and the city does not impose structure upon the individual. In the midst of such rustified decadence in 1965, two changes chanced into the permutations of City Hall to affect the area.

First was the grandson of a United States Senator, with the lugubrious handle of Augustus Stanley Owsley III. A refugee from Alexandria, Virginia, he arrived in California with two kilograms of LSD. Now you may think LSD stands for lysergic acid diethylamide but I just looked it up in my dictionary and it defines LSD as pounds, shillings, pence from *librae, solidi, denarii,* Latin words meaning pounds, shillings, and tenths. These subtle differences. Thus was introduced anew technology and materialism to a culture well acquainted with both.

The second big move was the coming of the galactic leather tongue. Rising out of the sea, it exerted such pressure that Richard Meltzer was heard to exclaim, in a dingy office on Canal Street, "I see the brothers and they spake in unknown tongues." So moved was he by the experience, that close intimates report it was the last coherent sentence he ever muttered aloud. On the horizon then was a showdown between the forces of theology and the forces of Mammon. Resolution slated to take place on the polo fields.

The first inland appearance of the tongue was an accented version. Sighted by famed limp critic Ralph Gleason at the by now famous appearance of the Rolling Stones at the Cow Palace, he called the phenomenon the buckskin brigade. The first group to pick up on this was the Charlatans. Since they couldn't play any instruments, they are important only for the mere costume move. And besides, their lead singer performed in cocktail clothes.

Approaching the problem from the other end was the Jefferson Airplane. They were playing at the same time as the aforementioned Charlatans and were about as good. Okay, so they were a silly millimeter better. But that ain't a hell of a lot. Their move, though, was to come on as *the* drug rock band. Maybe they were. For myself, I always preferred South Bend Silver.

Another group that knew the Lorentz transformation and

could keep up the tongue pressure had to be none other than Blue Cheer. The Airplane could never play live. The Blue Cheer could never make records. But live? What a different piece of horseflesh. Acid rock? Hell no baby, it was pure STP. Energy flowed freer than dope or cotton candy when they played in the park.

Big Brother knew buckskin. Better than most, not as well as some others. They had a real live injun in the group. Not the cigar store type, Gurley could curdle your blood with just one scream. But they weren't so hot either. Oh they played as well as most of the local bands, but that was not a particularly high standard of musicianship. What distinguished them and then destroyed them was Janis. Prancing around, shaking her boobs, letting her hair and her pants hang down, it was too much. Reversal of sexual adulation. All us horny bastards who weren't into Tina Turner had a new idol to form masturbatory images around. Give 'em head Janis. Only head didn't mean head; it meant head.

So much for the lows on today's weather forecast. Highs are abundant and prevalent in the five groups that dominate the quality (what an Aristotelian concept) aspects of the San Francisco sound. Country Joe and the Fish, Moby Grape, Steve Miller Blues Band, Grateful Dead, and the Quicksilver Messenger Service. The cream of the crop, the top of the wheat, or, as the Mexicans call it, the divine *collittas*.

Country Joe may not be part of it, but then again he may. Up in Massachusetts, people make a big deal about the difference between Boston and Cambridge, and even more that Brookline isn't a part either, but being there, you'd never know the difference. And even though Berkeley and San Francisco are separated by a Bay, they're connected by a bridge or two. And where Frisco was flower power and Berkeley was FSM, Country Joe transcended these limitations through acid power. The technological theology of his first album still makes visions of Edgar Cayce dance in any head's head. And what a head album! No acid trip is complete without "Bass Strings." Or even "Who Am I." La la la la la la lalala la la la la la lala lala la la la la la. And Joe even had the real Masked Marauder.

Zeno's first paradox states that you cannot traverse an infinite number of points in a finite time. There's some more words but that's the essence of it. A contemporary representation of this is Black's marble machine. Ultimately it reduces down to a ping-pong effect, much like the Dreyfus commercial. First there was the Byrds. The East Coast, not to be outdone, came up with the Lovin' Spoonful, cowboy hat and all. Back went the marble, this time landing a little farther north and whammo, presto socko, the Moby Grape. The Grape made four albums of which two are listenable or they made two albums of which four are listenable or they made one album with five guys, one with seven, one with four and god knows about the last. A group truly into mathematical complexities, giving them their Bach-like sound. And a little of everything for anything. When they had it on, they were a successful amalgam of the prevailing winds. A lot of times, though, they didn't have it on. But always they were pleasant, enjoyable and Skip Spence always had the most incredible smile. A good time was had by all whenever an appearance was made in the Polo Fields.

Steve Miller made his mark as a blues (read hard rock) guitarist. Everybody did. That was the basis of the psychedelic sound—the hard rock rhythms of the Rolling Stones imposed on different time signatures. The first time I saw him he was backing up Chuck Berry. The album that was released only shows where Mercury is at, not the respective artists. Hot and heavy was their trademark. And then they went into a studio. Maybe it was because Curly Cook had left. Maybe it was pure genius. Maybe it was pure THC. Whatever it was, *Children of the Future* was the first of four brilliant studio endeavors. Never departing very far from the blues, but never going too far in, Miller showed he could use a board as well as McGuinn. And just as technological, even if their roots were in different times, different places. "Lt.'s Midnight Dream" may be the best blues to come out of the whole rock thing and with Wilmer and the Dukes doing "Living in the USA" there's cross-pollination too.

The Dead. The divinely elegant Grateful Dead. In performance, they are the best rock has to offer. Acid, country, lemon and lime. As a life style, they are the best San Francisco has to offer. Noted for the electic eclectic electric quality of their sound, in three albums they've shown they can do it all. Lillian Roxon relates the information that the Dead's second album, *Anthem of the Sun* is a good companion for an acid trip. Rather, and right on, Lillian.

The highest of the high are the Quicksilver Messenger Service. All Virgos, of course they're brilliant. Two were born on August 24, and two on September 4. The later duo, both born in the same year, even hail from the same hometown. If you're into reading, you may not be able to do much with this data, but I'll wager they have some interesting numerological hangups. *Fusion* did a piece on them in its June 14 issue and what can I add to it? Pearlman won't listen to the album if he knows in advance it's QMS, but sometimes I can trick him into listening to it for a while and he'll dig it. And you know who else digs it? Commander Warp, the elegant dude, that's who. And the Commander sure knows his dope and his music. Quicksilver knows where buckskin is, they know where foreskin is. Acid, cocaine, speed, hash, mere grass, good grass; you name it, they have it for you.

Okay there you have it. San Francisco, a nice place. Good vibes, good music. But tell me who'll do a similar piece on Bernice, 'cause it's just the same, and I'll bet that by now there are even more groups there than I listed.

GEORGE RATTERMAN

Prepare yourself for a shockeroo. To musicians it may be even more than that. But the casual fan and total layman with or without ample curiosity can get a kick out of it too. Music, with a helping hand from science, has developed *two* sparkling ingenious *brand new shiny instruments* and revealed them almost simultaneously (at least they were on the same hour) to the general public via late night closed-circuit TV in a number of locations on both sides of the Canadian border. Instruments come and instruments go and instrument shows (particularly on closed circuit) often fail to ignite interest. But this time even an interesting program format was unnecessary (though it was a pretty good format as things go), for the DELGY and CICOTT are no ordinary instruments no matter what frame of mind you're in. The Delgy (a quite risky spelling which might lead the reader to pronounce it del-jee before it reaches common usage, it's actually pronounced del-gee as in Delguy, the proposed French spelling, and it's to be expected that a number of schoolboys who believe it to be a Delgee might spell it Deldgy if they're alert in their spelling rules and ignorant of the ways of music), with only one (rare) prototype model available on public exhibition in St. Louis, Missouri, at the low admission price of $1.75 (kids somewhat lower), is (it seems) a cross between a saxophone (a tenor to be precise), a tuba, a keyboard, a plastic cylinder, and a piano chair. It *seemed* that way and no further specifications were given (as the night was devoted to *music* pure and simple). It works by means of blowing into the tuba-sax reed-hole mouthpiece and the air getting bounced around the inside of the large transparent tunnel-like cylindrical tube after going through all the usual saxophone tube rigamarole and then there's further possible control over the eventual sound by means of the keyboard. Now the keyboard function may seem more than a little bit like some of the better things done by Lionel Hampton. If it sounds that way to the critics it's only because the man himself had his hand in the production. Well the sound *is* (in a way) already resolved before the keyboard goes into action, so the sound can be delayed or not as the player sees fit on top of the natural unpredictable delay-or-not already inherent in the mere superimposition of the keyboard hookup. And the keyboard *can* be disconnected (it's been done at least twice so far) from the horn channel by using a tool kit that could be found in any home and *that* sound is pure raunch (a lot like Lester Young and Ornette Coleman *no matter who does the playing!*) the like of which has been unseen and unheard of since the days of the alto flute stop on the Farfisa. Swing is a natural medium for the Delgy to be performed in and the men behind the machine (the instrument) wisely-or-otherwise decided and chose to have a man of the Zoot Sims school to do the honors and he stuck to the standards but added a few fresh touches of his own to the frequent flights of improvisation. "Suns of Sunette" was a particular knockout! And, to a lesser extent, so was the always subtle "Bags Groove." Another interesting fact is that, while the Delgy weighs less than the combined weight of (for instance) the usual tuba, tenor, keyboard and foot pedal unit combined, it weighs in at considerably more than the average European cathedral pipe organ. So much for the Delgy. On to the Cicott.

Consisting of little more than a drum set and a screen resembling that of an oscilloscope but with numbers on it attached to the Delgy chassis (it's attached to the whole thing for some undisclosed reason even though it has something to do only with

the keyboard and its innards, or so it seems), the Cicott (pronounced si-cott as in the soda) (thinking about a cicada may
help you remember) at first seemed to do far less than the Delgy
but that may have been due to the temperature of the fresh snare
drum head (which they had to admit hadn't had enough time to
be warmed up after replacing the original head broken earlier
that night by an overzealous musician-mechanic who was given
a sneak preview as well as an opportunity to get his dibs in even
though he had no business being there; apparently tensions were
soaring before telecast time and everything had to be just right,
but as it sometimes goes things can be *too* right) and eventually
their faith in the startlingly new percussion instrument was rewarded by something which can only be described as breathtak-
ing. Thought by many in the studio audience (you could see the
boredom on their faces during the overly wordy introduction to
the Cicott immediately after the apparently unbeatable Delgy
demo) (no commercials!) to be a weak younger brother to the
other one, it took the Cicott less than five seconds of its second
run-through to stand on its own as no innovation has stood on its
own since Haydn's early experiments with plagiarism or, perhaps,
Stuff Smith's fiddle moves of over a quarter century ago. No,
throw those references in the garbage bucket: THE CICOTT
STANDS ALONE.

Chosen just for the occasion should the first attempt fail,
Martin Denny IV took over from King Cluster (high on the
hog!) and plunged his way in after taking a quick tab of acid to
steady his nerve endings and sandpapering his sticks (for rub-
bing moves to increase friction upon contact). Although the
screen did so little for his predecessor it finally showed its stuff
under Denny's watchful gaze, calculating to within a hundredth
of a second and a thousandth of an inch (!) the nature of future
percussive sounds for the next four days from the Cicott sound
board (not all the sound comes out of the drums): you knew
what was coming and you couldn't help it and it was just too
much! Ed Blackwell (maybe because he saw a couple of appropriate movies when he was a kid) just guffawed his way into the
public eye by taking over from Marty in midstream (not actually

taking over, more like assisting and rejecting the assistance of)
and played himself up right nice with his own set of brushes
(how could the King have gone wrong, oh that's right, it was that
matter of the unwarmed skin) and he answered the Cicott's fiber
bundles with an immediately recognizable parody on the organ-
drum part of "Ruby, Don't Take Your Love to Town" and the
Cicott played along with him (apparently if your will is strong
enough or just if you play okay you can break the inherent rigid-
ity of whatever mess has been set up by previous Cicott misfits),
the interval of delay (shorter than with the Delgy) pumping
right along. Once in a while everything seemed *too* perfect, so
they stopped the whole show to show everybody there were no
wires connected to behind the scenes which might be controlling
everything to make it seem even better than it was. It was no
fluke, however. The Cicott was for real. But don't forget the
Delgy either. It's no slouch, even in comparison. So remember
them both: DELGY, CICOTT. A great potential is predicted for
both.

No kidding. Cynthia Bravo of the only Shell hidden camera
ad where they don't show the whole setup resembles not only
Denise the West Indian in Hair but also Red Morio's girl friend.

And George Ratterman he's the guy who used to be a hot shit
third string QB for the old (AAFC) Browns of Cleveland, Ohio,
and then he came outa retirement momentarily to be one of
about two or more ex-performers talkin up the action in the first
year of the now famous AFL and then he got caught with some
other chick (they even got a photo of it).

THE "I WANNA BE
WITH YOU IF YOU WANNA
BE WITH ME"
FICTION INTERVIEW

Summer '66 and the world destroyed Dylan. Not on some rocky road/ highway 61. Neck broken by harmonica holder cycling through village. Somewhere back in '65, maybe at Forest Hills, the crowd devoured his image while masturbating itself. But Dylan still exists hidden in Woodstock, New York, with wealth, wife, and piano. Stoned with Clapton one night, we visited. What remains is a residue of recollections.

Like why don't you come out?

The image. The image. Wearing a wig was a bad scene. All those people screaming and amphetamine. And where it's at. Grossman wanted me to ball Baby Jane Holzer for press.

With protrusions and pearls . . .

And chinese flutes.
Now I just compose and shop in supermarkets. The broken neck pr covered my tripping out. Man, those fuckin' gigs. England. A roomed life with wall-to-wall jokes. And people clawing to get inside of me and my shoes when all I know is the farmer's daughter.

What about your appearance at the Guthrie Memorial Concert?

What about it. The man was a genius. What I did was for him and no one else.

But everybody gets so excited. "He's wearing a suit," rehearses the audience . . .

And the band . . .

Friends. We just play together 'cause we're friends.

What about Baez?

Haven't seen her in two years—doesn't like my voice or somethin'. Electricity scares her. Morbid lyrics scare her. So she sings in the same pitch—records my songs 'cause she's too scared to record her own. In the old days. Beautiful. Used to wipe herself with an American flag after doin' it. Sure, I still love her even though she's straddled on peace and some punk ex-president from college-kid. Yeh, and the way she drops acid lying naked on ole Fats Domino records.

Love was just a four-letter word in *Don't Look Back*.

Right, man. Four years ago in some dogshit farce. When I was developing as an international noise. "Subterranean Homesick Blues" hit fourteen while posing for Pennebaker who positioned himself for the networks and the show must-go-on hype and Grossman's contractual constipation. Making me peeking through a keyhole down upon my knees . . .

And the electric transformation?

In Minnesota at seventeen when I played for food an' local ball I was into rock. Cut "Mixed-up Confusion" in '62 with electric backup. So for like three years I sang Caruso—hitting all the notes and holding my breath three times as long until "Like a Rolling Stone."
I was electric on the '65 European tour. Filmed me and the band doin' a little for another film called *Nine Below Zero*—don't think it'll ever be released though.

Why?

Look, I always wanted to be Little Richard. If ya don't believe me, look in my ole high-school yearbook. I used to stand there with a piano and scream and everybody laughed at the amps. I came to New York an' got into folk 'cause that's what was, man. I wrote what people wanted an' Grossman created the image with all this stuff about my leavin' home and stuff. Suddenly people were doin' me—I had the bread an' fame so like I reverted to high-school—eleventh grade to be exact. And there was me in this movie screaming in the Olympia in Paris and Grossman said cut the tracks but wait a few takes on the image, Bobbie.

You've always been aware of your image and public taste. Was your Woodstock seclusion just another bit to gather the tribes?

I knew it was time to stop, that's all. Someday I may be hung as a thief.

You're not copping out politically?

I say what I have to, man. The artist is the most political figure in society because he stands outside. *John Wesley Harding* is religious and political—besides, they're both the same. "Where another man's life might begin that's exactly where mine ends."

"He was never known to make a foolish move."

So "don't go mistaking paradise for that home across the road." Let's take that again. "All Along the Watchtower" contains an encapsulated "Desolation Row" in science fiction terms. "There must be some way out of here said the joker to the thief." What's political, man? Sorry I can't do that William Zan Zinger stuff anymore. Besides, "none of them along the line know what any of it is worth." Everybody wants to be inside my shoes and I'm married with three kids—where the fuck is Nashville in space?

But as a poet you must realize that people associate your musical thoughts with their existence. They want . . .

Did I hear product or me? They've pirated the basement tape, xeroxed Tarantula, and made me cut my hair off. But there's about eighty cuts that they ain't gonna hear because Columbia won't release 'em. Right now I'm into my existence and it feels good.

Has your voice changed? On Nashville Skyline it's higher and smoother . . .

That's because I'm higher and smoother.

I mean . . .

"Music is so much less than what you are." O.K.?

WEST COAST THEN
. . . AND NOW

West stretches north and south rather than east and west. And the biggest part of the West coast of the United States (where rock and roll got started sometime ago) is the state of California. And so California is south of what's the name of that place oh yeah Oregon and to the south is Tijuana. And I bet you thought rock and roll all ended with San Isidro, California. Well there's this really huge (and growing every day) wild crazy rock and roll scene way down south of the border. There are many excellent rock groups now (and even then) down there in sludge country Tijuana—all behind closed doors of course in some of them clubs they got there where they try to con you in from off the street (you know). Well here's just a partial list of all of the many several groups doing it down in old Me-hee-co: an unidentified group that does Jimi Hendrix routines, a group by the name of Los Macinac Busboys, also the Eleven Hombres, Sam's Mother & Sister, A Bucket of Steam, etc., etc. Not exactly. The last four groups mentioned above are lies: no such groups ever existed or played in Tijuana. But. But the first one did (you could hear their tunes coming out of the place a few doors away from the Woolworth's and guys were saying "come in heepies"—outasite) and, to my knowledge, they still do. Great scene huh? Well let's see, that makes three places where nothing's going on these days in the way of rock and roll music: San Francisco, L.A., and, last but not least, Tijuana (where they have lots of dope and also known for its tacos).

Okay, L.A. first. Well in L.A. they'll tell you that there are only two spots for young folks to stay nowadays, Venice and Echo Park. In Venice, where Morrison used to sleep on the beach, there's a pretty damn good bar with a pool table and beer and records and dancing and psychedelic colors and lights where you can now hear the entire Soft Parade any time you want (as long as they're open) ANY TIME YOU WANT. Okay and in Echo Park you can sit around on top of a hill and watch a guy watering his lawn on another hill or walk down to a burrito take-out place down the bottom of the hill ALL DAY LONG IF YOU WANT. Great scene! And other rock and roll centers too, like the Strip (guys wearing Nehrus in this day and age—too much!) and places where you can get yourself a tattoo if you want. So many great things out there down there in L.A. right? You guessed it.

Took care of Tijuana and L.A. already, that leaves only the great city of S.F. (famous for the gold rush and good eating). Well recently this summer a group of us kids (all of them rock and roll fans) went into the world-famous Fillmore Auditorium in San Francisco and it was in a different place from where it was last time (it was in a gym this time). And they had Ten Years After, Ike & Tina Turner, The Flock. Okay let's look at those groups, one by one. Ten Years After, as you probably already know, are limeys, not Californians, and they're dull but that's just etc. Next, Ike & Tina Turner are darkies and their whole super-duper Ike & Tina Turner Review Featuring the Ikettes you'd think might be a real big putdown of all this S.F. jive but it wasn't even 'cause it wasn't even GOOD but again that's just etc. Okay l(e)ast was the Flock, a pack of youths from Chicago (not only not California but not even from a coast and not even from an official scene like Boss-town so not even from a place where it's happening and not even from a place where it's officially not happening but only ambiguously connected to a possible scene/ non-scene 'cause after all there's Litter and Chicago Transit Authority and the great Midwest has the MC5 and) and who could give a crab about any of that. But they sure have good hot dogs inside the Fillmore and Hell's Angels from Ohio(!) who wear leather(!) and talk to guys who wear Mickey Mouse T-shirts, what a terrific rock and roll scene. And there's still the S.F. zoo and the aquarium and in Berkeley they have the new Country Joe album (what's the name of it?) in record store windows.

And as rock and roll goes, so goes the place where it comes from, you know the country or the city where it's going on. So of course not one single major league baseball team in either league on the West Coast managed to win the pennant this time and that includes San Francisco Giants, Los Angeles Dodgers, San Diego Padres, Oakland Angels and, no not Oakland Angels, Anaheim Angels (better known as California Angels) and Oakland Athletics. As rock and roll goes, so goes the city. And so goes the summer for its ball teams . . .

I may be a foreigner (as you could no doubt possibly have told from my use of the language), but I've been a rock and roll fan all my life and I got a good idea what's going on. True that my initial interest in California rock and roll (and in particular, San Francisco) was sort of 'cause, you know, well, I always figured U.S. rock was yrs and yrs behind English rock and so wondered if these S.F. rumblings were the big move to catch up or something like that or something. Well I was there then, and I was there again now. What was it like then? Well that was back when all of us were groupies more or less and I admit it sure was loads of fun getting to see Janis's nipples thru that mesh dress of hers and I'll have to admit that it wasn't that good a nipple but it sure was exciting catching it on the street down in the Haight. And that Grace Slick was sure one of the great machines of this or any other century. But there were several other things going on too.

Like one of the most popular of all rock and roll heroes of all of San Francisco (let him remain nameless) used to hit the sack with a number of lesbians who worked in a famous clothing store in the Haight. Not that he didn't do it with *all* available nookie on the scene. It was just that with lesbians he could spread his love to outposts previously impossible. So it wasn't just the usually interpreted mere abstract love scene. It was not just concreteness but *flashy* concreteness.

Around the time of Monterey, Gary Blackman (who handled
a lotta chores for the Airplane and even contributed the Jefferson
Airplane Loves You button—he wanted it to be Jefferson Airplane Tongues You but he settled for the former—as well as the
drawings on the inside sleeve of the Baxter's album) was kinda
hoping that the Airplane would get together as a true tribe in
tribal proportions for at least a couple a days at the Zen Center
(twenty miles from civilization—even by California standards—
on a twisting winding dirt road, and not just anybody was
allowed to go there but the Airplane was doing a benefit for them
so they were allowed in) 'cause even the Dead was more of a
tribe and they only lived not that many blocks away and sometimes all in one place. The Zen Center turned out to be such a
freakout of freakouts that nobody (including Casady) took any
acid while there (mud baths, and fresh air and stuff). Well a few
days later Casady walked downstairs from the third floor (he
lived on the third floor with Ginger who was once Kantner's
woman and once was a Merry Prankster too and, they say, once
got busted with Casady on STP) past the second floor where
Yuri lived (he was once the manager of the then famous Sopwith
Camel and was then a button dealer who rented cars all the time
but never got a license 'cause nobody does in California) to the
first floor there on Fell Street (it wasn't exactly the first floor
'cause it was elevated) where Bill Thompson (manager, oops
road manager, 'cause Graham was manager-manager of the Airplane) and a less famous but no less groovy guy (a heck of a
swell Joe who roomed with Marty Balin when he was Marty
Buchwald) lived at the time. All Jack wanted to do was borrow
the waffle iron but he was all dressed up anyway, wearing his hat
of that period and all. Bill's gal Judy said to him tell Ginger such
and such about the use of this particular waffle iron and there
was something about some stuff in the *Time* mag article on the
Airplane (so and so said that acid helped him compose). Posters
all over the wall and a whole lot of Thompson's own art work
things (crayon drawings of strange and unusual animals if they
were animals) and many, many Buchwald paintings (pretty
good, too, and some used string and other imaginative things) on
the many walls. And Thompson was wearing his Sgt. Fury & His

Howling Commandos T-shirt and they were buzzing about how great Jimi Hendrix had been the night before at Monterey and (Judy mentioned) how he balled his guitar. Everybody agreed that he would sure make a little history for himself that night at the Fillmore (in its original location), and of course they'd all be sure to be there anyway 'cause the Airplane was playing and so was Gabor Szabo (often mispronounced Zazbo).

That was nothing. Coming back from Monterey with this guy Julius (who handled Big Brother, no shit, just dig some guy named Julius handling Janis nowadays) who had lots of hash and a different kind of pipe (it had three holes in it rather than two) and coming back with this chick who ranked the daylights out of old Julius some time or other and they had lots and lots of Big Brother and the Holding Company buttons (a bagful). And no bird if it wasn't a darn purty ride up the coast back to S.F. and there were surfers every couple miles and if that didn't seem like a constant nothing did. And nothing did. But so, you know, and there's a story that (oh and Gary Blackman, at the motel in Monterey, was asked by this chick to see if Jim was at the festival site and if so to tell him his wife wanted him home—Jim *who?*: Jim McGuinn and that was after he became Roger and then there was the whole story about how he became Roger and Subud and all and the story took about half an hour) Big Brother's first East Coast appearance was not at the Anderson Theater but at a private party in Neponsit (they paid all expenses and all and saved money 'cause there wasn't any publicity: good idea).

Some time later, at the Columbia signing press party in New York City no less (ya see, they were already outstepping geographical restriction to the other coast, the coast of their homeland, or some of theirs). Peter Albin said that they once played an Angels funeral and Janis got some chocolate ice cream on her white T-shirt so she just took it off (letting her famous tits flop around in the breeze) and turned it inside out (then she put it back on). And he said that Love (the L.A. smash group) was really Hate if you asked him, they used to beat guys up. And one of the most fun guys to jam with was Corky Siegel of Siegel-Schwall and Casady was loads of fun too, he said.

And the Airplane once jammed with Paul McCartney and he

laid a tape on them of two *Sgt. Pepper's* cuts a few months
before it came out and they were mighty glad but breaking the
ice was rough and Marty said "it's tough figuring what to say to a
Beatle etc." and "Pooneil" was about then (an STP song) and it
seemed like just a *little more* flash was all they needed and they
catch England. Well here it was at least two years or maybe one
after that at the Fillmore *East* and Marty was with (it's true)
LINDA EASTMAN. That's some neat irony, huh? Well she was
with Peter Albin too . . . and Sam Andrew . . . and ———
——— ———.

"It's a Beautiful Day" was around then too (in the near
beginning) and so was a band by the name of The New Salvation Army Banned: the Salvation Army raised a stink so they
became just Salvation. And Pigpen was carrying his laundry
across Haight Street and there wasn't one single person on the
street who didn't know the whole Captain Trips story and feel
indebted to Garcia for having started the whole goddam thing.
And even earlier than that there was The Great Society with that
great twenty-five minute version of "White Rabbit." And The
Doors played the Avalon and John Dowd was there to see it and
he said that the girls couldn't relate sexually to Morrison nohow:
he was just plain weird! And more other things than you could
count (and Quicksilver was once the number four band in
town), as things began to categorically resolve and weirdness,
freakiness, and wholesomeness became distinctly separated stuff.
Who knows how many of the things back then were really the
Kingston Trio in disguise, or the Serendipity Singers, or the
Troggs? Only Moby Grape remains supreme. Or even remains to
tell the tale. A great group then as now, and it's good news
they're still kicking. And the Dead shot their wad, turning out to
be merely the best quality band from here to Yokohama, and
what's quality got to do with rock and roll? It (West Coast rock
and roll) was all a matter of discovery and revelation and the like
and once the whole show became obvious the possibility of discovery went out the window and that was showbiz and we all
miss it today.

Richard Meltzer

PYTHAGORAS
THE CAVE PAINTER

New questions. New questions? Really? Old philosophers, played out even then, novel even now. But just hear, hear, and listen to the beginning *before* you conceptualize the possibilities for the question "Now that you know who you are, what do you want to be?" actually to be a question as opposed to an even-though-you-know-what-you-know-I-know-that-I'm-ready-to-leave. Gargle with mercury but if you don't know what's coming off you'll never realize that "Third Stone from the Sun" is the *D.C.* version of the Silver Surfer on an asphalt trip: that is, you sure as hell have to be arrogant even if you don't particularly groove on ego trips.

Many are the means of allegorically expanding it all and summing it all up. Remember Plato's myth of the cave bit? SEE THE SUN FREE! And Nietzsche: groove on murkiness and Dostoevsky's vaginal pit extensions thereof. And more or at least a few, to name a few. But what happens when everybody has seen the sun and wallowed in the shit? That doesn't mean hey *Time* and *Newsweek* have written up the hippies even though John Canaday still doesn't understand Rembrandt or Andrew Wyeth. Or Genêt is welcome in *Family Circle* and *Family Circle* is welcome in your own home so what do you do now, now that Janis Ian has taken STP and avoids Clearasil. But: Well you just gotta be better in your all-encompassing bit and think and know that better is worth something and worthiness isn't a drag and that infinite regresses are okay. Enter: Jimi Hendrix, standing on his head and knowing what that means too.

Afterthought is a different slightly different story. Inches can be miles if you want them to be, and the ground between the Beatles and the Stones is far greater than that between Jan van Eyck and Hoagy Carmichael, the development from "Dandy" to "Que Vida" is awesomely greater than that bridging the gap between Hans Memling and Marcel Duchamp. Irony is ironically important, and ironically these proportions hold ground anyway. The Byrds *sing* "Eight Miles High"; the Beatles, Stones, Doors and Jimi Hendrix *are* far more than eight miles high, and, with the way up and way down being one and the same, they cover a lot of space, traversing it without moving. Still one place to go. Lastly through a hogshead of real fire. But come up the years, too, perhaps. Perhaps.

Okay, let's work on a logic of ascent/descent that's more fun and less fun than Fitch proofs or Nelson Goodman or even the famous Aristotle. Man like we can be so high that the high is irrelevant and so systematic that system crumbles so we might as well be structurally ready and readily structural so we can guarantee a good time for all total awareness freaks. Of course A and not-A. Of course, of course. Although she feels as though she's in a play, she is anyway. I can pick your face out from the front or behind. It really doesn't matter, if I'm wrong I'm right. And some people like to talk anyway, like Paul McCartney in *The True Story of the Beatles:* "John propositioned me. He told me that he thought the group could do nicely and anyway it was a lot of fun. He didn't talk about the possibility of turning professional. It was me, I think, who realized that skiffle could easily lead to some useful pocket money so that we'd be able to date the girls and maybe get a few clothes for ourselves. Remember, though, we were very young . . ." (a peculiar quotation for a paragraph on logic). Enter: Jimi Hendrix, pre-literate, post-articulate, proto-logical, bi-lingual (at least English and American), plurisignative. His major logical connective:

All you've got to work with at any time is your bank of memories and the state of the world as it is under all sorts of internal and external interactions and things like that. "I Don't

Live Today." Okay. Right. Present progressive time sense goes
out, future-oriented past and past progressive come in. Jump
from speaker to speaker, alternate sounds and silences, you're
finally conscious of all the implications of musical spatio-tempo-
rality. Fine. Spade rock was three years ago or now or the year of
the iron sheep? So? It's also in "Fire."

Law of identity fanaticism? Marvel comics too hung up on
the avoidability of the identity of indiscernibles; D.C. knows that
if you live on the planet Xzgronl#m you can tell your kid at the
ninth meal of the 67.3-hour Xzgronl#mian day that here on our
planet Xzgronl#m we eat purple potatoes and groove on
bizarre tautologies. Jimi Hendrix grooves on the earth's "strange
beautiful crescent green" with its "majestic silver seas" and
"mysterious mountains" which he wishes to "see close." And
somewhere guitars hum like bumblebees.

All this and déjà-vu transcendence too.

Double-standard science-fiction rock too. Byrds have to be
uninsulatedly "open" but not if they really knew that openness
means inevitable openness to insulation. Paul McCartney suggests merely fixing a hole in Dave Crosby's jewel forest closet,
and Jimi Hendrix wonders if maybe this chick's made of gold or
something and asks her quite politely, man there are still some
standard preciousness metaphors man.

Cage and Stockhausen might not really wanna play tennis
with Rauschenberg but Jimi Hendrix wouldn't mind eating Marianne Faithfull.

Are unknown tongues (units of change, awe, mere awe,
taxonomic urgency) still possible? Sure, but they might just be
about as significant as bottle caps. Bottle caps might be significant, however, too. The world is music but what is music but
what is the world too. And monism pluralism monism pluralism
too too. One of the alltime great traditional unknown tongues

occurs early in "Third Stone from the Sun" at the first eruption of the theme played at a random speed which just might be 45 or 33 rpm I guess. But that's not the point about the Hendrix tongue relevance board of directors (get your mind together, there are a whole bunch of you) that should be made to relate to post-Beach Boys ethnomusicology in general. For, along with Schopenhauer, we know that music is the metaphysical equivalent of all the nitty gritty power of nature, but along with Johnny and Brian and Jimi we know that music is also like the *World Book Encyclopedia* article on Brazil. Obviously Heraclitus contains Anaxagoras, but crystallization out of flux in music or in subway-car stability assertions might also be a different scene too. "Waterfall, don't ever change your ways" in "May This Be Love" is not only perfect Anaxagoreanism in a nutshell but even the perpendicularization of Heraclitus' river. The anti-tongue fadeout of "Foxey Lady" is the death of a guitar string. Best quotation tongue on the album: the Who-like beginning of "Love or Confusion." But how 'bout the beginning of "Hey Joe," a quasi-transitional passage which would be an awesome internal musical thingamajig in any Airplane context? That's nice too. And the first "Are you experienced?" is without doubt *the* definitive jack-in-the-box tongue. Morrison says, "Everybody loves my baby," right there in the middle of "Break on Through," right there conspicuously out of place. Lennon tells you in his book at the movies that he'd love to turn you on, right there where grass smells like World War II English newscasts. But Jimi Hendrix puts the question in the question slot, oh but where did the question slot come from and how did it get there?

"And the wind cries Mary" and "The Wind Cries Mary" sounds old, in a manner which peculiarly makes the whole album sound old for a while, not old in archaic or old like good-time music but old like a few years old. But just for a while, whatever a while is. And it's essentially appropriate that this actual real world introspective psychological time thing has the ring of "Queen Jane" by that groovy old temporally aware Dylan guy. Oh yeah, but on the other hand "May This Be Love" is reminiscent of great American Indian hits of the past as performed by the Crests. It could easily have been a hit as a direct followup to

Johnny Preston's "Running Bear" or as a release within six months before or after the Beach Boys' "Ten Little Indians" or as the track before "Tomorrow Never Knows." Anyway, a grandiose *specific* past-oriented temporal tidbit. Open your mouth and you are referential, play a guitar and you are trans-referentially a reference guitar scientist too. Fall asleep and you are lying on an archetype. Hear "move over Rover and let Jimi take over" (in "Fire") and you might just believe you've heard a brand new big dog-little dog variation. "Manic Depression" is a post-*label salvation* song. "Manic depression is frustratin' mess": labeled content already old hat and no longer solution; neat tension between former label as subject and latter as enunciated experiential predicate. Byrds *vs.* Yardbirds in "Purple Haze" shows you that any polarity is usable, any dualism is okay for two minutes or so. And "not stoned, but beautiful" is an excellent spur-of-the-moment neo-eternal I-don't-want-to-tell-you-this-so-I'll-tell-you-that readymade dualism. "*That's* what I'm talkin' about, now dig *this*" (in "Fire") was ironically written on the same soil as all that Russell-Moore constipation!

Music-noise pleasure/displeasure conditioning is a funny thing. By changing my seat at a Jefferson Airplane performance in Boston a few months ago I discovered that all guitar sounds, down to the merest of guitar sounds, sounded okay from behind the guitar, on the same side of it as the musician. Now I can listen to Jorma on record as if I were in his guitar position. Jimi Hendrix presents a multi-faceted problem with his guitar pluckin', one so vast that it ceases to be a problem as such on the same plane as mere irritations like the sociology of knowledge or medium-message stuff and it merits whole new conceptual schemata replete with matching jargon shoelaces. Like Roland Kirk. Like Jasper Johns. Hendrix's spatial relationship to his guitar transcends any standard finite batch of prepositions. It even requires a few new sexual position-process metaphors, like sychronized cunnilinguo-copulation, since he's obviously capable of playing notes with his teeth while outdoing the whole Bo Diddley-John Lee Hooker mild-mannered exhibitionism with his crotch.

In the case of listening to a standard guitarist on record, the actual audience-artist spatial relationship is epistemologically irrelevant, and aesthetically relevant only in a rather limited setup. Required is a mental picture of the guy facing you and occasionally moving around; in conjunction with this you visually change the situation and sit behind him or turn the stage around, or you put yourself right in his shoes. This requires a tunnel view of space with enlargement-contraction due to imagined distance and 180-degree reversals. Or you can give yourself an *a priori* behind-while-in-front-of sort of compressed tunnel space. But the ambiguity of the actual spatial relationship between you as a person positioned all over the place in the world and such items as the guitar cat at the moment of recording and the hi-fi speakers as apparently flat in front of (as the case just as well might be) you while you're listening x hours later is never much of a concern, simply because it is never much of a concern. Most people, even psychotics obsessed with 180-degree guitar reversals, simply couldn't care less about getting additionally hung up with the problem of determining (or being gripped by the impossibility of ever, ever determining) their *actual* spatial relationship to this guy far over the mountains years and years ago who happened to have recorded the original raunchy version of the tune they happen to be humming while they're facing east, right now (or is it north by northwest and some time other than now, since the *en soi* and *pour soi* just can't get together). Just think about this: Jimi Hendrix makes this new realm of aesthetic psychosis tenable, not only tenable but groovy. You can *care* about it because his space is not tunnel space but PAISLEY SPACE. Not just a cylinder of relevance or a cone of relevances extended to a sphere of relevance, but a *paisley*, metaphorically wondrous and elusive enough to be even more all-encompassing without the "of relevance" attached. Implicitly, the record-listening experience has *always* been far more complex than the in-person experience. The Beatles always knew that. Reversed fade-outs and multitracking even scared some San Franciscans into a preference for live performances. Now Jimi Hendrix has thrown it all into everybody's faces, even the faces of those who have not heard him live or on record and those who never will and those who are frogs.

A. Warhol

R. MELTZER INTERVIEWED

A, well-a, ya know, oh you wanna know all about the tongue, huh?

How big is it?

Imperceptibly tiny one could . . . say. . . .

Is it hot in the summer?

Only when it sucks pumice.

Why not upside down, or more directly in fact?

I want to tell you all about the UNKNOWN TONGUE.

In fifty-two cogently reversible words, what is an unknown tongue?

The basic unknown tongue is, if you care, you know you can sort of fit it out through all four levels of Plato's divided line, you know all those levels. It's increment of change, increment of awe, increment of mere awe, parenthetical awe, objectified awe or any of that, and lastly, increment of taxonomic urgency, you know like you just gotta label it *tongue*. You know: *there's* a tongue or there *was* a tongue right there. Oh it's a musical transition jargon thing.

How about the need for further analysis and delineation of the paradoxical unknown?

Oh balls, the whole analysis of music bit is sort of use a pack of words to tack onto a pack of sounds juxtaposed with a pack of words. Every creep who ever bothered with that sort of crap didn't really groove enough on how silly, in the good sense, the whole operation has to be. How do you *talk* about music, anyway, particularly when. . . . It's also a matter of temporality and analysis, that scene you know. Like Aristotle, the original pumper, did that whole thing with his *Poetics,* you know, give you a hunk of quasi-decent explicit categories that make it so that you alter the way you see drama forever, like you see it as Aristotelian sculpture drama which is a groove but it drags too. So you take the concept of the rock track: it's short, it's not a long tedious grinding thing-in-front-of-you that you not only gotta pay attention to to keep up with but where labels sort of imprison your whole temporal thing with the expectation bummer 'cause they're so easy to stick on legitimately. But you can piss at Sophocles anyway.

Wha?

Why I'll be glad to tell you. What I'm sort of dragging my way into is that rock is the best-worst suited for being verbally dissected 'cause it doesn't matter, and at the same time rock analysis, not any of that Paul Williams asswipe or any of that, can be validly insipid and harmless-harmful enough to be irrelevant to rock transition as music. Epistemologically it's nice too 'cause you can repeat the record quick and see if you spotted a genuine tongue if that matters and it don't matter if you scratch the record unless it matters. . . .

How does all of this affect your personal life?

Oh, aardvark tits! I guess I'm like an Arab in a burnoose standing almost near a telephone pole watching a swarm of red efts go by . . . anyway, historically, tongue jargon goes back to fall '63 when me and Memphis Sam were readin' this *Time* magazine article on Ray Charles and it said something about Southern gospel experts saying that he speaks the unknown tongue so we decided to find it. So in the Newport recording of "I Got a Woman" he starts off with something like "Oh sometimes, sometimes I get a little worried, oh but I just wanna tell you it's all right" then he does "be . . ." and takes his time breaking into "cause." The whole band comes in with ". . . 'cause I got a woman." Well that fragmentation of "because" is *the* definitive primal tongue.

Just to be mundane, can't any musical form whatsoever have the unknown tongue?

Sure, but the thing about rock is that it's really aware of the tongue as mere gimmick and mere structure and the use of any structure as ultimately mere gimmick, readymade or otherwise. With Country Joe, you've got recognition of the mere fact of music, all music. With the Beach Boys in *Pet Sounds* and the other one, you've got the mere fact of a specific *other* music, Beach Boys classical rock classical form. The Beatles' move, the big Beatle move in those days, initially, was the explosion of total tongue consciousness.

Well, why is there a tongue here as opposed to there?

You stupid or something? There isn't. It's all a matter of audience attention and that sort of thing. Like once I did a tongue demonstration for some guys and I put on "I Feel Like Homemade Shit" by the Fugs and everybody ignored the standard tongue points I was dealing with, they were just listening for the word "shit" behind all the gobble-gobble. As a moment of forced awareness the shit-point was a tongue.

Are there any other tongues besides *unknown* tongues?

You know there are. Scads of 'em. Implicit tongues are self-explanatory. Meta-tongue is nice. The title is okay because it's pseudophilosophical and hence self-playing out . . . a jargon that gets into self-bummer territory before the stuff it's describing and it can't help precipitate playing out the stuff. Listen to that George song on *Beatles VI*, "You Like Me Too Much," there's this part where they're building toward the tongue . . . that's something ya gotta clarify, what does it mean to expect the tongue; it's real post-surprise stuff or surprise-composition stuff, sort of just the thing in rock particularly after all that Ornette Coleman-John Cage goodies, you know rock irony and transcendental mere regularity . . . oh yeah, the meta-tongue. Well they go into "It's nice when you believe me, . . . if you leave me" and you sorta expect a drum-tongue by Ringo 'cause it's working that way, but Ringo pulls out and gets subtle as they go on into "I will follow you and bring you back where you belong." They do it twice, it's nice. There's the aquatic tongue transition into the big band in "Yellow Submarine," in fact the whole song bobs up and down like the waves of the standard aquatic tongue. You can handle the entire *Sgt. Pepper's* album as a meta-aquatic tongue field, oh talk about the meta thing altogether. It's when you have a different level of surprise, okay?

Okay, how about tongue fields?

Tongue fields are present most generally as entire tracks with constant tongue transition. Tim Hardin stuff, just because you say so so that they're not mere folk trash, use every note as tongue transition, even the fretting. Incidentally, you could take it as mere external folk trash qua tongue too. The Kinks are masters of the quotation tongue field, you know like transitions of reference abrupt and potent enough to do it; listen to "Where Have All the Good Times Gone." Tongue pressure is something else again, it's this setup with transition not merely within a single tongue field, but transition through tongue levels themselves, often with plenty of warning. To this day, "Doctor Robert" by the Beatles is still the only pure example of tongue pressure, although the break in Donovan's "Epistle to Dippy" has some degenerate tongue pressure. But tongue pressure is something like the anti-tongue too. The Association and Paul Revere and the Raiders are big anti-tongue groups. With the anti-tongue there's tension as to how that which obviously must be inevitably resolved musically will actually be resolved, it's like sticking overly obvious tongue indicators in your face so the multilevel thing can't be more than merely structural. But then again, tongue as mere structure is sort of the whole pre-rock musical scene anyway. And the Association is great at the irrelevance tongue, where you catch all the levels but many of them are too subterranean to matter except as setups for the ground and a little bit of flight, like with "Looking Glass," one of their great masterpieces. "Pandora's Golden Heebie Jeebies" is nothing short of an anti-tongue pressure field.

What else, oh and why haven't you mentioned the Stones yet?

Ah, the Stones have always been different from standard tongue orthodoxy, and that's swell. Oh yeah, except for their "Can I Get a Witness" with the break-reentry thing around ". . . yeah, yeah . . . up early in the morning." But they regularly use stuff like the Jagger Crescendo Principle instead of the strict tongue, so they get into second-orifice tongues by hitting you with tongues which appear such that the appearance itself is tongue-like, right? But I wouldn't call the Stones a post-tongue group, they're basically pre-tongue.

Who's post-tongue?

The Doors, Love, stuff like that. With Morrison, you've got verbal and vocal freakouts and explosions working at an intensity so different from the moves in the tongue structure of the instrumental thing that it hits too thick to be just a tongue, the tongue is overshadowed. But sometimes there's this overshadowing hitting in fusion with traditional tongue motif anyway. Love uses tongues which are irrelevant merely as tongues 'cause they have series of entire tongue universes standing around too big for the detail to matter in kind; Arthur Lee's tongues are not straight reference tongues but actually tongues by reference, reference to specifics, reference to the very fact of music as absurd. The San Francisco rock scene is sort of a scene of tongue avoidance if anything; it's sort of an attempt to work out a rock with a pre-rock tongue structure but without a tongue acceptance principle, like check out "Morning Dew" by the Dead, the tongues don't hit as hard as the hardest part of a song would imply by rock implication. That's sort of the opposite of what the Byrds do with Dylan's stuff. They take "The Times They Are A-Changin'" and give it a time sense that Dylan wasn't up to yet, time as musical time jam-packed with tongues, the nitty-gritty of all temporal perception by the way, and the Byrds leave out that self-conscious dissertation on the metaphysics of time that Dylan had in his last stanza.

Any more types of tongues, and can tongues involve merely words?

Oh yeah, words. The best example of the verbal tongue is the opening of "Eight Miles High," the transition covered by "Eight miles high . . . and when you touch down," and that's enough, even though it's musically reinforced anyway. Other kinds of tongues, well this interview is dull as dirt so I'll just give you one more: the beef tongue. Obviously, that's a real fat one. The first eruption of the theme in Jimi Hendrix's "Third Stone from the Sun" is a beef tongue.

More.

Um, the real masters of the tongue as a conceptual totality are the Beatles, they cover the whole spectrum, they even use tongues where other groups have attempted to show the impossibility of tongue interest. Take "2000 Light Years from Home," it's "Baby You're a Rich Man" without tongues and not far enough afield from the tongue universe to be beyond the tongue. Now if they did it as a move out of the tongue universe along with all other universes, getting progressively further away . . . but it's nice and homey that they don't and ironic as a chair to see the Stones homey. The great Beatle tongue chestnut is the beginning of "If I Fell": they go from John Lennon saying "If I fell in love with you would you promise to be true help me understand 'cause I've been in love before" and all that to the body of the song by a really spiffy Ringo drum roll that you can even see as a tap in *Hard Day's Night*. Love uses Michael Stuart for the same kind of drum stuff in "Red Telephone." Beatles, well. . . . Moby Grape's first album is as wide a tongue move as the Beatles and they even compress about three or four albums' worth of tongue maneuvers into one. Another thing the Grape understands is that part of the original basic rock move is the short track. It's easier to take a short track and pack it pumice-full with goodies than a long one, and then the long one takes on too much of the temporal ordeal drama aura. But some rock guys have been able to carry the move into that.

Who, for instance?

Well, Dylan of *Blonde on Blonde* works out everything into the muzak-tongue field, where periodic musical relief does the trick in the long horse, like in "Memphis Blues Again."

Why do you call it muzak?

Well, in muzak the focal point is wholesome tedious smooth sound strained to minimal interpretability and you gotta pull the notes out of it to make it the song you know it is and you wanna hear. You know. Dylan is a muzak master structurally, and the Left Banke carries it all the way back by somehow putting the whole thing back into the short track, accompanied by enough great non-essential-but-always-there-anyway muzak components to break through to hard-core muzak pressure because they don't and can't break through.

Got any analogies to elucidate this whole tongue thing? I still think you chew the root.

Okay, take the scenes in *Hard Day's Night* where the boys escape all the time by running away from the pack pursuing them and then, upon realizing there's no way out, they do it by going right back in the same direction they came from. Or you could take a photo of the earth and the moon and fold it in half and punch a hole in it and unfold it and stand in wonder. Good enough?

What's next in the tongue framework, what's gonna happen?

It seemed as if you'd need a cunnilingual receptacle principle for the tongue, but there's the diz instead, the diz for all who don't know yet being the cleft of the penis. . . . No it isn't.

Got anything concrete?

We got concrete pumice diz clefts and everything else. Anyway
there's a whole bundle of tongue transcendence and tongue
playedoutness too of course, tongues can become carpentry too.
What do you think "Bike Boy" is? Or the Soft White Underbelly?
Or "The Fool on the Hill"? Or "Surfer Bird," the oh-so-awesome
"Surfer Bird"? Screw the necessity of regularity elaboration and
distortion, and get with it with the non-move. That Stones
bummer, what's the name of it . . . oh *Satanic Majesties,* well
that's the groovy totally inadequate break-the-spell-of-Beatlistic-
tongue-enforcement that failed. The Underbelly won't fail, isn't
failing, will never fail. You don't know what it's like. You know,
music as avocado, but avocado as turquoise cardboard dead cat
run over by ivory toe. Okay, here it is in a nutshell: 1. crystallization in flux, fill in or at least do something with empty-full spatio-
temporal infinitesima in putty; 2. form as field, field as form,
—— as ——, tusk as brutal face, brutal face as nasty vortex,
nasty vortex as umbrella treatment scheme, but, all in all, umbrella treatment scheme as field qua field qua form. I'm sick of
talking, 'bye fans.

Another question. . . .

Another answer.

David Walley

MC5 INTERVIEW

This interview took place in the New York apartment of MC5's press agent Danny Fields, the day after the band signed their new contract with Atlantic Records. Present for the MC5 were Rob Tyner, Wayne Kramer, Fred Smith, Dennis Thompson, Michael Davis, and Brother J. C. Crawford.

WAYNE: We need to talk about music, because music really needs to be talked about. It's the most personal thing, the most important product.

DAVID: All right, how is the energy level of music concerned with the MC5's aims and goals? Is music a radicalizing tool?

WAYNE: Oh, there's no doubt about it. Music is, as you know, the killer efficient communication form. It feels good, it feels better than reading something.

DAVID: It's sort of like a cathartic effect.

ROB: (Laughter) We're from the Midwest—we don't know any big words . . .

DAVID: Where do you think this approach is going?

ROB: Structurally, music is going to become much more complicated—with much more content. Musically speaking, there are these many many traditional rules—you know, things that *are* supposed to be done with rock and roll and are *not* supposed to be done with rock and roll—all that's going to break down.

WAYNE: Well, I'll give you an example. Taking things beyond what they've always been. You know, it's the same musical problem that has been faced by every generation. You have this usually rigid network of rules and regulations, and people putting on music that doesn't mean anything. You have to go beyond. For there to be any progress in music, that has to happen. These old principles have to be surmounted with new principles, you know, and new ways of dealing with music, and new ways of conveying music, using music as a communicative, educational, creative, and recreative medium, which it is.

DAVID: A friend of mine said that he thinks rock music is just going to go into pure sound.

ROB: Oh, certainly. Pure sound energizes. The more energy in the sound, the bigger the sound that gets to you, the more intense the experience is, and the more intense the experience is, the more intense reality is—your metabolic reality at that moment, you know, an intensive feeling of your metabolism—that's where you find your reality. And music is equated on that level too, because it does make metabolic changes. Like on the stage, I notice metabolic changes at every instant. So fast—your heart beat and your respiration and everything, because you're using your body 100 per cent—that's what music is supposed to make you do.

It's supposed to use your body 100 per cent, so that you can force yourself out, put out as much energy as possible and make a perfect circuit so that there's an energy flow between the music and the audience, it all becomes one big thing, and it reinforces itself and everybody feels pure and clean.

We send it out, and they send it back to us, and we send it out harder and it culminates in a reaction—things happen in the room.

WAYNE: Can we take this back a little bit? I'd like to give you background, so you know exactly what we're talking about, as it came to us in terms of energy.

When we first started—ever since we were aware of music—we always knew that there was certain music, certain records, that really made you feel good. There was something there, something that just really hit you, you know? And when we started playing music, we just played the tunes that really moved us, that really made us feel good. And at that time we called them "drives." Made you feel good, you know. And so everything we did, music, all the arrangements, were always with this driving consideration. Because we wanted to have that drive.

ROB: We knew it felt good, that's all we knew about it. It feels good to play music like that, you want to be involved in making music like that. Rocking on—

WAYNE: So we met John Sinclair, and he helped us to the whole concept of energy which is essentially, man, if you take everything in the universe, take everything that the mind can conceive of, anything, everything, and break it down, you can only go as far as energy.

ROB: So you see, we make an analogy between that and the energy content in the music. The more energy there is, the closer you are to what things are actually made of.

WAYNE: In other words, energy is freedom. Energy is real, as opposed to a fantasy that exists only in somebody's head.

FRED: Because everybody knows that if we take as much energy as we can and put it towards doing one thing, then it'll get done. The more energy you put towards it, the more you get done.

DAVID: The more energy you raise, the more energy you get back.

WAYNE: So the parallel with music is that music with the highest energy is the most real music, that does the most for your meat, so we realized why energy music was *the* music, and the music that wasn't high energy, we couldn't relate to.

DAVID: But the music fuses all of you together.

WAYNE: Definitely.

DAVID: But the one thing I do get, leaving the music aside in some respects, is that you're so together, that instead of five separate energies, you're all *there*.

WAYNE: The energy is explosive.

ROB: Well, you take the energy in one person's body, you know it's X amount, but if you fuse it with X number of others, the power of the equation increases proportionately.

It's like you say you put in so much energy and you get something back, but it's increasing instead of decreasing—as far as like money goes.

DAVID: Yeah, I know, it's always an increasing thing, and like when you try—

FRED: There's a parallel there then to the whole Movement too.

WAYNE: Right, that each person who involves himself has received another person's energy, and it is only a matter of time until there's enough energy to . . .

ROB: To cover all levels. That's the basic principle involved here, all these different people, all these different groups, and different organizations are each covering a level; the Black Panthers cover a level, and the Motherfuckers cover a level, and the SDS cover a level.

Fusing all those energies together, it's going to spread. That's because everybody is jostling for position on these levels, you know, who's going to cover what level.

DAVID: Then you shouldn't have an argument about levels at all, it should just be power, but that's the thing.

ROB: That's the thing we've been talking about, that's the confusion that's always held people back on this planet. Everybody is involved with all this bizarre confusion and stirring up all kinds of lies and misinformation flying back and forth. That's the very thing that's held the people on this planet back for so many thousands of years.

DAVID: The realization has only become really apparent in the last twenty to thirty years.

ROB: Right, because we're a young race, and we're just now reaching puberty, so to speak, because there's so much emphasis on sex right now, and there's a whole thing building up, and we're just beginning to grow up; the race, the species is just going to grow up.

DAVID: When will this be?

ROB: It'll come when its time has come.

WAYNE: A whole new species.

FRED: Our kids, your kids—

ROB: Chromosome-damaged kids (Laughter).

WAYNE: And those kids aren't going to go through all the stuff that we've gone through, they'll just be starting off cool to begin with.

FRED: They ain't going to be repressed.

ROB: Right, exposed at an early, early age to their whole metabolic thing. You know, kids are hip to metabolism 100 per cent—they know what feels good and what doesn't feel good, and they're hip to energy blasts. Man, you see kids in a playground? I mean, you did it yourself when you were a kid, running until you were sweaty and just flipping out—it just felt so good. And you know, you'd cry for hours, man, until you were so pure that you couldn't stand yourself and went to sleep, just like that. You were into these high energy blasts all the time when you were a kid, but then it gets repressed as you get older because you have to grow up.

WAYNE: Not just repressed sexually, but repressed on all levels, and you rot inside, and you're no good after a while. All that energy that you should be pushing out, it's kept bottled up inside, it just burns you right out—you're a hulk.

DAVID: So you know, what I question sometimes is the method; you know, it's pure, the energy level, it's good energy—but how you channel it, because—

ROB: Nobody is in any position to tell people how to discipline their own personal energies, you know what I mean?

It's like when you become exposed to all that energy, you have to grow, to be that powerful. I wish I could say it more clearly, but that would take in all levels—it's like walking around with a gun in your pocket. Know what I mean? You have to be a gentle dude. When you have the energy of the universe burning through your meat, you have to be killer gentle, because you know that you can explode at any time; you can take care of anything on any level and be so intense that people would just be blown back from you. So you have to be cool; it's like Superman walking around.

DAVID: But we *are* supermen because we finally figured out—

ROB: Because we know how to get all the energy.

BROTHER J.C.: You finally figure out the whole key to judgment—because everything, everything on the human level, everything we go through, it's all a test, everything, everything. You're being tested every day. You're being tested by your boss, you're being tested by your teachers, and you're even being tested after you die, to see how much you leave behind. Being tested all the time. The whole thing is, make the killer judgment—judgment is what defines your actions, you know.

What you want is to receive a judgment so pure and so clean and righteous; you'd just always be doing the right thing, all the time, doing the right thing for you but at the same time the right thing for everybody else. Now it's all a matter of direction. If you're going in the right path, you're going in the right direction, getting further and further out to attain the killer understanding of yourself, yourself and your people, and your planet and your universe and your God, and your whole Mother being and whole Mother universe—either go in that direction centrifugally out—or you go centrifugally in, towards the planet, weighing yourself down with properties and fame and go down—right down—

ROB: And wind up buried.

J.C.: So you can only take that one direction, to reach out, to reach out to everything to everything. As long as you're going in that right direction, you'll be cool. Plants don't grow down.

ROB: Music can fuse with people, it can bring the people together. Music is an experience shared by all people. It's like water, know what I mean? Now, you can't tell anybody about water. They either drink it or they don't. If they don't have enough sense to drink it, then what can I say?

DAVID: Dig television—television hasn't gone anywhere—and the last person who did anything with television was Ernie Kovacs, and that was in 1960.

ROB: Even the people who have hold of it, man, aren't. They used to use the sapsucker to reinforce all the bullshit values. When I was a kid it was all about the war, all propaganda films on the Second World War.

I see movies now where they said, "Get all those Nip bastards," and it was just like that; I saw it on TV and you know, I dug it—I saw them Nips get shot right in the neck, man, and I loved it.

But the thing is, that was used to reinforce all their bullshit propaganda that they put out about the war. "Mom and apple pie" garbage.

DENNIS: They can't do it with the Vietnam war, though.

ROB: I know; they can't do it because nobody is going to buy it, so they don't even mention it, they don't hardly even mention it.

DAVID: Like nobody really fought in the Second World War, they never had real closeup shots of people actually getting . . . Like now, it's instantaneous and five minutes later it's on film and in the can—

ROB: And Mrs. Smith sees her kid on TV getting his head shot off—it's just about like that.

And it's just that supersonic nowadays, and it's just that close to home. Reality is creeping round the old front door and it's going to come barging through, man, with all the macabre and the bizarre behind it—until it begins the ultimate flash, man, until somebody leaps out of the TV screen and rapes their daughters right before their very eyes. And it'll get down to that, you know, because something else is knocking on everybody's door.

DENNIS: It's true, it's true.

ROB: Something else is knocking on everybody's door nowadays.

J.C.: You cannot escape it, you cannot purchase sanctuary.

ROB: True, where you going to run to, where you going to hide? So, you get down and get back—that's the decision. Man, I can't stand talking about governments, about war, shit like that, you know. I'd much rather talk about people and music, because that's the remedy for that whole thing right now. That's going to knock that thing down and fuse the people together, because it feels so much better than any other method that I can see.

DAVID: Some people are going to have to die.

ROB: Some people are going to have to die.

WAYNE: They all worry about what's going to happen when they die. The whole culture is based on that.

DAVID: On the belief in death.

ROB: In the killer death worship culture; but we're involved in the culture of life—life culture, and you're involved in it too. And we know what's righteous, and what's right. And we're just all trying to do whatever we must to bring about the righteous balance of the universe. Whether you call it that or not. We're trying to get the shit together, that's all.

WAYNE: Let's get down now to things that we really wanted to cover.

FRED: We wanted to talk about music.

ROB: Every time we go to an interview they want to talk about this and that, and we never get to—we have to talk about the revolution the whole time (Laughter).

WAYNE: Well, what we're talking about is taking music from stage to stage—I'll go through it historically, man, from the past, so you can see how we come to this stage, but originally we realized that we could just play, just start on a theme, and improvise. So we played and we got very aware of dynamics. In other words, we built up and up and up and up higher and higher, and better and better and harder and harder, more intense. Finally, we realized that we had to take things beyond Western music, music as we had known it before then, to other levels and other planes.

FRED: We didn't listen to any jazz musicians, the only thing we listened to was hard rock and roll. We didn't get into listening to jazz until we met John [Sinclair] just a couple of years ago. So we came through with the rock thing, and just took that out.

WAYNE: We realized that we had to get beyond the beat, beyond the key—into playing pure sound. As the expression—pure sound has a feeling; when you get into the sound as opposed to any progression of notes, you get a pure emotional reaction.

ROB: You get closer to the basic element of it.

WAYNE: You get a more intense emotional equivalent, more intense, and more pure. You realize that music has emotional equivalents; in other words, how it affects your body, and when you get into pure sound, you're beyond, and progression—it's emotion itself.

DAVID: Can you get beyond progression of emotions too?

ROB: New feelings should bring about new progressions. New progressions and new shadings and new everything. In other words, emotion has an unlimited potential. But our metabolisms are set up in such a way that they can be altered infinitely—you know what I mean? It's a very classic and beautiful and flowing thing that we're into.

It's so sensitive, this meat that we have on our bones—and you can feel so many different shades—and new progressions will bring about new feelings in people. New equations will bring about new awareness and new perspectives. It only follows, if your body is feeling a new way, then you're seeing things and getting impressions in a new way.

DENNIS: It leads to higher energy; the five of us would keep overcoming all of these inhibitions that we have through the past—and our energies are becoming more fused together, we're just getting higher and higher.

DAVID: It's like you don't have a structure any more, as much as the kernel of one pulsating mind.

WAYNE: Yeah, that's true. The music that we're talking about is not music—in the sense of music of the past. In other words, it's not music in terms of everything that people thought music was. We're talking about something else. We're talking about going beyond standard, accepted forms.

FRED: It took the media a long time to pick up on it—

DAVID: The media doesn't listen to music, man, they listen to money.

FRED: Right, and what I'm saying is that three years ago we were playing stuff that would still be pretty far out today to these people. It's still contemporary, but by the time the media got onto it, it was three years old, and they're just picking up on it now.

ROB: Yeah, but the thing is the longer they left it alone, the stronger it got. We became more convinced that we were right.

DAVID: What a modern musician has to do, a rock musician or a jazz musician—

ROB: A musician has to become familiar with not only his instrument, but the people he's playing with and to, that takes time.

DAVID: But you know, it's always been a question of priorities; true musicians always suffer. Look at jazz musicians, they've been suffering for years.

ROB: Really, look at Sun Ra.

WAYNE: But now, now things have moved around to a position where we can bring the change about, where we can put things in more proper perspective. In other words, we can talk into this tape recorder, and it'll show up in *Jazz & Pop*, that these people should listen to Sun Ra, they should listen to Pharaoh Sanders, they should listen to John Coltrane. It'll save your ass.

FRED: It's true, no doubt about it. It's the most powerful motivating force.

DAVID: It's the most concentrated form of cultural change. It's power, it's the most powerful force in our minds and I know it's the most powerful force in all our lives.

FRED: The Establishment has never recognized the common people anyway, and especially the common people's music; it just wasn't news that these niggers down in the ghetto were playing this music. And the poor people's music has never made it because it's never had a chance to get exposed.

DAVID: We've always been hung up on imitation European culture anyway.

ROB: European culture is such bullshit—quite frankly. But today there's this other culture; it has its own media, its own ways of getting the word around, its own music, own life style—we're basically subversive.

The mere fact that some people wear all the outside manifestations of a rebellion against all that bullshit—the long hair, and being dressed bizarre and things like that—they ought to be taking in other levels, also, but they're not utilizing their position; therefore, they're the Pigs, because they're in a position to reach a lot of people and just by default, by not utilizing their potential, they're repressing the others.

That's a decision that we all had to face, to make an alternative for ourselves; and we had to construct one.

DENNIS: Are you going to be the solution or the problem?

WAYNE: Either the problem *or* the solution. Can't be both, because if you go on being both, there'll still be a problem, you have to be 100 per cent the solution. And you'll be doing what's right and what's just. Suddenly, here's the concept of being either problem or solution, that naturally makes them consider—well, what does that mean? What problem, what solution? In relationship to what? Which brings about a whole new awareness.

DAVID: Well, it's just then like making somebody think: *if* you can do that. Nine-tenths of the education in this country militates against anybody thinking at all.

ROB: We're not for people thinking, we're for people doing.

FRED: People have called us the problem . . .

DAVID: Who called us the problem?

FRED: Well, we're all a bunch of troublemakers except maybe you—(Laughter)

WAYNE: See, that attitude there would be the attitude of your regular on-the-street honkie.

FRED: Well, listen—we go across the country, we go to a lot of colleges, clubs, and there is a lot of good people there in all these places—the people want to talk to you, they want to talk to you about the revolution and they want to talk about getting together, and they'll talk about it, and this is revolution. We have to be doing these things.

ROB: The thing is that there are still a lot of people sitting around and not thinking about it, and not doing anything constructive or useful with their bodies outside of working on a job for the Pig. You know what I mean? And wondering when they're going to get up enough balls to quit, to start doing something that's really them. There's a lot of people right now in that position, it's a decision they have to face. Borderline cases.

DAVID: Well, how do you kick them over?

ROB: Nobody can kick you over, man. I can't tell you who to sock it to. All we can do is to make the information available to them, and be an example, a living model, working out the problem.

WAYNE: We'll continue doing what we can do.

FRED: You just have to be righteous and ready to testify at any time—

ROB: And keep in metabolic contact with the universe, and you'll know whether you're righteous or not. You have to keep in—the universe talks to you more plainly than anything, man. When you drink too much wine, you're going to be crawling around in your own vomit, Jack, and that's how the universe talks to you.

J.C.: You can blaspheme against God and the Mother, man, and still attain eternal happiness. You can blaspheme against the sun and still attain happiness. You blaspheme against the Holy Ghost, the laws of the universe, and you get your comeuppance, Jack—right there.

ROB: You jump out of that window—you meet concrete reality, actual reality. You violate those laws of the universe, it talks to you real plain; and you know, that very concept applies on all levels. If you do too much of one thing, if you are day-to-day fucked up, it'll talk to you like that—know what I mean? Too much scag, Jack, the universe will have words with you. It will have words with you, and it's not pleasant when it speaks to you like that.

FRED: You're just not doing the things that the universe wants you to do.

ROB: Yeah, and that's the kind of righteous stuff you have to keep your eye on, because that's heavier than praying, God speaks to you physically on a metabolic level, and the universe runs the shit to you and tells you what's righteous and what isn't.

And, from that, you can infer how to take care of the rest of your day, man, how to take care of the rest of your whole life, just by following those simple basic laws. It takes a lot of fumbling around until you get them down to the natural facts, basic natural facts.

WAYNE: But it's necessary.

ROB: It's necessary, it's the killer experience and the purge: purification and a resensification on all levels. Resensify you back to your meat, because that's the way you take it in. Your meat is your senses, because your senses are made out of meat. And if you don't keep in contact with your meat . . . that's why all these straight people are so fucked up, man, 'cause they let their meat loaf—and it just rots, it rots.

DENNIS: Too fat to fuck.

J.C.: It's true, it's true. All these dudes walking around with their dick in a holster on the side, know what I mean?

ROB: Yes—and they're all on the rag all the time, and you can't have fun when you're on the rag. Everybody knows that. These people have always been on the rag and they don't know what it's like not to be on the rag, and they're scared of it.

DAVID: It's being scared of facing themselves.

ROB: Yeah, right, it's like scared of 'fessing up, scared of testifying, scared to get down because you might hurt yourself.

DAVID: I wrote a thing which I think ought to get printed some time, and I said, this government spends billions of dollars every year on tapping people's wires—and all they have to do is to turn on the radio.

WAYNE: Yes, Jesus, if they knew really what was happening, they'd shoot us. They would drill us with machine-gun fire in the streets.

ROB: This is the real world, and they oughta come on out and check it out—it's far out, but they have a whole other definition of what's really happening in the world. But, you know, we all came from that.

FRED: Right, it's true, we did. I know.

ROB: But it isn't impossible to realize your position in the universe, man.

WAYNE: It isn't impossible at all, but I tell you, the older you get the harder it gets. You're never as pure as the day you're born.

DENNIS: And you're really open then, you're really pure.

DAVID: But, man, you get slapped on your ass when you come out.

ROB: That's natural, in order to breathe, man, that slap on the ass—that's a good thing. People need a little slap on their asses—and very shortly the whole species is going to get a little slap on the ass and start breathing and checking it out, because we've been holding back much too long, too long.

DAVID: I live in the East Village, man, I walk down the street, and I can feel, all through my body, I just feel this energy, and I see the Man do his thing with his club—instant bringdown. I'm not saying that all cops are bad—there are certain cops that are really into it—but a pig, right? Okay, I see these guys who cruise around real slow, just checking you out, hassling you, and you think, what are they *doing?*

ROB: Man, they're just exhibiting the extreme of the honky culture; you know what I mean, the honky culture blended and refined down to one specific—at all levels. If you give them a chance. They're all like that, though, and they're all starting to get into that thing. They're all becoming super-cops, because this is the supersonic age. We got supermen walking through the streets, man. We got super-black militants, we got super-freaks, super-Puerto Ricans, man—and they just *have* to be super-cops.

It's getting like that everywhere, because it's a hip thing to do in the cop circles. That's what they do, that's the thing to do. They got super-equipment? We're going to get super-equipment too, man.

DAVID: They've got bazookas, things like that—

ROB: Yeah, right, but we got music and the power of the almighty blessed universe behind us, man. There ain't no bazooka can stop that, not none. Because the universe will have its say, and it's about to speak real loud to everybody.

J.C.: When it happens, you get down, and you go right with it, man. You either get down or get back.

ROB: But we're just playing around, we're just dicking around with this stuff. Look what they're doing with TV, they're just dicking around with it, they're not using it for what it could be used for. It's a beautiful medium, just like rock and roll. Rock and roll's a perfect medium to get information to people, and like nobody is using it. They're just dicking around with it, because they don't know its potentialities and they don't understand their own energies as it applies to those potentialities, you dig?

FRED: It was a very big thing when they discovered the wheel too.

ROB: That was only yesterday, you know—that was only yesterday. I want to keep re-emphasizing we've only had two million years of history on this planet. This species as we know it only has two million years of history.

We're on the hip planet, man, a billion years from nowhere, on the fucking rim of the galaxy; the inter-galactic worlds are infinitely older than we are, and the people and the species on it must be right in proportion with that. You know what I'm talking about? They've had more time to develop because they're close into the middle of the galaxy, and we are a young species. Dinosaurs ruled this planet and lived as almost the sole life on this planet for 160 million years. Now that's 160 million compared with 2 million—when the dinosaurs' history was 2 million years into it they were just little things.

DENNIS: Well, it's like that; the more time to develop, the more time you spend in reality, the more you have to dig it.

DAVID: With all the equipment we have, all the potentialities.

ROB: I know, and the thing we're talking about is giving Superman the TV camera. And you're not handing it to no chimpanzee, you're handing it to Superman; and he's going to begin throwing out some flashes, man, that are going to be heavy flashes. You know what I mean?

THE BEST OF ACAPPELLA

It used to be that you could only find it in little, out of the way places. There was a cut on the first Captain Beefheart album, an Anglicized version by Them on their first effort, another on the Amboy Dukes' *Migration*. Or you might hear it in the midst of a jam session somewhere, flowing out amid laughter and shouts of hey-I-remember-*that*, a little I-IV-V progression and then into "Teen Angel." Frank Zappa once devoted an entire album to it (*Ruben and the Jets*), but fell prey to the too-easy temptation to parody.

But now the rock and roll revival is fully upon us. The music of the First Phase is all around; Chuck Berry is at the Fillmore, Fats Domino just recently had an almost-hit record, the Coasters are again recording and appearing. On another level, there was a Pachucho record hop at the Family Dog a while ago, Cat Mother is singing about Good Old Rock and Roll, and a group named Sha-Na-Na played oldies-but-goodies at the Scene to screaming crowds and rave reviews. We're almost back in 1958 again, with people starting to dig out their old 45's, immersing themselves in such as Dion and the Belmonts, the Big Bopper, the Earls and the Fascinations, doing the ol' hully-gully as they walk down the street.

It's nice to see rock nostalgia happening; more than that, it's nice to see something *past* nostalgia happening. The old values seem to be on their way back; as the decency rallies proliferate, we are slowly entering a new phase of the old outlaw days of rock and roll. The cycles are turning, my friend, around and around once more, and we're coming home at last. Goodbye, Fillmore East; hello, Brooklyn Fox.

But I don't really want to write a thing on late fifties/early sixties rock and roll: that topic deserves a book and (sadly) will probably get one in the near future. Rather, this is about a stream within a stream within a stream; a little thing that happened once a long time ago, something that began, went round in its own little circle, died after a time. Call it a movement if you will—art historians would like that term. Call it a sub-culture, or maybe a microcosm of a much larger rock society—sociologists would like that. Call it an "experiment with the polyphonic possibilities of the human voice within a set and limited structural framework"—musicologists would like that. Or call it a genre, or a style, or a fad. Anything your little heart desires.

But I call it Acappella music, which is what it was known as then, though all of us had to have the word explained at one time or another. "Hitting notes," in the language of the street, and this is probably the most fitting title, since it was born on the street, on the corners of the small cities and large metropolises. Somebody tried to make it a Star once; they almost succeeded, but it ultimately toppled over from its own weight, coming back, in the end, to the very place where it was born, the place where it probably still remains today.

This, as they used to say in the movies, is its story.

The formula was very simple. You would be at a dance (or a party or just sitting around on somebody's front stoop), and things were draggy so you would go in to the bathroom (or hallway or stay on the same old stoop) with four (or six or twenty) other guys and sing (and sing and sing). The songs were standards; there was "Gloria" (of course), and the lead singer's voice always cracked when he reached for the falsetto part. There was "Diamonds and Pearls," a must from the Paragons, then "Valerie" for the crying and melodrama, "What's Your Name" 'cause it had a boss bass part, finally into "Stormy Weather," that perennial old classic:

> Don't know why
> (a-don't know why)
> There's no sun up in the sky
> It's Stormy Weather
> (Stormy wea-ther, wah-doo) . . .

Acappella, not to be confused with the classical *a capella*, means "without music." We were told that on the first all-Acappella album ever released, called *The Best of Acappella, Vol. I.* (Relic 101). They weren't quite right, as it turned out—there was very definitely music involved. What they really meant to say was that there was no musical accompaniment, no background instrumentation. Acappella groups had to rely solely on their voices (helped a bit at times by an echo chamber), using them to provide all the different parts of a song. This tended to put a greater emphasis on the role of the back-up part of the group, pushing the lead singer into a slightly less prestigious position. There was none of this limp Supremes background humming that is so prevalent today—Acappella groups really had to work, nearly scat-singing their way through the highs and lows of a song.

The movement began sometime in late 1962 or '63 with a group called the Zircons. The original Zircons (for there was a second, less creative group later) were probably together for about five days, at least long enough to cut a record which ultimately became the first big Acappella single. It was called "Lonely Way" (Mellomood GS-1000A), and sold somewhere above three thousand records. In these days of the Big Huge, three thousand really doesn't sound like much, but for an Acappella record, appealing to a limited audience in a limited area, the number was quite substantial. There had been a few other groups who preceded the Zircons (notably the Nutmegs who had made a lot of practice tapes in the style), but it was they who broke the initial ice, receiving some air play on AM stations and promptly breaking up over it.

"Lonely Way" was, and still remains, one of the finest Acappella songs produced throughout the entire history of the style. Many of the later productions had a tendency to be hollow; there were holes in the arrangements and you really missed the presence of the back-up music. Not so with "Lonely Way"—the harmonies were full and vibrant, the arrangement tight and tasteful, everything working together toward a melodious whole. I had the record for two weeks before I even realized they were singing alone.

After the Zircons, the Acappella movement went into full swing. In what surely must be a famous first, the style was not fostered by radio air play, by record companies, or even through personal appearances by the groups themselves. Instead, the driving forces behind Acappella, those who promoted, financed, and ultimately pushed it, were by and large *record stores*. And to fully understand this (though it occasionally will happen down South among specialty blues labels), we must do up a little background history.

Rock in the fifties, though it followed somewhat national trends, was basically regional in nature. Southern California birthed a peculiar brand of pachucho-rock; Tex-Mex had the Buddys—Holly and Knox; Philadelphia gave the world dances, American Bandstand and Fabian, and New York had the groups. The groups, together for a day or a year, often recording under a variety of names, sprang up at record hops or teen variety shows, here today and gone tomorrow. As a conservative estimate, I would say that close to ten thousand records by fly-by-night groups on similar fly-by-night labels were released in the late fifties and early sixties. And slowly, again mostly around New York, there grew up a little fandom around these groups, calling itself by various names—"oldies fans," "R 'n B lovers," etc.—who became really involved with the kind of music these groups were producing. In time, as the Top 40 began to play fewer and fewer of these combinations, the movement was pushed underground; groups like the Ravens, the Moonglows, the Five Satins, the Paragons slowly became the chief proponents of the older music. At a time when most radio stations were slowly sinking into the morass of Bobby Vee and Tony Orlando, groups like the Cadillacs and the Diablos were busily keeping the faith alive.

This fascination with groups has carried over to present-day rock and I've always been at a loss to figure out why. Even today, a group stands a better chance of being listened to than does a single artist; there is more glamour, more . . . well, *something* about a group that calls forth stronger loyalties. Whatever, this rock and roll underground, though it had no connection with the radical movements of the day and indeed was probably very hostile toward all outré forms of behavior, resembled very much the early days of progressive rock. There was the same sense of boosting involved, the same constant grumblings that the *radio* played *shit* and if *only* they would program some *good* groups . . . And if you can remember turning people on to the Airplane, (or even grass) for the first time, you might be able to imagine what it was to turn someone on to Acappella records. ("Now here's this fine group," arm around shoulder, slowly leading toward the record player, a weird glint in the eye . . .) You were simply doing missionary work—taking care of God's business here on earth, and you just *knew* that He looked down and that He saw it was good.

In the true spirit of supply and demand, this group-oriented underground spawned record shops designed to meet their needs. Even at the height of their popularity, there were still only a few, maybe one or two per city, sparsely spread in a ragged line from New York to Philadelphia. In New York there was Times Square records, later followed by the House of Oldies and Village Oldies on Bleecker St. In Hackensack, New Jersey (soon to be a major center of Acappella—no foolin'), was the Relic Rack. Newark boasted Park Records, which gave away free coupons so that you stood to gain one record for every ten, and Plainfield had Brooks records, a store which had the dubious

honor of having the dumbest salesgirls in existence. There were
also a few in South Jersey, mostly around Trenton, one in Philadelphia whose name I can't remember, and maybe two or three
others. The Acappella underground was not exactly a mass
movement.

Times Square records, located in the 42nd Street subway
arcade, was the biggest and best. It was run by Slim, a tall,
gangling man who knew everything there was to know about
rock and roll, assisted by Harold, who knew nearly as much. Slim
was a strange character, looking for all the world like a Mid-
western con man, always ready to show you this or that little
goodie which he had just gotten in. He used to write for some of
the little hectographed magazines that sprang up around the
movement, little rambling columns that talked about the health
value of Benson and Hedges, his ex-wife, all the new records
Times Square was going to find and sell at outrageous prices. In
a sample column, from *Rhythm and Blues Train* #5, he
covered tapes that you could have made from the Times Square
files, the fact that no one brought in "Saki-Laki-Waki" by the
Viscounts on Vega label so that the cash price they would pay was
now two hundred dollars, a few upcoming inventions of his
(including air-conditioned streets), and finally finished with a
joke about the best thief in the world, who stole a tire off one of
the wheels of his car when he was doing fifty.

Slim really came into his own when he had an FM radio show
which appeared in odd corners of the dial on occasional Sunday
afternoons. He used to play some fine music, new Acappella
releases, also rarer records from the Times Square stock. "And
now," he would say, "here's 'Sunday Kind of Love' by the
Medievals, worth ten dollars at Times Square records." And then,
"pop," there it would be, probably the first time it had ever been
on a radio station, rescued from some dusty old file of DJ
records. (This is all past now; Slim died a while ago, and maybe
this could serve as a belated good-bye from at least one of his old
fans.)

But if Slim was a world in himself, his store was a veritable
universe. Records lined the walls, sparkling in all manner of

colors. One of the sneakier ways to make a record rare in those days was to release a limited number in a red (or green, or yellow) plastic edition. Times Square had them all, Drifters 45s in purple, a copy of the long sought-after "Stormy Weather" by the Five Sharks in a full five-color deluxe edition, others in varying hues and shades. Alongside the rows of hanging records were huge lists, detailing the prices Times Square would pay for rare records. Elvis Presley efforts on the Sun label went for ten dollars; "Darling, I'm Sorry" by the Ambassadors would bring the bearer a princely two hundred dollars. The rarest record of all, which Slim never actually succeeded in obtaining, was the old 78 version of "Stormy Weather" by the Five Sharps, complete with sound effects of thunderstorms and rain. (In the end, he was forced to gather together a collection of drunks and name them the Five Sharks in order to re-cut and re-release the record.) If you had the Five Sharps version, you could have made yourself an easy five hundred dollars.

The nicest thing about Times Square records, or any of the shops for that matter, was that they never minded if you just hung around the store, listening to records, rapping, trading and buying on your own. The clerks loved to talk, loved to show you obscure oldies, loved to find out if you could teach them anything in return. After a while, the stores became regular meeting halls, places where the groups hung out, where the kids brought their demos, where you could hear any number of versions of "Gloria," or "Pennies From Heaven," or "Ten Commandments of Love." It was a big club, and you could join if you had ever even remotely heard of Sonny Till and the Orioles.

But though Times Square was the headquarters, the Relic Rack actually started the whole thing off. Hackensack, New Jersey, is an unlikely spot for anything resembling a music center. It's dumpy, stodgily middle class, right on the outskirts of the pleasant pastoral spots of Secaucus and Jersey City. Yet its one asset was that it had a fine record shop, one where you could find nearly anything you were looking for and one which had the same set of vibes as Times Square records.

The Rack, in the person of Eddie Gries, had experimented for a time with bringing out re-releases of some of their rare oldies on their own label, Relic. They had some success and so nearly simultaneously Times Square followed suit. After a time, there was an assortment of things out on these private labels, some Acappella and some not, all managing to do moderately well. The important thing here, though, was not so much in the labels themselves, but in the fact that when the Zircons proved Acappella could actually *sell,* at least in a limited circle, the labels were already in existence to push and provide a vehicle for the music. Which brings us, finally, to the Star itself.

Acappella music grew out of the fifties rock underground, which coalesced around an assortment of loosely termed R 'n B groups all held together by this series of specialty record shops. The music itself was primarily more a style than anything else, using basically interchangeable words and phrasing. Like blues, the thing was not in what you did, but rather how you did it. To generalize, we can divide the output into two main types, notably, the Fast song and the Slow song. The Fast song was up-tempo, lots of sharp vocal work in the background, heavy emphasis on the bass, lead singer on top merely filling up the rest of the balance. In the context of Acappella music, it had more of a tendency to fall apart since even the most spirited singing could not usually make up for the loss of rhythm instruments. In these fast songs, all the holes could never really be filled adequately and the result, except in selected instances, was usually choppy, sounding weak and thin. Its good feature, however, was that it usually provided the most freaky vocal effects then present on record. In their push to clean up the loose ends, back-up vocalists were really hard pressed to find suitable accompaniment. Some of the results are like the Del-Stars' "Zoop Bop" (Mellomood GS-1001B), a song which is easily five years ahead of its time. Consisting of little more than a collection of indecipherable syllables, rhythmic effects and skillful use of the echo chamber, the record comes off as one of the first psychedelic golden oldies.

The Acappella form truly found itself, however, in the Slow song. Essentially a ballad, it was soft, the background singers filling out the lead vocal, coming in over, under and through it at various times. When successful, the effect could be haunting in its starkness and purity. The Vi-Tones once made a record called *The Storm* (Times Square 105A) which is nothing less than unearthly, minor in mood, creating feelings I know I could never put down on paper. Acappella was really a true return to essentials, finding the emotions that could be represented by simple harmonies, using only the human voice as its instrument. When it was done well (something that often eluded the dozens of groups who relied on showy vocal pyrotechnics), it could be incredibly gripping and powerful.

We could get really hung up in drawing analogies to present-day rock here, but it's much too tempting to find any number of parallels in the rise and fall of Acappella and compare them with what has been happening over a like period of time in rock. Acappella began with a handful of groups, all highly polished in a crude sort of way, proud of their craft and creating a superior collection of recordings and performances. Then, as the movement's sense of self increased (much as in the curse of Marcuse's One-dimensional Man), the quality began regressing. It began to be self-conscious of what had formerly been unconscious and the contrived results were hardly listenable. Pale imitations sprang up, filled with sloppy singing and off-key harmonies. Strangely, all this happened at a time when Acappella was actually increasing in popularity; the amount of good stuff simply decreased in a kind of inverse ratio. And Acappella, not having the numerical power nor the resiliency of rock, could not afford to have its strength so diluted—it *had* to keep being produced at a high level in order to survive. But once the downfall started, there was no stopping it. When Acappella finally died, there were few left around to mourn it.

But all that is much nearer the end of the story. Acappella's Great Groups come well at the beginning, and most managed to retain their high positions until the whole thing began to fade out of sight. We've already spoken about the Zircons; the newer group that sprang up to take their name was not nearly as good, producing one fine song ("Silver Bells," Cool Sound CS 1030A), and then concentrating on shlock versions of "Stormy Weather" and the like. This newer group actually got around to producing an album (on Cat-Time label), but it was significant only in the negative.

But the other large groups of Acappella managed to stay together, and several of them kept on producing more and better stuff. The Young Ones, who became popular almost at the same time as the Zircons, were probably almost as well known, maintaining a high quality in their records (with resultant rise in reputation). The group was from Brooklyn, ranged in ages from eighteen to twenty and managed to coalesce one of the truly unique sounds in Acappella, thanks to a lead singer who had the capacity to sound nearly *castrato* at certain times. Their first record, on the Yuusels label, was called "Marie," a near-standard stereotypical Slow song:

> *He made the mountains*
> *He made a tree*
> *And He made a girl*
> *When He made Marie* . . .

But for whatever reason, the Young Ones took this song and really did a Job on it, creating out of it one of the most moving records of the whole period. Though "Marie" contained some musical background, the Young Ones soon moved over to Slim and the Times Square label and began producing Acappella records.

While there, they came up with several passable songs and two truly Great ones. The first of these was easily the finest version of "Gloria" (Times Square 28A) yet available, a tremendous reading of a song which had been done over and over and over, sometimes nearly to death, by some huge number of groups. But even better than that was their Acappella version of "Sweeter Than" (Times Square 36A), a remake of the Passions' oldie of "This Is My Love." From the opening note to the final, bell-like harmonic rise at the end, the song had Classic written all over it.

If the Young Ones represented some of the best that Acappella had to offer, the Camelots certainly showed the versatility of the style. For one, they produced the best up-tempo song, "Don't Leave Me Baby" (Aanko 1001), a record that featured a bottom line any present-day bass guitarist would be happy to make his own. The Camelots' success was mainly due to their incredibly rich harmony, a sound which brooked no faltering or loose moments; they were on top of their material at all times. Of all the groups, they made the best effort to go commercial, recording for both Laurie and Ember records, but, like the others, they have long since disappeared.

Underneath this top layer of groups were three or four secondary combinations, all of which had varying moments of excitement to them. I have a warm spot in my heart for the Savoys, hailing from Newark, who came out with some fine material on the Catamount label. They and a group called the Five Fashions were the stars of the best Acappella album ever put out. *I Dig Acappella* (Cat-Time LP 201A), featuring a cover photo of a plump girl in a bathing suit overseeing gravestones with the names of the groups on them (*I Dig* . . . get it?), contained some twenty cuts of sheer Acappella proficiency. There were the inevitable bummers, of course ("She Cried" by the Rueteens, the Zircons' "Unchained Melody," but on the whole, it was the finest statement that the Acappella movement had yet made. It still *is*, by the way, and I can think of no better way to introduce anybody to music "without music" than to play them any one of half a dozen cuts from the album.

It would be nice to report that the other albums that came out were as consistent as *I Dig Acappella*. *The Best of Acappella* series on Relic only lived up to its name with the first volume and continued downward from there. Except for selected groups (The Citadels, a revival of the old Quotations, a few others), the series degenerated into a collection of poor imitations, flat har-

monies and gimmick groups. They would feature Joey and the
Majestics—"A twelve-year-old lead singer!"—songs done in
barber shop harmony, the first Acappella song done in a foreign
language, any number of other superficial hypes. My personal
favorite from all of these winners was a group called Ginger and
the Adorables, who appeared on the cover of Vol. IV, five chicks
who really looked as if they could roll your back until it began to
break. Unfortunately, they couldn't sing worth a damn. In the
liner notes, we were told that

> *Ginger and the Adorables (also known as the Lynettes) are from
> West Orange, New Jersey. They were discovered by Wayne Stierle
> while singing outside a local candy store. Lead singer is Ginger
> Scalione, 16; 1st tenor is Jill Tordell, 16; 2nd tenor is Gail Haber-
> man, 14 . . .*

The period of decadence was about to set in.

A group that was beyond decadence, though, indeed was
beyond just about *anything* one could name, was a combination
from New Jersey called the Velvet Angels. They released a few
singles, had a few cuts on some of the anthologies, and were
always rumored to be the pseudonym for a famous group cur-
rently slumming it. Whatever, the Angels' biggest claim to fame,
aside from having the deepest bass in existence, was that their
records always carried the notation that they were recorded in a
Jersey City hotel room. It would say: "This Acappella recording
was made in a Jersey City hotel room," and you would listen and
say, yup, it sure sounded like it. But they were good, one of the
better, and so above any sort of this petty teasing.

Withal, you could feel Acappella slowly fading away. It was
losing steam, fighting a weighted battle against a nearly overwhelming onslaught of crap. But in November of 1965, as the
whole thing was entering its twilight, Acappella had its finest
moment. The occasion was the first Acappella show, sponsored
by the Relic Rack, featuring all the groups that we had heard but
never seen, people like the Savoys, the Five Sharks, the (new)

Zircons. It was to be quite an Event; except within a small home-town radius, Acappella groups almost never appeared anywhere. They were simply much too esoteric and obscure. As the night drew closer, it seemed as if a huge party was about to take place; good feelings were spread all around.

As it would happen, the night was fated: the entire East Coast was struck by the Great Blackout. But Hackensack, for some unknown reason, was one of the few remaining pockets of light. And it was exciting to be at the theater; a kind of community existed between the people who came, a spiritual bond which said that there is one thing that binds us all together—one thing that we have that the Others outside don't even know about. There was a sense of belonging, of participation in a small convention of your own personal friends. We were all together.

Now I suppose that it would be logical to describe a pseudo-mystical experience at this point, complete with stars and flashing red lights. It would bring things to a dramatic finale, tie together all the differing streams of narrative we've started up and left hanging, round everything off in a nice, warm ball. But I can't do that, simply because it just didn't happen. The groups came out; I remember seeing the Five Sharks, a new group called the Meadowbrooks who did a few nice things, maybe a couple of others, but the air was never charged with the feeling that something Wonderful was taking place. The music was good, we all liked it and applauded like mad, but the Magic simply wasn't there.

The reason that nothing like that could happen was because the people on the stage were essentially no different than us. There was no charismatic distance between us down here and them up there, no feeling of the performer and his relation to the audience. These people weren't professionals; they were only doing the same things that we had been doing all along, leaning up against the wall, laughing a lot, trying to sing. They might have done it a little better than we could, but that was irrelevant.

It was fun. Like a sing-along, or a hootenanny. Like being in one of those 1890s ragtime places where people get drunk and sing the old songs. Like being home. And so, when it was over, we left and said it was fine, 'cause it was, especially when that big bass hit that riff, *damn* he had a low voice (trying it) *bah-doo bah-doo* and what about the falsetto from the Sharks *oo-whee-ee-oo-oo* yeah but remember . . .

There was another concert somewhere along the line, a lot more records, more groups, more everything. But toward the end, no one really cared very much. Acappella died because the confines of its own small world could not contain it when it became too large; it simply could not keep up enough quality per record. Toward its final days, when people like Stierle were producing Acappella's brand of bubble-gum music, when groups like the Autumns recorded limp versions of "Exodus," when it became nearly impossible to separate the good from the bad, many of the old fans began drifting away. And I was one of them, picking up on the Beatles, the Stones, on newer things with the vitality that Acappella once had, but somehow lost.

But because I still remembered, I went down to Times Square Records the other day, just to check it out, to have some sides played, to find out what had happened in the years I had been away.

There was a sign on the door, saying the store was to be closed soon. It had moved from the old large location to a smaller, very cramped hole in the wall. Slim was gone, of course, and skinny little Harold was gone also. All that remained was a pale junkie behind the cash register who would doze off each time I would ask for a record. I wandered around inside, feeling fairly lost, remembering how things once were and irrationally wishing they might return again.

I asked the guy at the store what had happened. "Nobody likes the old music anymore," he told me. I said that was sad. He shrugged and dozed off again.

I left a little while after that. He was right, of course. Even the rock and roll revival will probably pass right over Acappella music, over the Five Satins, over the Orioles, even over the rainbow. Which is really too bad. In passing over all of them, it'll miss the heart of the whole thing, avoiding the meat and picking up some of the filler, bypassing a lot that might be nice to have in these days of giant festivals and supergroups.

Acappella was not the stuff of which you could make mountains. It was simple music, perhaps the simplest, easy to understand, easier to relate to, and so maybe it's not so bad that Acappella will be passed over after all. It would be lost at the Fillmore or the huge stadiums, swamped by the electrical energy that is so much a part of the contemporary scene. Acappella is meant to be personal, music for street corners and bathrooms, for happy memories and good times.

A stream within a stream within a stream. Folk music of a very special kind.

NO EXPECTATIONS NO. 2

Nothing has really happened all summer. Fact is now fiction and fiction is now fact. There are, as you've no doubt sensed, periods in history of progress and periods of no progress. That is to say, there can never, never be any historical certainty of progress. When all stands still (. . . they are standing still: Revolution No. 9) as it seems to in 1969, one can look around and all that one really sees is what happened up to this point. The present defies us but there is a way to get at it. One way, through our pop time machine, shows all our heroes since 1962 in retrospect. We desperately trace the story of them and us, the living people, and speculate on how we ever got to this God-awful point in time. Some of these heroes are still out there. They look a bit tired, a bit jaded, but these heroes have enough money that they don't need to kill themselves with overwork. That much the Mod revolution did succeed in accomplishing. Clapton is rich, Beck is well-off now, Jagger works when he wants to. They can fly to beautiful vacation spots. I recently saw a photograph of George Harrison at one of these places, in "an exclusive part of Sardinia." Man. He looked healthy.

POLITICAL FOREWORD

This article is an article on two levels. It is about the polarization of the United States into two camps and why I don't like this. It is, in a second (and peculiarly personal way), about the death of some of the people like Brian Jones, involved in public life, who represented—in the 1960s—the MIDDLE to these two emerging extremes; why they died; what might have happened if they hadn't; and why, for a strange reason, people don't pop up to replace these fallen people, and restore the middle way to the prestige it used justly to have.

Michael Horowitz, one of New York City's young writers, has called the moving, dynamic center-of-the-road VIEW to culture, politics and people by the very correct (accurate) yet emotional phrase: THE LITERARY RADICAL MIDDLE. At its height of power, the literary radical middle (LRM) was represented by publications as diverse as *The East Village Other* and *Ramparts* (both of which, last year, went over to the Left-Political Bag), and it (of course) had nationally known political figures such as Robert Kennedy, Martin Luther King (B.B. King too), and its most powerful spokesman, and most beloved personage, John F. Kennedy. Yes: the corpses of the LRM are impressive. Now, today, the literary radical middle is literally dead.

(". . . who killed the Kennedys when it was you and me" . . . Mick Jagger)

The LRM manifested itself in rock and roll and pop music mainly through certain musicians: B.B. King, Buddy Holly, Jim Morrison, Bo Diddley, Brian Jones, Paul McCartney, none of them extremists. Rock musicians are themselves some of the greatest humanitarians, humane by their very choice of *music* rather than *war* as a profession, and by their frequent commitment of themselves to roles *as social leaders,* even at their very young ages. They are nonetheless activists, without being extremists. Activists in the John Lennon-Mick Jagger sense.

John Lennon, for example, said recently that he is still "fighting against the same people. Before, it was my teachers . . . now it's just a bigger fight." The fight, this fight against linear authority (what college students have labeled "the system") has become a very big deal for this generation, so much that the extremists have forgotten that this system (linear authority) is just an extension of people's minds. "Infiltrate," says Lennon. "Confront," says one extreme; "law and order," says the other.

There you have the fission of our times. This fission leaves J. W. Lennon inside the two extremes and part of the LRM. He wants change, he speaks English articulately, he rejects destruction. These three characteristics make him of the LRM.

It is obviously in the way to fight linear authority that the LRM and SDS disagree. This is the big distinction (and record company executives should note this) between the message of pop music and the methods of political activism. The music scene is not so threatened by political trends as the music business quietly fears. Instead it should be noted that SDS is a non-literate extreme. It is boring, a boring extreme, and it did not become popular until the real heroes of the sixties died in the name of moderation. If the LRM grows again, SDS will simply disappear.

Not surprisingly, the LRM's current surviving lights are few and comparatively getting weaker in their impact on kids. Most of the survivors are not the political LRM people, but writers and musicians, who are all coming into increasingly intimate contact with one another. Jim Morrison, in a recent *Rolling Stone*, said he admires Norman Mailer.

If, however, there don't seem to be any more politicians in the public eye who embrace the middle ethic (other than Mailer), don't wonder why. The politicians all seem to get killed. The weight of agitation for change is thrown, load and all, onto a few writers and musicians. (Dylan knew this when he wrote "The Weight.") And now, we come up to date and the question of Ted Kennedy. Is Ted committed to the LRM?

Ted Kennedy had been so political all his career that one didn't know where he stood. But ever since Bobby's death and his becoming a U.S. Senator, there is no doubt that he is with the LRM. The recent doubt cast on his career is bullshit. The death of Mary Jo Kopechne should not be equated with any lack of judgment on his part. (In the U.S., one cannot condemn people on circumstantial evidence.) Free him from gossip's web, and Ted is a committed man. That is what counts.

Rock music, as you no doubt know now, is all caught up in this political web. It has lost its original purpose as a culture separate from the Establishment. And that is why this windy introduction to the music of today and the Rolling Stones' new songs is justified and necessary. For to talk about the Stones now as just a band would be the tritest nonsense. To talk about the metaphysics of joy and compassion in their songs "Honky Tonk Women" and "You Can't Always Get What You Want," is, on the other hand, terribly valid. *The Stones songs must be seen as living culture, culture that moves with today's fast-moving people, today's moving targets, today's minds.*

Life is a gypsy barroom queen in reverse.

YOU CAN'T ALWAYS GET
WHAT YOU NEED
Fallen idols and left-over culture heroes

But one golden hero is dead and more are to fall. The first of these fallen heroes was Brian Jones, the Golden Stone of the Golden Age of Rock. "The Victim of pop culture," cried one English scandal sheet, *The People.* First his health failed him and then his nerve, people said.

Brian Jones was like a movie actor's version of a blonde, tow-headed English middle-middle-class country youth, with a short vocabulary and a long, lean smile, the kind who makes good through rock and roll and then becomes a twenty-two-year-old man who is our leader and will lead us out of the wilderness our parents created.

But who was Brian? Was he a middle-class hero for the middle class? Was he more huggable and kissable than your favorite chick??? Was he a stereotype: i.e., all rock and rollers (and that means sexy males) from England are blonde and are called Brian. What's in a name? Here's a list a friend of mine from Yorkshire once gave me:

BRITISH PROLETARIAN NAMES
Cheryl
Mary
Linda

John
Paul
Richard
Brian

BRITISH MIDDLE-CLASS & ARISTOCRATIC NAMES
Margaret
Michael
Anthony
Charles
William
George
Brian

Brian worked hard to be a Rolling Stone. If Mick Jagger was the Stones' engineer, and Loog Oldham their publicity man, Brian was their quiet musical genius, their charmer (like Paul in the Beatles), their hidden asset, their soul. He started in 1962, having left his hometown of Cheltenham in Gloustershire where he had just completed his training as a junior architect. In London, he supposedly made the Soho scene, and he met Mick and Keith, who were from the other side of London, the area where mod and middle and tough all intersect and one town looks like the other. The area sat through Viking raids and German bombs and became a fair recruiting ground for the local weirdos to head for London, to get out of their dead-end town.

There is a large Ford motor plant in Dagenham, and there are towns even there, far from the sooty, tweedy north mill country, those towns in London suburbia where there is flat land and claustrophobia. So one went to London.

The teddy boys had died out there and the Beat scene (with its art school fans) was at its peak when it all started. What made this new thing work simply was that it was an Up aesthetic.

One former British pirate radio DJ said "it" always happens in cycles. The 1962–63 beginnings were in a way miracles, but they were also a stock market-like upturn, a bull market.

SIX YEARS PASS
The up cycle becomes the down cycle
and the culture heroes become the fallen idols

Rock was a Zeitgeist, a period of time in history when people influenced each other and listened to each other. With 1970 approaching, I think of them all as the fallen idols. (Will Pope Paul VI become more popular than John Lennon?) And I think everyone under twenty-five should know who these fallen idols are and who they were in their hey-day of bell-bottomed melifluosity.

In the working-class life—which many people really lead— there are not gritty salt-of-the-earth people ("Factory Girl" gets closer to it) . . . these are middle-class fantasy images . . . the people are just working class—the lottery and raffle, and good luck to one of their class is cheered as upward mobility. When one worker makes good, it is a sign of possibility for another. It is a ray to heaven. And the working class knows they can't all get out and they cheer their fellows who do.

This doesn't quite explain the Beatles and Stones (though the Beatles thoroughly won the hearts of lower-class Liverpool long before 1964, and the Stones won the hearts of the lower-middle-class Mods who used to hang around the Crawdaddy Club in Surrey supersuburbia southwest of London) but it explains the motive.

The Beatles became *knights* and the Rolling Stones became *Robin Hoods* mainly because they were at the same time typical *and* extraordinarily confident kids. And the motive was always the same with English musicians. Simply stated, it was to triumph over boredom.

But things have changed. You can't shop in the same store anymore if the price goes up too much. "You Can't Always Get What You Want" is more than a Rolling Stones song; it is the watchword of now, the song of this essay.

THE NEXT THOUGHT
The Stones as left over culture heroes

The Stones have become the number one rock group of the world, as somehow (in general) through Lennon's plastic incorporation of Yoko Ono into the Beatle framework, the Beatles have withdrawn (voluntarily) from this *role,* the role of number one.

The Stones, who failed tactically in 1967 and 1968 to put their power through to us, who failed to lead enough people to their ideas (ideas like "No Satisfaction"), failed to win their *Beggar's Banquet* album cover dispute, are now making it O.K.

The Stones now are world's number one rock group, despite the fact that they have never once completely gotten their message across . . . with the possible exceptions of "No Satisfaction" and *Beggar's Banquet.* Whether the message is for all of us or not (i.e., for mass consumption) is beside the point. How have the Stones gotten so far without being understood? Or, *are* they, in some mysterious way, understood?

The Stones are against marriage, in favor of old-age pensions, against mental cruelty, for drugs (but only in the sense that no one has the right to be against drugs), in favor of having children outside marriage. In fact, they are in favor of everything hip people in America already do.

But they are also Shakespearean—and Elizabethan and bawdy and tawdry and 25,000 other Shakespearean things. They love nouns, substantive nouns, and substantives talk about substance, which also means something of value. Words pop up continuously in Stones songs, like "connection," "obsession," "satisfaction," "confession," . . . not just because these works are essential to the Stones' song story lines, but because each of the noun-words in itself says atomically simple things.

I would not bother to repeat the words of "You Can't Always Get What You Want," except for the superb accuracy of this song in describing the way most of the avant-garde, musicians and young writers alike, feel about the way the youth revolution has gotten fucked up. Two years ago, it *did* look like you *would* get what you wanted. Now you can't. So Jagger's song *stresses* the obvious. And makes, in so doing, the reality of it more potent, more believable, more necessary to accept.

SUICIDE

Despite the official "accident" version of Brian Jones's death, all the musicians I've talked to think Brian Jones did not die, but committed suicide. His death seemed to bring out suicidal feelings in a few of his fellow artists. His private confessions on pop culture (like: I wish I never left home) are scary. His childlike sweetness going to death reminds us of Keats and Shelley and Byron and of Elizabeth Barrett Browning's "No doubt I'll love thee better after death."

The avant-garde in Boston and New York (if they haven't sold out already and are still honest and have integrity) are experiencing a temporary but strong death wish. No way out of this. Conservative era. Nixon's setting the pace. Bad vibrations. David Silver met Nixon in an elevator and said the man's impossible. Nixon is vulgar, vulgar in the Latin sense of ordinary, mediocre. The avant-garde is beautiful and always risking its skin by its very deeds. No wonder it says to itself: "We who are about to die salute you."

Why is the avant-garde, so-called, not changing then? Why is it clinging to its death wish?

The Rolling Stones' newfound popularity here is a strange clue. The Stones now are beginning to be recognized as profiles in courage . . . the rest of us, by contrast, are afraid. There is a feeling that *we* (all of us) should have made it five years ago when it was easier, so we could be courageous now too. But *we* didn't. (Some of us.) And *they* did. And yet we can admire the Stones' courage without being jealous of it. The Stones could have led this whole generation of the 1960s instead of the Beatles. Yet, they blew it up to now. Nineteen seventy is here and it is very, very ugly. Even the record companies sense this—even with the record industry amounting to 1/870th of the gross national product, a firm economic anchor indeed. The Stones have blown it a little less than us. And they remain what they are: culture heroes with two feet on the ground.

> *She was standing with a glass in her hand*
> *She was waiting for her connection*
> *And her feet weren't quite in command*

NEXT

Camus says man's daily choice is to live further or to commit suicide. Suicide, Durkheim says, is a cultural phenomenon as well as a psychological one. People kill themselves because they want to leave a culture that doesn't offer them anything. Fighting against Zeitgeists is a violation of the Freudian Law of Economy of Energy. You get tired.

> *They all look so pale*
> —*From* Beggar's Banquet

ASIDE COMMENTS

Rolling Stone magazine had a stupid cover of Brian Jones. *He,* Brian, is-was not the devil. It was *Jagger* who played the "sympathy for the devil" role.

There is little mystique left in pop culture, but the Stones are splendid examples of musicians who are not acting their roles out of any particular desire to be mysterious. Leave that to Count Dracula. But, if the shadows get darker, my obsession will be your obsession and we'll all be together confessing. And if things get brighter, we'll think back some time in 1975 and say: yeah, the Rolling Stones. I don't dig them anymore, but I sure liked them when I was bitter."

How can we progress out of the slime of events that have surrounded us, like entrails dropped out of the sky—and how can we move on? Decentralization, birth control, honesty in media, cultural patience, hard work, therapy (most rock critics are now undergoing psychotherapy), more therapy, some aesthetic interests supported by your meager pocket money.

The brilliance of "Honky Tonk Women" (by now surely a *Billboard* No. 1), as a street song about a man and a woman is due to its potency. You come when you hear it, and you remember how "Back Street Girl" and "Lady Jane" seem to be from another era. Next to Stupid Girls stand the Honky Tonk Women, the women of New York, Memphis and the bedroom.

America has it easy to feel abandoned, but it's sort of nice that Mick Jagger wrote a song about American life. Thank you Mick. This country isn't used up after all, you might think. And it did once have a mystique.

So, if I don't see you at your favorite record store so much now, don't forget to meet me at the election polls in November, 1972. And in the meantime, hope those Honky Tonk Women get around.

WOODSTOCK NATION

I looked at my watch, I looked at
my wrist,
I punched myself in the face
with my fist;
I took my potatoes down to be
mashed—and made on over to that
million dollar bash.

—DYLAN

The Woodstock Music and Art Fair wasn't held in Woodstock; the music was secondarily important and the art was for the most part unproduced; and it was as much of a fair as the French Revolution or the San Francisco earthquake. What went down on Max Yasgur's farm in the low Catskills last weekend defied categories and conventional perceptions. Some monstrous and marvelous metaphor had come alive, revealing itself only in terms of its contradictions: paradise and concentration camp, sharing and profiteering, sky and mud, love and death. The urges of the ten years' generation roamed the woods and pastures, and who could tell whether it was rough beast or speckled bird slouching towards its Day-Glo manger to be born?

The road from the Hudson River west to White Lake runs through hills like green knishes, soft inside with good earth, and crusty with rock and wood on top. What works of man remain are rural expressions of an Other East Village, where the Mothers were little old ladies with sheitls, not hip radicals with guns. There's Esther Manor and Siegel's Motor Court and Elfenbaum's Grocery: no crash communes or head shops. Along that route, a long march of freaks in microbuses, shit-cars and bikes—or on thumb and foot—passed like movie extras in front of a process screen. On the roadside, holiday-makers from the Bronx looked

up from their pinochle games and afghan-knitting and knew that
the season of the witch had come.

"Beatniks out to make it rich": Woodstock was, first of all, an
environment created by a couple of hip entrepreneurs to consoli-
date the cultural revolution and (in order?) extract the money of
its troops. Michael Lang, a twenty-five-year-old former heavy
dealer from Bensonhurst dreamed it up; he then organized the
large inheritance of John Roberts, twenty-six, for a financial base,
and brought in several more operatives and financiers. Lang does
not distinguish between hip culture and hip capital; he vowed to
make a million before he was twenty-five, beat his deadline by
two years, and didn't stop. With his Village/Durango clothes, a
white Porsche and a gleaming BSA, he looks, acts and *is* hip; his
interest in capital accumulation is an extension of every hippie's
desire to rip off a bunch of stuff from the A&P. It's a gas.

The place-name "Woodstock" was meant only to evoke cul-
tural-revolutionary images of Dylan, whose home base is in that
Hudson River village. Woodstock is where the Band hangs out
and the culture heroes congregate; it's where Mick Jagger (they
say) once ate an acid-infused Baby Ruth right inside the crotch
of a famous groupie. A legend like that is good for ticket sales,
but the festival was always meant to be held in Wallkill, forty
miles away.

By early summer, Woodstock looked to be the super rock
festival of all time, and promoters of a dozen other summertime
festivals were feverishly hyping up their own projects to catch
the overflow of publicity and enthusiasm: Rock music (al fresco
or recorded) is still one of the easiest ways to make money off the
new culture, along with boutique clothes and jewelry, posters,
drugs and trip-equipment, *Esquire* magazine, Zig-Zag papers and
Sara Lee cakes. But the Woodstock hype worried the burghers of
Wallkill, and the law implemented their fears by kicking the bash
out of town. Other communities, however, were either less uptight or more greedy; six hard offers for sites came to the promoters the day Wallkill gave them the boot. With less than a
month to get ready, Woodstock Ventures, Inc., chose the 600-
acre Yasgur farm (with some other parcels thrown in) at White
Lake, N.Y.

Locals there were divided on the idea, and Yasgur was attacked by some neighbors for renting (for a reported $50,000) to Woodstock. But in the end, the profit motive drove the deal home. One townsman wrote to the Monticello newspaper: "It's none of their business how Max uses his land. If they are so worried about Max making a few dollars from his land they should try to take advantage of this chance to make a few dollars themselves. They can rent camping space or even sell water or lemonade." Against fears of hippie horrors, businessmen set promises of rich rewards: "Some of these people are short-sighted and don't understand what these children are doing," one said. "The results will bring an economic boost to the County, without it costing the taxpayer a cent."

The vanguard of freaks started coming a week or more before opening day, and by Wednesday they were moving steadily down Route 17-B, like a busy day on the Ho Chi Minh Trail. The early-comers were mostly hard-core, permanent dropouts: Their hair or their manner or their rap indicated that they had long ago dug into their communes or radical politics or simply into oppositional life-styles. In the cool and clear night they played music and danced, and sat around fires toasting joints and smoking hashish on a pinpoint. No busts, pigs or hassle; everything cool, together, outasight.

By the end of the next day, Thursday, the ambience had changed from splendor in the grass to explosive urban sprawl. Light and low fences erected to channel the crowds without actually seeming to oppress them were toppled or ignored; cars and trucks bounced over the meadows; tents sprung up between stone outcroppings and cow plop. Construction went on through the night, and already the Johnny-on-the-Spot latrines were smelly and out of toilet paper, the food supply was spotty, and long lines were forming at the water tank. And on Friday morning, when the population explosion was upon us all, a sense of siege took hold: Difficult as it was to get in, it would be almost impossible to leave for days.

From the beginning, the managers of the festival were faced with the practical problem of control. Berkeley and Chicago and

Zap, N.D., were the functional models for youth mobs rampaging at the slightest provocation—or no provocation at all. The promoters interviewed eight hundred off-duty New York City policemen for a security guard (Sample question: "What would you do if a kid walked up and blew marijuana smoke in your face?" Incorrect answer: "Bust him." Correct answer: "Inhale deeply and smile."), chose three hundred or so, and fitted them with mod uniforms. But at the last minute they were withdrawn under pressure from the Police Department, and the managers had to hire camp counselors, phys ed teachers and stray straights from the surrounding area.

The guards had no license to use force or arrest people; they merely were to be "present," in their red Day-Glo shirts emblazoned with the peace symbol, and could direct traffic and help out in emergencies if need be. The real work of keeping order, if not law, was to be done by members of the Hog Farm commune, who had been brought from New Mexico, along with people from other hippie retreats, in a chartered airplane (at $16,000) and psychedelic buses from Kennedy Airport.

Beneath the practical problem of maintaining order was the principal contradiction of the festival: how to stimulate the energies of the new culture and profit thereby, and at the same time control them. In a way, the Woodstock venture was a test of the ability of avant-garde capitalism at once to profit from and control the insurgencies which its system spawns. "Black capitalism," the media industry, educational technology, and Third World economic development are other models, but more diffuse. Here it was in one field during one weekend: The microcosmic system would "fail" if Woodstock Ventures lost its shirt, or if the control mechanisms broke down.

The promoters must have sensed the responsibility they carried. They tried every aspect of cooptation theory. SDS, Newsreel and underground newspapers were handed thousands of dollars to participate in the festival, and they were given a choice spot for a "Movement City"; the idea was that they would give hip legitimacy to the weekend and channel their activities "within the system." (They bought the idea.) Real cops were specifically barred from the camp grounds, and the word went out that there would be no busts for ordinary tripping, although big dealers were discouraged. There would be free food, water, camping facilities—and, in the end, free music, when attempts at crowd-channeling failed. But the Hog Farmers were the critical element. Hip beyond any doubt, they spread the love/groove ethic throughout the farm, breaking up incipient actions against "the system" with cool, low-key hippie talk about making love not war, the mystical integrity of earth, and the importance of doing your own thing, preferably alone. On the other hand—actually, on the same hand—they were the only good organizers in camp. They ran the free food operation (oats, rice and bulgar), helped acid-freaks through bad trips without Thorazine, and (with Abbie Hoffman) ran the medical system when that became necessary.

The several dozen Movement organizers at the festival had nothing to do. After Friday night's rain there was a theory that revolt was brewing on a mass scale, but the SDS people found themselves unable to organize around the issue of inclement weather. People were objectively trapped; and in that partial aspect, the Yasgur farm was a concentration camp—or a hippie reservation—but almost everyone was stoned and happy. Then the rain stopped, the music blared, food and water arrived, and everyone shared what he had. Dope became plentiful and entirely legitimate; in a soft cool forest, where craftsmen had set up their portable headshops, dealers sat on tree stumps selling their wares: "acid, mesc, psilocybin, hash . . ." No one among the half-million could not have turned on if he wanted to; joints were passed from blanket to blanket, lumps of hashish materialized like manna, and there was Blue Cheer, Sunshine acid and pink mescaline to spare.

Seen from any edge or angle, the army strung out against the hillside sloping up from the stage created scenes almost unimaginable in commonplace terms. No day's demonstration or political action had brought these troops together; no congress or cultural event before produced such urgent need for in-gathering and self-inspection. The ambiguities and contradictions of the imposed environment were worrisome; but to miss the exhilaration of a generation's arrival at its own campsite was to define the world in only one dimension.

Although the outside press saw only masses, inside the differentiation was more impressive. Maybe half the crowd was weekend-hip, out from Long Island for a quick dip in the compelling sea of freaks. The other half had longer been immersed. It was composed of tribes dedicated to whatever gods now seem effective and whatever myths produce the energy needed to survive: Meher Baba, Mother Earth, street-fighting man, Janis Joplin, Atlantis, Jimi Hendrix, Che.

The hillside was their home. Early Saturday morning, after the long night of rain—from Ravi Shankar through Joan Baez—they still had not abandoned the turf. Twenty or forty thousand people (exactitude lost its meaning: it was that sight, not the knowledge of the numbers that was so staggering) sat stonily silent on the muddy ground, staring at a stage where no one played: petrified playgoers in the marble stands at Epidaurus, thousands of years after the chorus had left for the last time.

No one in this country in this century had ever seen a "society" so free of repression. Everyone swam nude in the lake, balling was easier than getting breakfast, and the "pigs" just smiled and passed out the oats. For people who had never glimpsed the intense communitarian closeness of a militant struggle—People's Park or Paris in the month of May or Cuba—Woodstock must always be their model of how good we will all feel after the revolution.

So it was an illusion and it wasn't. For all but the hard core, the ball and the balling is over; the hassles begin again at Monticello. The repression-free weekend was provided by promoters as a way to increase their take, and it will not be repeated unless future profits are guaranteed (it's almost certain now that Woodstock Ventures lost its wad). The media nonsense about death and O.D.s has already enraged the guardians of the old culture. The system didn't change; it just accommodated the freaks for the weekend.

What is not illusionary is the reality of a new culture of

opposition. It grows out of the disintegration of the old forms, the vinyl and aerosol institutions that carry all the inane and destructive values of privatism, competition, commercialism, profitability and elitism. The new culture has yet to produce its own institutions on a mass scale; it controls none of the resources to do so. For the moment, it must be content—or discontent—to feed the swinging sectors of the old system with new ideas, with rock and dope and love and openness. Then it all comes back, from Columbia Records or Hollywood or Bloomingdale's in perverted and degraded forms. But something will survive, because there's no drug on earth to dispel the nausea. It's not a "youth thing" now but a generational event; chronological age is only the current phase. Mass politics, it's clear, can't yet be organized around the nausea; political radicals have to see the cultural revolution as a sea in which they can swim, like black militants in "black culture." But the urges are roaming, and when the dope freaks and nude swimmers and loveniks and ecological cultists and music groovers find out that they have to fight for love, all fucking hell will break loose.

J. Oliphant

BUFFALO SPRINGFIELD:
A Round

Schools (taught) augment: Berkeley vs. Bob Jones → (Give to the college of your choice). Schools (thought) sustain: Hamilton vs. Burr → (If your heart's not in America, get your ass out) → the FBI *is* J. Edgar . . . born in Wash. D.C. 1895 → has he left yet? → a Darwinian prototype hung upside down. Or, to go on: Hegel; eye for an eye → turn thy cheek → love thy enemy* →. To still other fronts (same revolution), cruising with Ruben and the Jets is a Newtonian dodo bird.

THE RADISH AS A WEED

Rock as Drama (Pop): you + I → us
or
"Love Me Do" + *"Ask Me Why"* + *"Please Please Me"* & *"Thank You Girl"* + *"I Call Your Name"* + *"You've Really Got a Hold On Me"* + *"I Want to Hold Your Hand"* + *"Till There Was You"* + *"I Wanna Be Your Man"* + *"I'm Happy Just to Dance With You"* & *"I'm a Loser"* + *"I'll Be Back"* + *"Baby's in Black"* + *"I'll Follow the Sun"* + *"You Like Me Too Much"* + *"I Don't Want to Spoil the Party"* & *"I Never Needed Anybody's Help*

---

* See *Buffalo Springfield Again*

in Anyway" + *"Another Girl"* + *"We Can Work It Out"* →
"Think for Yourself" + *"Say the Word and You'll Be Free"* +
"I'm Looking Through You" + *"In My Life"* + *"Run for Your
Life"* & *"I'm the Taxman"* + *"I Look at All the Lonely People"*
+*"She Said She Said"* I know what it's like to be dead + *"For
No One* + *"Tomorrow Never Knows"*→

> *And it really doesn't matter if I'm wrong*
> *I'm right*
> *Where I belong I'm right*
> *Where I belong*

"I'd love to turn you on" →
"All You Need Is Love" →
I am he as you are he as you are me and we are all together →
"Hey Jude" → Revolution One →

> *One kiss leads to*
> *An Other:*

Rock as Conflict (R&B): you *vs.* me → them
as
"It's All Over Now" + *"I'm All Right"* + Don't play with me
'cause you're *"Playing With Fire"* + *"Spider [vs] and the Fly"* +
"You Better Move On" + *"Get Off My Cloud"* + Look at that
"Stupid Girl" + This could be *"The Last Time"* + *"Gotta Get
Away"* + *"She's Under My Thumb"* + *"Doncha Bother Me"* +
Just be my *"Back Street Girl"* + Good-bye *"Ruby Tuesday"* +
"Take It or Leave It" + *"You're Out of Time"* → *"Something
Happened to Me Yesterday"* → Why don't we *"Sing This All To-
gether"* + *"She's a Rainbow"* → Please allow me to introduce
myself + *"Street Fighting Man"* + *"Stray Cat Blues"* + *"Factory
Girl"* → *"Salt of the Earth"* → (*"Back Street"*—*2000 Light Years
From Home"*—*"Salt of the Earth"* →)
and another:
Rock as Narrative (Folk): I + HE → (man)
wherein "Masters of War" → "Mr. Jones" → *J. W. Harding* →

BACK TO SCHOOL

Evolution of art: 1700–1969: (short form)

Classicism → Romanticism → Realism → Impressionism → Expressionism → Abstraction → Reaction to Abstraction →

Historical Perspective (An episode)

Among Claude Debussy's close associates numbered Mallarmé and Verlaine—prime movers in the Impressionist and Symbolist movements. What they did to words Debussy attempted with music: "I desired for music that freedom of which it is capable perhaps to a greater degree than any other art, as it is not confined to an exact reproduction of nature, but only to the mysterious affinity between Nature and the Imagination."

His method: suppression of detail, emphasis on atmosphere, and (above all) a "peculiar" subtlety.

His tools: Dissonance as an end to itself (no longer an episode en route to consonance); use of modal scales: ("What Shall We Do with a Drunken Sailor"); the pentatonic scale: (black piano keys only—many Western folk songs); and use of the whole-tone scale (limited melodies, numerous harmonic implications) . . . one root of modern harmony.

ROCK AS ATTUNE

Buffalo Springfield as a collective shrug:

> *Is it strange I should change*
> *I don't know*
> *Why don't you ask her.*

No one song was ever written entirely by someone other than a member (independence yet reciprocal, from within). The Beatles recorded "My Bonnie," "Till There Was You," "A Taste of Honey" (they shudder), and like the Rolling Stones, mirrored their beginnings through Chuck Berry. The Stones also went to Sam Cooke, Hank Snow and Arthur Alexander.

Reaction (Bonnie—Julia) (Red Rooster—Stray Cat) is inevitable/welcome (i.e./e.g., Elvis Presley is a "has been" who still is → burn down Atlanta with your music and move to movies).

The Springfield's music suffered little cultural shock (from without or within) and changes were/are subtle and ethereal—as opposed to Dylan's turnabouts (he went rock!) wherein he leads the band wagon and when they join it he drops out. And as the Springfield trilogy was self-assured it was also certain → too good to let go → go on → rest (union). Buffalo Springfield, Buffalo Springfield Again, Buffalo Springfield Last Time Around, and their circle is completed. Is there anywhere else to go? One more record, a few more ideas perhaps, but there are other ideas to be performed somewhere else.** Three. A perfect number. The beginning. The middle. An end. Say it and get out.

Their longest cut, "Broken Arrow," is 6:13 and most are under three minutes. Say it and get out, because sometimes words don't work (A-start–Z-stop! or the alphabet is framed).

Don't conclude, allude.

> *His mother had told him a trip was a fall*
> *and don't mention babies at all.*
>
> *Did you see him?*
> *Did you see him?*

But lyrics are equipped with music and Buffalo Springfield makes you feel, sets you in YOUR corner and stares:

> *Do you think you love her . . .*
> *Do you think at all.*

They make you feel through a trinity of words + notes which always equal mood. (Built by association.) Lyrics suggest, music supports, and the resulting texture (mix) convinces you. She IS a Rock & Roll Woman. I am a child because the song maintains its beautifully simple nature and idyllic perceptions throughout:

** See (listen to) *Emperor of Wyoming*

> *You are a man*
> *You understand*
> *You pick me up and*
>   *lay me down again*
>
> *You make the rules*
> *You say what's fair*
> *It's lots of fun to have*
>   *you there.*
>
> *I gave to you*
> *Now you give to me . . .*
> *I'd like to know what you like.*

All accompanied by That Incredibly RIGHT guitar like "Blue-bird" has T.I.R.G. Impressions are homologized and the design is constructed in terms of tone rather than object. (I.e., Songs are about *Something* rather than you and I—reaching you from underneath instead of head on.) The only songs—aside from "I Am a Child"—which are direct, say things like:

> Sit *down* **I** think **I** *love you*
> **Anyway** *I'd like to try* . . . [*boldface mine*]

and perhaps their raison d'être:
   Do I have to come right out and say it(?)

BACK TO CLASS

As Debussy realized that dissonance can become an end in itself—there is no *absolute need* for resolution (cinema verité vs. Hollywood): Springfield do the same with lyrics . . . and music . . . tell me about "Bluebird"—or any of their songs—in terms of Intro-Climax-Resolution. No songs end so logically (Dylan) or so finitely (Beck's crashing conclusions) that the ear/mind can anticipate their motion and (thus) you stay with them note for word. "I Am a Child" doesn't END, it starts up again only to slowly fade out. "Rock and Roll Woman" just ends. A heartbeat concludes *Again* and "Kind Woman" fades ever so slowly.

There are a number of ways of going: (AAA supplies you with a direct route and a scenic tour) . . . you can strip to the essentials (return of the three-man group) or add a drop to the measure—Buffalo Springfield consists of three guitars: two leads—polyphony, i.e., counterpoint (melody) and one rhythm (harmony).

Harmony is "simple" enough. There are the supra-logical progressions of the barber-shop quartet and its female counterpart, the Lennon Sisters. Four voices become one tone . . . or try to. It can also become dispersed, stretching outward and becoming more complex (Everly Brothers) . . . one less "monotonous" tone. Or it can be figured—one or more parts of a piece move, during the continuance of a chord, through certain notes that do not belong to that chord (Mamas and the Papas). All harmony consists of employing consonance (pleasing to the ear) and dissonance (unharmonious) . . . *strict* harmony requires resolution to satisfy the ear. Too much of the former is stultifying—too much of the latter is "confusing."

The Springfield's unique sound (i.e., nobody sounds quite like them) is achieved through a balance of various musical principles . . . rather than being technically oriented (he's a "good drummer," "what a great bass line"), their approach aims at the total . . . the whole is greater than the sum of its parts . . . effect. Their refusal to use the major scale (pop ballads) and often the minor scale (numerous folk songs) leads to application of unusual modes (Dorian, etc.) combined with their ability to harmonize in numerous variations: displaced harmony in minor scales as well as the more unfamiliar scales. Their modulation (transition of keys) is obviously different (as opposed to the logical—often tedious—progression of the blues . . . tonic, dominant, leading tone, which has the strong tendency to move back to the tonic) and their melodies often employ deceptive modulation (ear is deceived and led into an unexpected chord). This can carry over to the timbre of the music (the banjo in "Bluebird" . . . the wide unexpected shifts of "Broken Arrow").

Add to the equation abrupt modulation (sudden change into keys not closely related to original key . . . and its antithesis, i.e., the tone which ends "Everydays" and begins "Expecting to Fly"). The result is that Buffalo Springfield is always "up there somewhere" in a melodic understatement. Even with their affinity for dissonance they seem to level off at just the right storey. The middle path . . . neither an ascetic nor ruler be.

The two lead guitars—polyphony (counterpoint) support of melody by melody as opposed to chords (harmony) . . . guitar and banjo in "Bluebird" voices in "Hung Upside Down."

RECORDS ARE ROUND

Not many people own Buffalo Springfield's initial album. There are a number of notable songs on it, and the beginning now seems like a statement of intention (attitude):

> *There's something happening here*
> *What it is ain't exactly clear*
>
> *I think it's time we stop, children*
> *What's that sound*
> *Everybody look what's going down.*

There have been thousands of songs with a similar theme, a similar tone: Something is wrong. "Eve of Destruction" is a soap opera, and even "Nowhere Man" is an encyclopedia. The Springfield sing and you can take it (them) for what it's worth. No lectures. Ever.

> *Sit down I think I love you*
> *Anyway I'd like to try . . .*

Their last album, *Last Time Around,* moves back into the country, and the contents are more consistent . . . lazy, down to the ground, almost shuffling. *Again,* their second album, is more a collection of fine singles than a uniform work . . . individual*

* See *Buffalo Springfield Again*

pictures become a collage.* The album—as does most of their music—gently seduces the listener's ear. And all seductions, of course, are mutual.

> *They married for peace and were gone—*
> *Did you see them*
> *They were there to wave to you. . . .*

* See *Buffalo Springfield/Last Time Around*

ROTO-ROOTER

ONE: BOB DYLAN

From the beginning, Bob Dylan's songs were about nostalgia ("Song to Woody"). But Bob was such a dilettante. He'd mix 'n' match all the nostalgic technologies . . . *The Free Wheelin' Bob Dylan* (Columbia CS-8786) had "Don't Think Twice," which belongs on *Nashville Skyline* (Columbia KCS-9825), "A Hard Rain's Gonna Fall," which belongs on *Blonde on Blonde* (Columbia C2S-841), and "Oxford Town" which belongs on Phil Ochs . . . At the beginning all the Bob Dylan periods already coexisted. Then in 1965, Folk-Rock came in, and Bob specialized, went for a Muzak form. No Cosmic Muzak like the Byrds had, but, it was visionary and mythic . . . Although Bob's titles were *Bringing It All Back Home* (Columbia CS-9128) and *Highway 61 Revisited* (Columbia CS-9189), only a few sharp ones recognized this visionary and mythic Muzak as a *method* to induce nostalgia in the public, in other words, a nostalgic technology . . . But, after all, all that Bob's glamorous *adjectival* technology did was glamorize (i.e., justify as visionary) things considered *both* irretrievable and special (i.e., objects of nostalgia): Glamorous adjectival technology like, "With your mercury mouth in the missionary times and your eyes like smoke and your press like rhymes and your silver cross and your voice like chimes, oh who do they think could bury you?" Why, if nostalgia's a compliment paid to the past, the compliment's gotta be justified . . .

In '66, following McGuinn's lead singing one year earlier (the Byrds' "Mr. Tambourine Man" version), Bob took all the edge off his voice, warmed it up, and, so to speak, let the Humboldt current caress it . . . on *Blonde on Blonde* he invented a drone mellow Muzak voice ("I Want You," "One of Us Must Know," "Sad Eyed Lady of the Lowlands," etc.). Like McGuinn or Byrds' harmony, this voice is seamless and by no means dramatic, and seamlessness is the biggest Muzak move. Bob's Muzak music technology made for unprecedented cumulative effects, for Muzak's spirit's nothing less than the inevitable total occupation and organization of all available sonic space, i.e., silence denial. By inevitable, I'd mean, every Muzak sound is absolutely predictable. The music lacks surprise to a supernatural extent. Such inevitability spells perfection on a visionary scale. ("Visions of Johanna" is visionary accumulation.) Into this repetitious field Bob introduced an apparent principle of contradiction, a visionary technique, *the unknown tongue*. Unknown tongues are musical forms with unpredictable inevitability or inevitable unpredictability or something like that . . . visionary music technology par excellence. Oh, the tongue's so paradoxical it's glamorous and everything it strikes is transformed . . . You can't predict where it'll strike next, but, once having struck you can't live without it . . . So couldn't a good tonguing transform the merely irretrievable into nostalgia? So Folk-Rock went out with nostalgia as tongues as *Blonde on Blonde* showed the highest density of tongues on record: Muzak tongues, yet, like all Muzak, they're repetitious, yet, paradoxical (the paradox of the unpredictable inevitable or the inevitably unpredictable). There's the "I Want You" chorus, the "Oh Mama can this really be the end, to be stuck inside of Mobile with the Memphis blues again" chorus, the "Sooner or later, one of us must know" chorus and *historically* the "How does it feel, to be on your own, with no direction home, like a complete unknown, like a Rolling Stone" chorus,—all of 'em fat Muzak tongues, in fact all of 'em Turkey Tongues, internalized within the tunes, wherein, the verse acts the set-up or "Turkey," to be shot down by the chorus. Only Muzak can internalize the Turkey Tongue.

John Wesley Harding (Columbia CS-9604) followed Bob's overrated accident by about 1.75 years, and showed nostalgia as mythic structure. There were many sparse myths: Tom Paine, St. Augustine, "The Wicked Messenger," the "Drifter's Escape," "All Along the Watchtower," Frankie Lee and Judas Priest, etc.; and, John Wesley Harding himself: "John Wesley Harding was a friend to the poor. He traveled with a gun in every hand. All along the countryside he opened many a door. But he was never known to hurt an honest man." And who could forget the strummed acoustic guitar, the bass, and lead harp, the occasional pedal steel guitar, the drums, the simple music, so portentous/pretentious, to have simplistic mythic grandeur like minimal art? For the first time in years Bob sacrificed music technology moves to be duller and do something else. It signaled Bob would sound like an old man for the next few years. The roots of the tunes aren't merely visible, they've been transferred directly to this barely electric content . . . here's an L.P. not only about, but also *with*, some aggressively traditional nostalgia, in the childish (i.e., Child Ballad), Woody Guthrie's "Ballad of Tom Joad" (which some people still brag to know *by heart*), word expansion, mode. Yep, word expansion, since this *simplicity's* found to expand words to their *archetypal* grandeur: "A friend to the poor," a friend to the poor? That's the typical trick of all simplistic and repetitious mythic dialects (i.e., Biblical language). And nostalgia's the sensation that follows the glamor, automatically imposed, on the *irretrievable exploits*, of the heroes in the tunes, by the structure of Bob's mythic dialect. That these tunes aren't merely structure and, therefore, abstract is only because a mythic dialect is a visionary dialect, and, therefore, the tunes *surpass* themselves through their grand and significant associations (i.e., word expansion). The purity of *John Wesley Harding* doesn't consummate in mere structure or abstraction, since these myths seem all too glamorous.

Popular nostalgic *words*, the hard-core ready-made language of sentiment, are so repetitious, they run to formal structures, recognized as those phrases we see and hear all the time: "I loved that dog," etc. . . . This overexposure means that phrase (and the others) doesn't mean a thing. Sometime back that phrase went blank. Its emotional implications, which were its popular meaning, disappeared beneath overexposure, which nothing can withstand. What remains is an arrangement of the words, i.e., the structure. Then popular nostalgic words have this advantage: they say no more than they *say,* imply nothing additional, *signify only their own structures* . . . But such simplicity's certainly baffling and abstract. The meaning of things is drawn from outside 'em. If they're blank, baffling, and, wholly abstract. The blatant gets densely mysterious before the eyes . . . For example what does this mean: "They say that you've been seen with some other man. That he's tall dark and handsome and you're holding his hand . . ."?

Nashville Skyline—its dull purity indicated purification by selection and not fire. This Bob Dylan L.P. has nostalgia as abstraction. And its dull ready-mades, of language and music, induced that abstraction. Bob's purified with a return to a root in blatant commercial C & W. (At least the commercial move was conceptually wise, but did it work out?) Ordinary, popular nostalgic stuff. But Nostalgia's extracted as a *visionary sensation.* Your Unknown Tongue, your Child Ballad, they're visionary technologies, that impart visionary energization necessary to nostalgic glamour. So "Lay Lady Lay" *nearly* reminds me of Skeeter Davis and *could* pry some tears under the right conditions, but this perfect little gem (a short and tight tune, like all the L.P.), sacrificed accumulation to perfection and its tongues (if any) are so short lived:

> *His clothes are dirty . . .*
> *But his hands are clean*
> *And you're the best thing that . . .*
> *He's ever seen.*

Abstraction's occurred when a structure remains mere structure, and so implies itself only. But nostalgic structures *must* imply more than themselves. Bob, always fond of a decent paradox, returned to somebody's root to make an L.P. about nostalgia that isn't nostalgic.

TWO: JOAN BAEZ

Smack on *Time* Mag's cover at the height of her craze back in, I'd say, '62 . . . Joan Baez didn't let success go to her head 'til a full four-five-six years later with *Noel, Joan, and Baptism* (Vanguard 79275) . . . A big star for those *earlier* days, yet she held out for a strict "one album a year." *Life* magazine said: "the finest new singer of them all, Joan Baez . . . a stylistic purity that places her in a class almost by herself . . . she sings with rare sweetness and clarity." Joan's corruption was delayed 'til *Noel* in '66: An Xmas album, contemporaneous with that "Beatles" album *In My Life,* (*Elektra* 74027) by Judy Collins, which made Judy both corrupt and ready-ripe for a subsequent big star ("Both Sides Now") . . . Joan's corruption descends from lacking versatility, a high-altitude (rarefied) stylistic purification which can't cope—but only interfere—with the Muzak spirit. Unable to relax her vocal tension (i.e., purity), unable to limp or croon, how could Joan coalesce with such Muzak conceptions as *Noel, Joan and Baptism?* What went wrong with Joan's corruption wasn't the corruption per se, but that it didn't consummate. Why, Bob Dylan's full Muzak, rotten to the core, on *Highway 61* and *Blonde on Blonde,* and, thereby launched himself a second stage career. Vis-à-vis Muzak, Joan's purified reticence can yield degrading interference . . . With Joan it's always been *non-versatility,* exactly "It's the singer not the song . . . ," that is, the singer's maintained style, which imposes a *form* of *purity* upon the songs. Joan Baez doesn't interpret a song. Like the Doors or Byrds, her imposed form *automatically* provokes mandatory interpretations from the audience. Joan's high altitude style is imaginary. The case of Joan Baez first seems simple—but her roots *are* imaginary. Like the Doors, Joan recalls (and could've been influenced by) certain wide and silver screen aspects, exact, Scottish and Rural English scenes of the seventeenth to eighteenth to nineteenth centuries (*Far from the Madding Crowd,* etc., movies . . .). Joan's gotta vision outta her very first old English Child Ballad. This vision's basically nostalgic and mythic, equipped with appropriate mandatory associations. Her style's another absolute contextualizer. When applied, it transfers its objects, no matter what (Phil Ochs *or* Classical Music from Brazil), to a mythic-nostalgic context, via the nostalgic technology of Joan's voice. (The regular Dialectic-Response pattern.)

Any Day Now: (Vanguard VSD 793067) "This is a collection of Bob Dylan's songs sung by Joan Baez," said Joan Baez on the cover. Well, songs from all periods, including such early Bizarro Childs as "North Country Blues" and "Boots of Spanish Leather." And the periods of Bob Dylan are each nostalgic technologies. "Recorded in Nashville," oh, the benefit of that nostalgic technology: i.e., Country Music. This density of nostalgia, "Love Minus Zero No Limit," "North Country Blues," "You Ain't Goin' Nowhere," "Drifter's Escape" are the first songs, in that order . . . For example, Dylan's own "Drifter's Escape" version has the hometown *dramatic* vocal which at "Oh, stop that cursed jury" recalls nothing so much as Dickens' fairly obscure ghost trial tales, while Joan's has vocally automatic stylistic nostalgia. Throughout the tunes Joan avoids dramatics and sentiment. Her high altitude habits prove there's no necessary connection between nostalgia and sentiment. This sets a rare example of nostalgia as automated form. So unknown tongues prove few and far between. Muzak tongues are tricky enough. But unknown tongues are like charisma (undisciplined) and could disrupt the automatic formal functions. (But there's one good autobiographical Turkey Tongue at the transition for an *a capella* "Tears of Rage" to "Sad Eyed Lady of the Lowlands.")

THREE: THE BAND

There're posters now circulating, which you can actually buy, of Al Kooper, who happens to sing like a Woodchuck: Al Kooper "Liberty" (Al as the Statue) and Al Kooper "Tyranny" (2 Als in the back of a staff car, Hitler's in front, "Greetings from Buenos Aires" it says . . .). As for the Band, they too sing like Woodchucks, but their favorite shot has 'em in odd, not funny, hats, with an aura of the Old West as it was getting old (1890–1905). (No excess, though, . . . they even play with a slight aura of incompetence.) But integrity; that's the word for the Band.

Though they sing like Woodchucks they're obviously good hu-
mored and not too anguished and, therefore, sound somehow
noble. That's just the nobility to guarantee nostalgia in what they
say. Like Bob Dylan, their old stable mate, the Band's songs are
about nostalgia: "We can talk about it now. It's that same old
riddle. Only start from the middle. I'd fix it but I don't know
how." But their typical visionary technology is nobility. Sometimes it even seems all their songs derive from "Long Black Veil."

Of course, the Band's by no means electric. Most of their
arrangements are conceptualized, and could be executed acousti-
cally. (The Pentangle's an acoustic Band.) There're no miniature
arrangements, but I'd say only "Chest Fever" and "This Wheel's
on Fire" need artificial energy. The Band's amplifier complement
is shameful by modern standards. When I saw 'em they put
sixteen mikes, through the P.A., on all the instruments and voices,
just to be heard. But then, more and better amps might be
conceptually unfortunate. Talk about integrity and roots, the
Band's avoidance of the modern volume scene makes 'em a
unique case of arrested development. (There's archaic charm in
arrangements which extract the simplicity from complexity and
vice versa . . .) Rather than transform the root strains of their
music, the Band just transplanted 'em. A true faithful transplant
and unique, their roots changed context but resisted the change
in form. They avoid the consequences and, harder to believe, the
spirit of technology in music. Man, the Band's music is less about
nostalgia than nostalgia itself, embodied.

FOUR: THE FLYING BURRITO BROTHERS

In an era of real old and mature groups, like aging Dylan or the
Band, man, the Flying Burritos are one of the few to at least
sound and sing like real teen-agers, like mere kids; reminds me
how some Byrds' freaks would call Chris Hillman "the Kid."
". . . A bunch of great kids, nice, decent, conscientious boys,"
said Nudie, of Nudie's Rodeo Tailors, their tailor, and tailor to
Buck Owens. I hear this Nudie's appeared on TV with the boys.
. . . Why I'd guess Burrito's most honestly self-conscious line

must be, "Then an angel appeared she was just seventeen . . . ,"
from "Juanita," a song they do. Even the real nobility in their
voices is teen-aged. And yet Sneeky Pete, the Burritos' great
pedal steelist must be the oldest White Rock Star. . . . A contradiction typical of the Burritos. With so much youthful spirit, they
make seeming random coalescence work like clockwork. The first
Burrito album starts off where their parent Byrds ended, at
C & W. And like the Byrds, they can move modules. For into a
standard (nine originals, two oldies) C & W tune-form they've
plugged Sneeky Pete! The astounding Sneeky Pete. Only one of
the greatest musicians to Rock 'n' Roll. With Sneeky, and Chris
Elhridge on bass (formerly of the Judy Collins Band), this band's
instrumental potential's beyond belief. . . . Already it's some
challenge to current concepts of form. Though Sneeky plays
pedal steel guitar, the *typical* C & W instrument, he plays no
mere C & W. Rather he's exaggerated those stock licks into a
technological sound . . . leads on, oh say, "Christine's Tuner" or
"Hot Burrito #2," oh boy. This is the Burrito's random coalescence, their challenge to form, perhaps it'll usher in some real
and not assimilated eclection. In assimilated eclection (i.e., the
Byrds), assorted forms are subordinated to a form, but real
eclection juxtaposes forms in some random coalescence whose
strength is just juxtaposition: For example the moving "Hot
Burrito #2" is nominally an R & B number with '50s style R & B
keyboards, but Sneeky's guitar technological *and* Graham Par-
sons' vocal is literally lonely boy. In so many ways, the Burritos
are a big return to '50s Rock practice wherein juxtaposition for
bizarre excitement was the big move: i.e., the Coasters, or the Du-
Tones' "Divorce Court" (flip side of "Shake a Tail Feather").
The Burritos lack the typical modern fear or respect for form.
. . . As a band they're real rabble. And Graham actually performs in high-heeled rhinestone booties, with Chris Hillman
often nearly asleep on the Leslie or Hammond cabinet. . . . And
they treat their favorite form, C & W, as a sorta soulful recognition factor upon which they can juxtapose exciting, pleasing
modules for a random coalescence. So their music's quite ornamental. They don't chew the C & W root at all, but treat it like a

structure for ornamentation, a structure to be ornamented (see "Hippie Boy") man, like an Xmas tree. And in the end even the noble nostalgia of the C & W form, as they do it, even nostalgia, turns out as ornament or icicle if you like. The Burritos are in no way dull and may create infinitely, since they lack a form that enslaves . . .

Felix Dennis & Jim Anderson

ROCK QUIZ

1. *"Rock 'n' Roll is a means of pulling down the white man to the level of the Negro. It is part of a plot to undermine the morals of the youth of our nation."*

   The Secretary of the North Alabama White Citizens'
   Council
   Richard Daley, Mayor of Chicago
   Judy Garland

2. *"I don't know anything about music. In my line I don't have to."*

   Yoko Ono
   Elvis Presley
   Timothy Leary

3. *"Viewed as a social phenomenon, the current craze for rock and roll material is one of the most terrifying things ever to have happened to popular music. Musically speaking, of course, the whole thing is laughable."*

   Billy Cotton
   Frankie Vaughan
   Steve Race

4. *"Nothing really affected me musically until Elvis."*

> Eric Burdon
> John Lennon
> Donald Peers

5. *"The kids accept almost any form of rock and roll, even the lowest and most distasteful . . . It seems to encourage sloppy clothes that become the accepted uniform. It's one step from Fascism!"*

> Malcolm Muggeridge
> Mitch Miller
> The Editor of the *New Musical Express*

6. *"I am one hundred per cent Christian and everything I do is done with my religion in mind."*

> Billy Graham
> Little Richard
> Cliff Richard

7. *"It's so fabulous being young and a girl and you can have nice clothes and can dress up, and that's the nicest part about it, being famous and people admiring you."*

> Sandie Shaw
> Mrs. Jeff Banks
> Sandra Goodrich

8. *"In the old days you'd drag your old man out on the lawn and kick the shit out of each other, and he'd say, 'Be home by midnight!' and you'd be home by midnight. Today, parents don't dare tell you what time to get in—they're frightened you won't come back."*

> Dick Gregory
> Frank Zappa
> Simon Dee

9. *"The same goes for my stripper routine. Nobody has ever objected . . . why should they? All that happens is that the stripping music plays and then I take off my jacket and . . . "*

Engelbert Humperdinck
Janis Joplin
Danny La Rue

10. *"The effect of rock and roll in young people is to turn them into devil worshippers; to stimulate self-expression through sex; to provoke lawlessness, impair nervous stability and destroy the sanctity of marriage. It is an evil influence on the youth of our country."*

R. D. Gaiman, Public Relations Officer to the Church of Scientology
Rev. Albert Carter, Minister of the Pentacostal Church
Marjorie Proops

11. *"Uh-oh, I think I exposed myself out there . . ."*

P. J. Proby
Jim Morrison
Judith Durham ("Big Boobs" to her friends)

12. *"Too many people are becoming obsessed with pop music. The position of rock and roll in our sub-culture has become far too important, especially in the delving for philosophical content."*

Mick Jagger
Tiny Tim
Jann Wenner

13. *"Pop's not a culture, it isn't an art. If rock and roll is a culture it's a great big boil and when it bursts it will leave a nasty scar."*

Mick Farren
Simon Dupree
Che Guevara

14. *"When I perform am I producing art? Am I fuck!"*

Mary Hopkin
Terry Reid
Jimi Hendrix

15. *"Pop is the perfect religious vehicle. It's as if God had come down to earth and seen all the ugliness that was being created and chosen pop to be the great force for love and beauty."*

Mike Heron
Donovan
Liberace

16. *"I had a banana band in high school."*

Bob Dylan
Duane Eddy
Sir Malcolm Sargent

ANSWERS TO QUIZ

1. The Secretary of the North Alabama White Citizen's Council. May 1956
2. Elvis Presley. April 1957
3. Steve Race. May 1956
4. John Lennon. February 1967
5. Mitch Miller. November 1957
6. Cliff Richard. April 1969
7. The three alternatives are Sandie Shaw's maiden, married and stage names. December 1967
8. Frank Zappa. June 1968
9. Engelbert Humperdinck. May 1969
10. Rev. Albert Carter, Minister of the Pentacostal Church. October 1956
11. Jim Morrison. March 1969
12. Mick Jagger. February 1969
13. Simon Dupree. April 1969
14. Terry Reid. January 1969
15. Donovan. 1968
16. Bob Dylan. June 1966

ABOUT THE EDITOR

JONATHAN EISEN is a free-lance writer and editor who lives in New York City. He is editor of the *Age of Rock* and (with Dennis Hale) of *The California Dream*. Formerly an editor with Pantheon Books and on the staff of *Commonweal*, Mr. Eisen was a founding editor of *The Activist* at Oberlin College.

ABOUT THE AUTHOR